WHITE CITY
BLACK CITY

Sharon Rotbard

WHITE CITY
BLACK CITY

Architecture and War
in Tel Aviv and Jaffa

Translated from Hebrew:
Orit Gat

The MIT Press
Cambridge, Massachusetts

First published in Hebrew by Babel, Tel Aviv © 2005
First published in English by Pluto Press, London © 2015
MIT Press edition, Massachusetts Institute of Technology © 2015
Sharon Rotbard © 2015

Publication of this book has been supported by a grant from the Graham Foundation
for Advanced Studies in the Fine Arts.

GRAHAM FOUNDATION

Translation edited by Ben Du Preez.

MIT Press books may be purchased at special quantity discounts for business or sales
promotional use. For information, please email special_sales@mitpress.mit.edu.

Every effort has been made to trace copyright holders and to obtain their permission
for the use of copyright material. The publisher apologizes for any errors or omissions
in the above list and would be grateful if notified of any corrections that should be
incorporated in future reprints or editions of this book.

This book was set in Arno Pro by Melanie Patrick and was printed and bound
in Canada.

Library of Congress Cataloging-in-Publication Data

Rotbard, Sharon, author.
['Ir levanah, 'ir shehorah. English]
White city, black city : architecture and war in Tel Aviv and Jaffa / Sharon Rotbard.
    pages   cm
Includes bibliographical references and index.
ISBN 978-0-262-52772-9 (pbk. : alk. paper)
1. Tel Aviv (Israel)—History. 2. Tel Aviv (Israel)—Architecture. I. Title.
DS110.T357R6813   2015
956.94'8—dc23
                                                                    2014045554

10 9 8 7 6 5 4 3 2 1

To Mor and Adam

The book will kill the edifice

Victor Hugo

Contents

לגור על החולות

העיר הלבנה של תל אביב
אתר מורשת עולמי

Part I

WHITE
CITY

They told me that the city is white. Do you see white? I don't see any white.
French architect Jean Nouvel standing on a Tel Aviv rooftop,
looking at Tel Aviv for the first time in his life. November 1995

If you will it, this shall not be a legend.
Theodor Herzl, *Altneuland*, 1902

In July 2003, UNESCO's World Heritage commission recommended inscribing the 'White City' of Tel Aviv in the organization's list of World Heritage Sites. The official text[1] supporting this endorsement argued that

> *The White City of Tel Aviv is a synthesis of outstanding significance*
> *of the various trends of the Modern Movement in architecture and*
> *town planning in the early part of the 20th century. Such influences*
> *were adapted to the cultural and climatic conditions of the place,*
> *as well as being integrated with local traditions.*

Almost a year later, in the spring of 2004, the UNESCO declaration was celebrated in Tel Aviv with a series of events, exhibitions, ceremonies and conferences. This was a culmination of a twenty-year historiographic campaign. The implications of this historiography go far beyond the architectural history of the Modern Movement or its (dis)integration with local traditions, and are rooted in the political history of the Middle East and the State of Israel. This history of Tel Aviv, presented for a moment as an architectural history, can be seen as a part of a wider process in which the physical shaping of Tel Aviv and its political and cultural construction are intertwined, and play a decisive role in the construction of the case, the alibi and the apologetics of the Jewish settlement across the country.

In that sense, exploring the story of this architectural history of Tel Aviv not only reveals some of the true political colours of both modernist and Israeli architecture, but also demonstrates how history can alter the geography.

'Tel Avivians walk around with their heads up … And now the whole world knows why!' advertising campaign for the UNESCO announcement celebrations. *Haaretz*

President Moshe Katsav congratulates Tel Aviv in the ceremony commending its declaration by UNESCO as a World Heritage Site. Fredric R. Mann Auditorium (Heichal Hatarbut), Tel Aviv, June 2004. Photograph: Nadav Harel

Book of Paper, Book of Stone

Cities and histories are constructed in a similar manner – always by the victor, always for the victor, and always according to the victors' record.

As with any given history, a city neither greets everyone equally nor satisfies everyone's desires. To physically alter a city and to write history takes a great deal of power, and power too is never distributed equally. Both the physical and cultural space of a city is always subject for challenge and struggle. It is likely that those who control the physical space often control the cultural space, and they are never those who have lost the battle over history. Those who have the power to shape the physical space to suit their needs can easily shape it to suit their values and narrative – not only to obtain for their values and narratives a hegemonic stature, but also in accordance with them, to reshape the city. We may formulate this simple state of things in the following paradoxical rule: a city is always a realization of the stories that it tells about itself.

One of the most common means of realizing the stories a city tells about itself is through conservation, and in its reverse, through demolition. Accordingly, whatever is done, not done or undone in the physical body of a city is also a form of historiographic deed because the decision to demolish an old building or to conserve an existing one defines what is fated to be forgotten and what is worthy of remembrance. A city may decide to highlight certain parts of its story deemed worthy of a particular mark by adding a commemorating plaque, erecting a monument, arranging a walking axis, by conservation, restoration or even the reconstruction of a particular building; it can also decide to turn the page, to send in the bulldozers and simply to

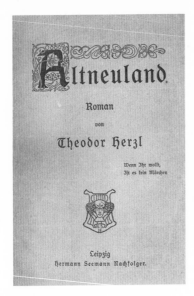

First a book, then a city. Theodor Herzl, *Altneuland*, the first edition, 1902, in German and 1904 in Hebrew.

forget. The relationship between the history of the city and its geography is a direct and necessary one – the geography of a city will always tend to conserve the stories to be remembered and to erase the stories to be forgotten.

Since the process of the physical building of a city is unavoidably interwoven with the processes of its cultural construction, control over the cultural construct of the city may be proven even more effective and profound than any other political governance or programme. Unlike other forms of authority, cultural hegemony is not only ubiquitous but hidden: it is defined by the unthinkable, suggested by the obvious, cloaked behind the *common sense* of the rulers and their subjects, and relayed through stories, legends and fables; the cultural construct of a city composes what we tend to designate and identify as 'normality'.

However, this normality may be challenged: a city can change merely by being seen or looked at differently, only because its story is told differently. Therefore, victors or vanquished, whoever wants to change a city must first change its story.

Born in the pages of a novel, Tel Aviv may be the only city in the world named after a book. Theodor Herzl's visionary novel *Altneuland* ('old-new country') was first published by Herman Seeman in Leipzig in 1902. The novel depicted an imaginary Eretz Israel/Palestine established according to Herzl's previous publication *Der Judenstaat* ('The Jewish State') (1896), in which he had detailed a total, utopian programme of a European liberal Jewish settlement in Palestine. The Hebrew translation appeared in Warsaw two years later under the title *Tel Aviv*, borrowed by the translator Nahum Sokolov from the book of Ezekiel (3: 15). It may not be a coincidence that Tel Aviv was at first a book and only later, a city[2] – after all, Zionism's two main goals were the revival of the Hebrew language and the building of the land of Israel. In that respect, Tel Aviv, a full-size realization of Herzl's oxymoron,[3] stands as living proof that books can erect buildings and establish cities.

To understand this transformation from paper to stone, it is necessary to start with the victors' architectural narrative of the 'White City', the urban legend served up whenever Tel Aviv speaks about itself. Occasionally it is delivered with a preface detailing the construction of Neve Tzedek, the first Hebrew neighbourhood *inside* Jaffa (the one-time Arab capital of Palestine which borders Tel Aviv but which now falls under its municipal jurisdiction). Sometimes an explanation of Ahuzat Bayit, Tel Aviv's first neighbourhood built *outside* Jaffa, is also added. But the standard blurb thereafter, the legend all inhabitants of the city should know, runs as follows:

In the 1920s, in a small town, in the Weimar social-democratic republic named Dessau, there was an architectural school called the Bauhaus. An avant-garde, international atmosphere dominated its teachings and its students. Among its alumni there were many German Jews and sons of Jewish pioneers from Palestine. The Bauhaus philosophy and International Style it advocated was built on the premise that it was possible to sculpt a better and more just world. In 1933, Adolf Hitler came to power in Germany and shut down the academy. Its teachers and students were forced to disperse in all directions. The Jews among them fled to 'Little Tel Aviv', 'a small city with few people',[4] filled with 'eclectic' architecture, where they revived the Bauhaus style and built themselves a White City.

The theme of a White City in Tel Aviv had already appeared prior to the International Style's arrival to Tel Aviv in early Hebrew novels such as Aharon Kabak's *The Riddle of the Land* (1915), Aaron Reuveni's *Last Ships* (1923) and Yaacov Pichmann's *Tel Aviv* (1927).[5] However, as an architectural narrative, this White City legend started to spread only when it received its official, 'scientific' and historical stamp of approval in the summer of 1984, with the exhibition entitled *White City* and curated by the architectural historian Michael Levin at the Tel Aviv Museum of Art.[6] In the context of Israeli culture, it was nothing short of a revelation. The exhibition succeeded in highlighting a coherent ensemble of high-quality modern architectural sites across Tel Aviv and championed a number of the architects who had been active in the area during the 1930s. These included, among others, Erich Mendelsohn, Richard Kauffmann, Dov Karmi, Karl Rubin, Zeev Rechter, Aryeh Sharon, Shmuel Mestechkin and Sam Barkai.

But the *White City* exhibition was much more than your average architectural exposition; it was the first concerted attempt to construct a history – *the* history – of Israeli architecture. Within this historiography, the White City of Tel Aviv and its composition were established as an inaugural point zero – the moment when Israeli architecture began. By default then, the *White City* exhibition itself became a defining moment in this story and today arguably stands as a, if not *the* central reference point for any debate on Israeli architecture.

It was a reflexive moment: the first time that Israeli architecture had spoken of itself and to itself – the first time it had demarcated its own 'history' and understood itself as history. The relevance of this instance, especially in light of the reigning historicist tendency within architectural circles since the 1960s, should not be disregarded. But the particularity of this moment in Israel was that while European architects harked back to the medieval city, to the renaissance and the baroque, or to vernacular and local traditions, the Israeli gaze towards the past rested on the very recent past, fixating on what would otherwise be classified as the most modernist moment in architecture.

In other words, the singularity of postmodernism in Israeli architecture lies not in its historicist gaze backwards but in the distinctive rebound which occurred as soon as it reached its modernist progressive moment naturally defined by it willingness to look forwards. If in Italy the postmodern architects longed for the baroque city or neo-classical architecture (which was longing for another past), Israeli postmodernism yearned for European modernism. Perhaps the best demonstration of this paradox is evident in the fact that the architect Shmuel Mestechkin, one of the few graduates of the Bauhaus school to make it to Israel, argued that no building deserves conservation, Bauhaus or otherwise.

Twenty years following the *White City* exhibition, it is impossible not to recognize Michael Levin's achievement. He succeeded not only in bringing the International Style architecture onto the Tel Avivian and Israeli architectural agendas, but also, as it turned out, promoted it on a global platform as well. Armed with only a small exhibition space and a thin catalogue with a short, modest text, Levin succeeded in doing what no Israeli curator had done before him. The *White City* exhibition went beyond profoundly influencing the work of architects or the taste of designers; much more significantly, it changed the way Tel Avivians looked at their own city, the way they introduced it to outsiders, and the way they have sought to shape it ever since. Unsurprisingly then, this mental transformation has had sweeping cultural, economical, social and political consequences.

Cover of the exhibition catalogue, *White City: The International Style Architecture in Israel, A Portrait of an Era*, curated by Michael Levin. Tel Aviv Museum of Art, 1984.

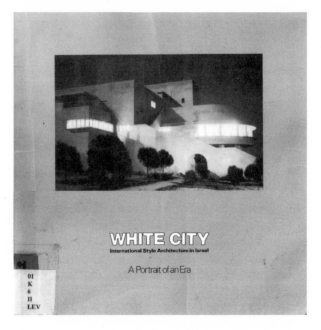

In the aftermath of the *White City* exhibition, things advanced almost by themselves, and it is likely that even Levin himself could not have foreseen what was going to happen. The story soon deviated from the cultural and academic circles, and made its way from the museum into the newspaper. Sparking immediate interest, popular architectural critic Esther Zandberg begun to dedicate a special place to Tel Aviv's own 'local International Style' of architecture in her regular *Environment* column, which had been appearing since the mid-1980s – first in *Ha'Ir*, a local, weekly Tel Avivian magazine, and later in *Haaretz*, the national daily. Under the title *White Box*, Zandberg published a series of articles in which she presented International Style buildings in Tel Aviv, explaining to the Tel Avivians how to look at them, why they are beautiful, what could be learnt from them, and why they should be preserved.

As the only architectural critic writing regularly in the Israeli daily press during this period, Zandberg had a unique role in promoting the values of International Style architecture to the larger public. Despite her familiarity with the history of architecture, she did not write as an 'architectural historian' so much as a chronicler. In this sense, her writing touched the present reality and was deliberately civilian, even 'feminine', in its analysis. Given the garish display of power being exercised by forces of business and state over organization of the country's environment during the 1980s imposing upon Tel Aviv a long series of megalomaniac, hallucinatory projects, there was perhaps no other alternative *but* to adopt such a sceptical, utilitarian stance and to confront great architectural visions with small, practical, pedestrian or household questions.

Intrinsically then, Zandberg portrayed the local International Style architecture as neither part of a great historical movement nor a revolutionary aesthetic, but primarily as a useful model for everyday city life, as a vehicle to promote values such as usability, economy, modesty, cleanliness, logic and common sense. Tel Aviv had only just begun to digest Israel's post-1967 war testosterone-pumped architecture and its huge megastructures, like the Atarim Piazza, the Dizengoff Center and the New Central Bus Station. With the corporate offensive of the 1990s already emerging, such 'effeminate' values were certainly needed.

Zandberg helped set the moral ground for the transformation of the White City narrative from being an academic chapter in an architectural journal into an integral part of the city's urban agenda. Her *White Box* expressed first and foremost the priority of a civilian and human scale and of traditional values of urbanity and domesticity. This humble standard of a

Tel Avivian house and a Tel Avivian street became the mark of a new liberal, ecological, civilian agenda that put the citizen up top as the first priority. Soon these civilian and domestic values of the White City became an integral part of the consensus and a factor not to be ignored. The traditional urbanism of Tel Aviv, which had been set in the 1930s and was based on streets and small apartment buildings, became Tel Aviv's default option, the logical and reasonable state of things not to be altered unless some credible and convincing explanation could be provided otherwise. Zandberg's conception of the White City became an effective tool for any civilian campaign against wild real estate initiatives. If it retained any ideological or utopian aspect, it was mainly expressed as a striving for normality and banality, as a longing for a Tel Avivian world where one could find a street, a grocery shop, a backyard or a staircase. In the context of the aggressive urbanism that governed the city throughout the 1960s and 1970s, the (re)birth of the White City in the 1980s could be regarded as the (re)invention of a Tel Avivian normality.

Conservation

With the onset of the 1990s, a new figure appeared in this story. The architect Nitza Szmuk, who turned the conservation of International Style buildings in Tel Aviv into her life's work, would become one of the most influential characters in solidifying the White City's story in the written and built reality.

Born in Tel Aviv, Szmuk returned in 1990 after studying and working in Italy, where she had specialized in conservation architecture. Soon after her arrival she was appointed the first chief conservation architect in the municipality of Tel Aviv. At this position, and over the course of the next decade, she initiated an ambitious project: Szmuk located, identified and classified buildings constructed in the 1930s, in order to set a list of buildings that were to be conserved. She drafted a conservation plan of Tel Aviv, in which she had defined the perimeter of the White City. She prepared and submitted the city's conservation plan (2650b), prescribed conservation regulations and technical specifications, and inspected projects and derogations.

But she did not stop there. She also extended her professional and administrative activity to engaging in the public and cultural spheres, adopting the role of Chief Spokesperson for the conservation of the local International Style architecture in Tel Aviv. She published her research in newspaper articles and a book,[7] led guided tours, and lectured in both public and professional forums. In the summer of 1994 she organized the 'Bauhaus

Nitza Metzger-Szmuk, *Dwelling on the Dunes*, English–French edition (Paris: Éditions de l'Eclat, 2004).

Book cover for Nitza Szmuk, *Houses from the Sand: International Style Architecture in Tel Aviv*. (Tel Aviv: Tel Aviv Development Fund and Ministry of Defense Publications, 1994).

Nitza Szmuk, *Bauhaus Tel Aviv: Plan of Conservation Sites in Tel Aviv*, photographs: Yitzhak Kelter. Bureau of Architects and Engineers in Israel, with the aid of the Tel Aviv Municipality Engineering Administration. Early 1990s (n.d.).

in Tel Aviv' festival, featuring a large international colloquium with leading international architects and a host of architectural, design and art exhibitions across the city centre. Towards the end of her tenure at the municipality, she initiated, formulated and submitted the White City's application for the UNESCO's World Heritage Sites. After the UNESCO declaration, Szmuk was one of the organizers of the celebration events in May–June 2004. On this occasion, she was unavoidably one of the event's main speakers and a guest of honour, with the curation of her *Dwelling on the Dunes* exhibition at the Helena Rubinstein Pavilion, in the Tel Aviv Museum of Art.

Whitened City

It created a buzz. The story of the White City and its Bauhaus Style percolated all sectors of Israeli public life and slowly became an integral, and then a natural part of Tel Avivian vocabulary. Despite the fact that no specific academic research associating the Bauhaus school to Tel Aviv or anything in reverse had actually been published yet, the two titles – 'Tel Aviv' and 'Bauhaus' – were mentioned synonymously in hundreds of thousands of articles, lectures, tours and conversations. Levin's exhibition catalogue soon seeped into wider public consciousness after its official validation from the political establishment. With this stamp of approval, the narrative was recycled back onto the streets themselves via real estate agents, renovation contractors, souvenir shops, billboards and even in notes on trees.

The Tel Avivians liked the story. Having lived in the shadow of Jaffa's rich four-thousand-year-old heritage for just under a century, they had suddenly, out of nowhere, been presented with their very own 'old city' and 'historic centre' (phrases which would pepper Mayor Ron Huldai's electoral campaign in 1998). It became instantly easier to differentiate the White City and its inhabitants from the grey rabble of the suburbs. But most persuasive of all was the fact that, overnight, these little white boxes had become goldmines; for all the highbrow cultural oratory, the crudest translation was a real estate boom born out of thin air.

The Bauhaus Style seemed to blend the spark of utopia with the patina of tradition, and fuse the radiant whiteness of the European avant-garde with a dazzling Mediterranean light. It enabled many Tel Avivians to conduct wealthy bourgeois lifestyles, and at the same time to expose a socialist and progressive façade, to take solace in the assurance that while their city was clearly grey and faded, it was *actually* white and clean; that although it was no more than a provincial Western outpost, it was as international as the International Style; and that although it was modern, it was historic. In this sense, the White City and the Bauhaus Style narratives with all their contradictions were a perfect extension of Herzl's own oxymoronic vision for Tel Aviv – *Altneuland*, the 'Old-New Country'.

During this same period throughout the 1980s, another, concurrent urban legend surrounding Sheinkin Street helped cement the White City/ Bauhaus Style mythology. Despite its location at the geographical epicentre of the White City area, the aura which enveloped Sheinkin Street during these years had been produced by the city's 'fringe'.[8] With the Tat-Rama art gallery and café as its hub – a space opened in 1984 by brothers Dani and Uri Dotan, a punk rock singer and an artist respectively – Sheinkin Street helped foster the perception that the White City was not only classical and European, but also a cosmopolitan, metropolitan mini-New York. Here too, the Bauhaus label suited everyone; the landlords and white-collar workers of the city's most celebrated street, Rothschild Boulevard, had no qualms about associating with the socialist vision behind the Bauhaus Style; while for the black-garbed youth on Sheinkin Street itself, Bauhaus were first and foremost a popular progressive 'new wave' British band who performed regularly at the 'Dan Cinema' rock venue. The municipality tapped into trendy, youthful vibrations around Sheinkin and re-branded the area the 'Heart of Tel Aviv' (*Lev Ha'Ir*). Armed with this new title, they then set about positioning the heart of Tel Aviv in the designated White City catchment zone, and a series of grand administrative and planning actions followed in order to shore up its economic and cultural relevancy.

With its establishment as a local hallmark, the Bauhaus Style began to infiltrate outside Israel's borders, this time as a national claim for an international recognition. Soliciting this approbation internationally involved a certain degree of emotional extortion, as if to say: 'You didn't want us in Weimar – please accept us in Tel Aviv.' After all, the Jews, the Weimar Republic and the Bauhaus were all victims of the Nazis.

In this somewhat perverse game, the German architectural community dutifully played their part, not least because they appeared pleased to rediscover themselves within a new Mediterranean decor. Many German academic commentators began to regard Tel Aviv as an extension of German cultural and architectural heritage or as some kind of 'New Dessau'. Over the next decade, multiple articles, books and exhibitions appeared in Germany, each retracing the Tel Aviv/Bauhaus connection and honouring those German-Jewish architects who had fled to Palestine.

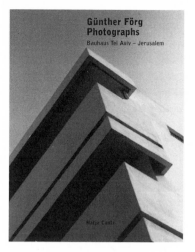

Klemens Klemmer, *Jewish Architects in Germany*, Stuttgart, 1998. On the cover: Erich Mendelsohn, Schocken Department Store, Stuttgart.

Cover of book: *Günther Förg Photographs: Bauhaus Tel Aviv – Jerusalem*, Tel Aviv 2002.

This use of the memory of World War II could be considered to be part of another similar and even more important tendency in the Israeli culture of the 1980s, that of the 'Second Generation'. The idea of a second generation of Holocaust survivors consisted of the late discovery of trauma among the descendants of the Jewish survivors of the Holocaust. As a cultural phenomenon, 'the second generation' syndrome appeared for the first time in 1986 in David Grossman's most successful novel *See Under: Love*.[9] This novel treated the image of the Holocaust through four different moments in the life of Momik, a child in Jerusalem, the son of Holocaust survivors, who is to become a novelist obsessed by the Jewish-Polish writer Bruno Schultz. *See Under: Love* granted Grossman not only the status of being the most important novelist of his generation, but also the stature of a saint. In contrast with the general attitude of repulsion, contempt and even disgust manifested by Israeli society towards the Holocaust survivors since the 1940s, the theme of the second generation was adopted by the ('white'/ Ashkenaz) Israeli public with enthusiasm. In the late 1980s, the theme of the second generation was developed by many Israeli artists and writers, and became a popular subject of academic works in psychology, education and social studies, enabling Israeli society to wallow in self-victimization while the Israeli army still occupied Lebanon, and in the Occupied Territories the First Intifada was breaking out.

Tel Aviv in the Tracks of the Bauhaus, an exhibition at the historic Haaretz building, curated by Rachel Sukman. Tel Aviv, 1994.

City with Concept: Bauhaus in Tel Aviv.
Stack of postcards, 1990s.

Bauhaus: Tel Aviv – Jerusalem
Photographs by Günther Förg,
Tel Aviv Museum of Art, 2003.

With the return of the Labour Party to government in 1992, the White City officially moved from the opposition backbenches into the corridors of power. Dovetailing with the new administration's aspirations to see Israel reaccepted into the family of nations after the Oslo Accords, the city's local International Style was seen as a means of propelling the country's integration into an increasingly globalized world. In 1994, the 'Bauhaus in Tel Aviv' festival signalled the beginning of a series of daring attempts to push this narrative into the international canon of modern architecture. It was allotted this crucial role in the national re-branding because in order to fully participate in the globalization process at hand, to become the next stop on David Bowie's or Madonna's world concert tour and to entice wealthy investors and tourists from abroad, it was necessary to transform Tel Aviv into a 'global city'. Membership of the existing exclusive club of cultural and economic capitals – made up of the likes of Berlin, London, Paris, New York and Toyko – necessarily demanded two things which, up until that point at least, Tel Aviv had been lacking: a corporate hub and a historic centre.

With the onset of the 1990s then, it was possible to witness the simultaneous erection of the industrial office towers of 'Ayalon City', a concrete-corporate sprawl engulfing the banks of Tel Aviv's Ayalon Highway, and the parallel hyperinflation of stories affirming the lasting historical pedigree of the White City. So intertwined did these two projects become, that they formed two items on the same municipal programme for functional zoning; consumption and offices would move to Ayalon City, housing and leisure would define the White City. Ayalon City eased the corporate demand for high-rise buildings in the White City and, in order to obtain something of a construction détente, various mechanisms and procedures were invented to develop an interdependence between the two. This included, for example, an agreement whereby the municipality was able to evacuate offices from its new 'historic centre' (either by encouraging promoters to prove tenants were using them for business or by expanding the building rights in new high rises on the other side of the Highway) and relocate them over to Ayalon in exchange for what were loosely defined as 'public tasks' – namely, the continued finance for the conservation of Bauhaus Style buildings in Tel Aviv's 'old city'.

Over the course the 1980s then the Bauhaus Style and White City mythology fully evolved from a seemingly inconsequential art exhibition into a cultural and economic lever, significantly transforming different localities across the city. At first these changes manifested themselves in the city's consciousness as opposed to its physicality, and were discernible in both the city's busy real estate market and the quotidian language heard in and around the heart of the city. Before long however, conservation plans were given precedence and a municipal body was formed to classify and supervise the preservation of selected structures. Things have come so far since Michael Levin's opening night that today, the White City of Tel Aviv has entered the pantheon of humanity for its achievements in the domain of architecture; with the support of its national community of architects and designers and a successful application to UNESCO, Tel Aviv has been declared a universal architectonic asset.

White Lies

However, the urban legend of the White City and its Bauhaus Style houses reveals some inaccuracies. Perhaps the most obvious surprise concerns the colour of the White City itself. As the French architect Jean Nouvel noted, with unmistakable disappointment, on his first visit to Tel Aviv in 1995: 'They told me that the city is white. Do you see white? I don't see any white.'[10] Indeed, Tel Aviv could legitimately be described as grey – pale at best, a dirty, dull monochrome at worst, but certainly not white. Moreover, the restoration programme implemented within the new city centre under Nitza Szmuk's supervision included the conservation of a rainbow array of different coloured buildings. So much so, it is doubtful if the area has ever been white or ever will be so again in the future.

Another contentious issue relates to the White City's location. The areas earmarked for maintenance hardly correspond with a municipal manifesto determined to preserve all buildings constructed in the International Style. According to the municipality's conservation programme, the geographical perimeters of the White City wind around Allenby Street, from Petach Tikva Road in the south-east to Jerusalem Beach in the north-west. According to this map, there are two zones that separate the White City from Jaffa, which despite their architectural irrelevance to the 'White City's narrative, have been practically annexed to the White City and to its historiographic rules. These include a mini-'Red City', made up of the Ahuzat Bayit, Shabazi and Neve Tzedek neighbourhoods (which are distinctive for their shingled roofs), and Kerem Hateimanim (the Yemenite quarter), which, as we shall see, is a district deserving of a status of its own. Glued together, they consti-tute the official White City and anything beyond these boundaries does not exist in the annals of Tel Aviv.

Thus, by design or otherwise, there is an almost complete overlap between those borders which delineate Tel Aviv's 'historical centre', its 'border of history', and the historical and conceptual borders which divide the municipality in half. Retracing each other perfectly, these lines run parallel to the city's now defunct train tracks, adjoining with Jaffa-Tel Aviv and Petach Tikva Roads, respectively. In doing so, they mark the boundary between orchards in the south and sandy beaches in the north, reinforcing the impression that Tel Aviv was originally born, *ex nihilo*, from the dunes.

And yet, just a glance at other Tel Avivian neighbourhoods constructed around the same time as the White City (or even earlier) – environs like Florentine, Neve Sha'anan, and Chlenov – reveals a wealth of diverse building styles, from the Colonial and Oriental, to the much sought-after International Style. If we acknowledge that the International Style of the 1930s was common *throughout* Tel Aviv then there appears no logical reason why these quarters have been pushed out from the boundaries of the anointed 'historical city'. Furthermore, having acted as the region's cosmopolitan centre up until 1948, Jaffa contains quite a considerable range of international and modern styles of architecture, which had not been included in the story of the White City.

It is important to acknowledge that almost all professional architectural accounts of Tel Aviv, Michael Levin's included, presented a reasonably balanced description of the varying influences at work during the 1930s. In fact, no one to this date has published a study of Tel Aviv focusing solely on its relationship with Bauhaus works or has produced any comparative examination arguing that the city's architectural origins lie solely in Dessau or Berlin and not, for example, with Le Corbusier in Paris or even more likely with Patrick Geddes in Bombay. Nevertheless, the Bauhaus legend is omnipresent in such commentaries and nearly always predominates, flowing through these texts like an underground current. In 1981, preceding the *White City* exhibition Michael Levin published an article in the prestigious Hebrew journal *Kav,* entitled 'The Architects Who Brought the Bauhaus to Israel',[11] in which he highlighted three Bauhaus graduates who were active in the 1930s: Aryeh Sharon, Shmuel Mestechkin and Munio Weinraub-Gitai.

In the catalogue which accompanied his show three years later, Levin tempered this concentration on Bauhaus-trained engineers and designers, referring to other influences on the city, such as: Le Corbusier, Erich Mendelsohn, the MOMA International Style exhibition curated by Philip Johnson and Henry-Russell Hitchcock, and even locally schooled architects, such as Dov Karmi and Zeev Rechter. In an effort to explain the public's attachment to the Bauhaus label, Levin advanced a dubious claim that its students constituted the largest group in the architectural community in Israel during the 1930s.[12] On the other hand, Nitza Szmuk in her book, *Houses from the Sand: International Style Architecture in Tel Aviv*, noted that the majority of the city's architects had studied in either France or Belgium, and not in Germany, but still managed to only discuss the Bauhaus school and its influence at length.[13]

All of the city's architectural chroniclers agree that, rightly or wrongly, the Bauhaus Style is the term most commonly used to describe the style of architecture produced in Tel Aviv during the 1930s. To his credit, Levin has always been more cautious than most in reminding his readers that the Bauhaus teachers unanimously opposed the use of the word 'style', let alone 'Bauhaus Style'.[14]

Such checks have done little however to quash wider usage of the term Bauhaus Style and its emergence, as if by popular demand, in local and folk historiography and theory. The weight given to this popular demand has tended to vary from one author to the next. Each tends to reveal, albeit in their own way, the extent to which they respond to the will of the people, often qualifying it in such a manner which enables them to ultimately adopt the story without actually endorsing it.

In the same spirit, the term Bauhaus Style appeared like an undisputable fact in the catalogue introductions which accompanied the *Dwelling on the Dunes* and *White City* exhibitions, written by the artist Dani Karavan and Director of the Tel Aviv Museum Marc Scheps respectively.[15] Nitza Szmuk was outstanding in this respect for being the only architectural commentator willing to take a risk and attempt to provide something akin to an explanation:

> *The Bauhaus was a pillar of the Modern Movement, advocating a rational approach to design and planning in combination with a social concept of architecture.*
> *In addition, the school insisted on the need for full control of the production process in order to arrive at architecture, furniture and product design characterized by clarity and simple, functional details.*
> *The Bauhaus was finally closed by the Nazis in 1933; the school's teaching staff and pupils left Germany, and disseminated its ideas in the United States, Britain, South America – and Palestine.*
> *Tel Avivians tend to single out the Bauhaus as the main source of influence for the Modern architecture that evolved in their city in the*

pre-State years. Terms like Functionalism, Rationalism or the International Style did not take root in the local vernacular, and the most common designation was – and remains – 'Tel Aviv Bauhaus'.[16]

Both Levin and Szmuk acknowledged that one of the few principles agreed on by all members of the Bauhaus school – an interdisciplinary centre and educational institution made up of a multitude of different individuals from varying backgrounds – was the accepted opposition to using the term 'style'. And yet, Tel Aviv stands alone as the only place in the world where a Bauhaus Style is said to exist.

No doubt equally irksome for Bauhaus teachers and alumni was the fact that the primary form of housing erected in Tel Aviv throughout the 1930s – the petit bourgeois three-story apartment building, rising over a ground floor of columns – did not conform with any of the concepts of social housing which formed the cornerstone of Bauhaus ideology, as taught by Bauhaus visionaries Walter Gropius and Mies van der Rohe. The overwhelming majority of buildings constructed within the White City area in the 1930s were what we would classify today as 'contractor buildings', or projects forced into construction by contractors looking to turn profit. Utopian social-housing-for-all did not really come into it. The exceptions to this rule were the workers' housing developments, which represented aberrant spaces at odds with the urban fabric of the city and its rhythm. In fact, the only replications of Bauhaus public housing to make it to Israel in the same form as those found in Dessau, Berlin and Stuttgart, came about in the 1950s and 1960s.

The official history of the White City mentions only four Israeli Bauhaus graduate architects.[17] The first was the architect Shlomo Bernstein, who spent two semesters there before returning to Tel Aviv, where he spent most of his professional life working for the municipality's Engineering Department. The second was Munio Weinraub-Gitai, who returned from the Bauhaus to work in Haifa and across northern Israel. There he produced a series of unique structures in the spirit of Mies van der Rohe that stood out prominently from the staple architectural designs being implemented nationwide at the time, and were notable for their focus on detail and construction technology. But such was his regional exclusivity that Szmuk makes no mention of Weinraub-Gitai in her book on Tel Aviv. The third Bauhaus student was Shmuel Mestechkin, who constructed several apartment buildings in Tel Aviv during this period (Szmuk only refers to one), but who was committed to his work for the Haganah, the underground resistance organization, and the kibbutz movement which was spread nationwide. The only local, Bauhaus-trained

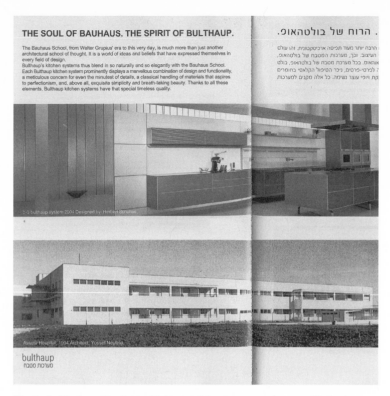

THE SOUL OF BAUHAUS. THE SPIRIT OF BULTHAUP.

The Bauhaus School, from Walter Grupius' era to this very day, is much more than just another architectural school of thought. It is a world of ideas and beliefs that have expressed themselves in every field of design.
Bulthaup's kitchen systems thus blend in so naturally and so elegantly with the Bauhaus School. Each Bulthaup kitchen system prominently displays a marvellous combination of design and functionality, a meticulous concern for even the minutest of details, a classical handling of materials that aspires to perfectionism, and, above all, exquisite simplicity and breath-taking beauty. Thanks to all these elements, Bulthaup kitchen systems have that special timeless quality.

. הרוח של בולטהאופ.

הרבה יותר מעוד תפיסה ארכיטקטונית. זהו עולם
התעצוב. וכך, מערכות המטבח של בולטהאופ,
אוחאום. בכל מערכת מטבח של בולטהאופ, בולט
לכרטי-פרטים, ניכר הטיפול הקלאסי בחומרים
קת ויופי עוצר נשימה. כל אלה מקנים למערכות

bulthaup
מערכות מטבח

'The Soul of Bauhaus. The Spirit of Bulthaup'. Advertisement and sponsorship for the White City events, in the exhibition catalogue for *Dwelling on the Dunes*, Summer 2004.

architect to conclusively leave his mark on Tel Aviv (and arguably on Israel as a whole) was Aryeh Sharon. In terms of shoring up Tel Aviv's urban legend, the major problem with Sharon is that, as a dedicated student of Bauhaus ideology, his straightforward and pragmatic structures have always been at odds with the stylized boxes which have come to be associated with Tel Aviv's Bauhaus Style. Sharon's most significant contributions to Tel Aviv in the 1930s, the workers' communal housing developments which were truly inspired by the Bauhaus teachings, were quite exceptional in their scales and programmes compared with the usual Tel Avivian apartment buildings. Tel Aviv's perceived Bauhaus Style, based largely on private enterprise and the free market, is contrary in both ethos and design to the way in which the Bauhaus ideology interprets social housing.

If there were any place in Israel where Sharon himself would consider the Bauhaus spirit to live on, it would almost certainly not be in Tel Aviv.

The ideal Tel Aviv in the *White City* exhibition catalogue: Engel House, planned by Zeev Rechter on the corner of Rothschild Boulevard and Mazeh Street, Tel Aviv, 1933. The Engel House is beyond doubt the most emblematic International Style building in Tel Aviv. Owing to the novelty of the raised building on pilotis, Tel Aviv became a 'town on pilotis' according to Aryeh Sharon. Few living people have seen the Engel House in its original state, as the necessary funds for its renovation were not allocated from the sums spent on advertising for the white city since Levin's exhibition in 1984, and the building had been in poor shape for years, neglected and disintegrated, with its ground floor closed up.

'The definition needs to be changed. Bauhaus is not a term nor a uniform institution,' said Aryeh Sharon in reply to Yigal Tumarkin's question concerning the Bauhaus architecture in Tel Aviv.

The cover of Aryeh Sharon's book, *Kibbutz+Bauhaus*, Stuttgart and Tel Aviv, 1976.

THE BAUHAUS MASTERS

Gropius: The name architect implies "Master of the Arts," one who will make gardens out of deserts. Kandinsky: Analytical drawing is training in exact seeing and exact rendering of the constructional elements of an object, its logical forces or tensions. Klee: Without intuition we can do a lot, but not all. In the beginning, one is concerned with the functions, later on, one learns to look behind the facade, to grasp the root of things, to dig down, to uncover, to analyse. Moholy: Spatial design is an interweaving of shapes into well-defined space relationships; shapes, which represent the fluctuating play of tensions and forces. Albers: From the study of materials we learn which qualities are important: harmony of balance, free or measured rhythm, central or peripheral emphasis. Students and teachers learn from each other continually, otherwise teaching is a sour bread. Breuer: Let our dwelling have the imprint of the owner's character. The architect, creates only half a dwelling; the man, who lives in it, the other half. Hannes Meyer: The architect must be backed by the scientist, the sociologist, and the psychologist. Architecture is not the individual emotional activity of an artist. Building is a collective activity. Hans Wittwer: He never "talked" architecture — but was a sensitive designer and a remarkable architect. Mies: Less is more.

DIE MEISTER DES BAUHAUSES

Gropius: Der Begriff „Architekt" bedeutet „Meister der Künste"; einer, der Wüsten in Gärten verwandelt. Kandinsky: Analytisches Zeichnen übt akkurates Sehen und exakte Wiedergabe der Elemente eines Gegenstandes — seiner logischen Kräfte oder Spannungen. Klee: Ohne Intuition sind wir zu vielem, aber nicht zu allem fähig. Zunächst befassen wir uns mit den Funktionen. Später lernen wir, hinter die Fassade zu sehen, tiefer zu schürfen, aufzudecken, zu analysieren. Moholy: Raumentwurf ist eine Verflechtung von Formen, die ein Wechselspiel von Spannungen und Kräften darstellen. Albers: Die Materialstudie lehrt uns, welche formellen Eigenschaften wichtig sind: Harmonischer Ausgleich, freier oder geregelter Rhythmus, Betonung des Mittelpunktes oder der Peripherie. Schüler und Lehrer lernen ständig voneinander; sonst wäre Unterrichten ein sauer verdientes Brot. Breuer: Unsere Wohnungen sollen der Persönlichkeit der Bewohner entsprechen. Der Architekt schafft eine Wohnung nur zur Hälfte; der Mensch, der in ihr lebt, schafft die andere Hälfte. Hannes Meyer: Der Architekt muß vom Wissenschaftler, Soziologen und Psychologen unterstüzt werden. Architektur ist nicht das individuelle, emotionelle Wirken eines Künstlers — Bauen ist ein kollektiver Vorgang. Hans Wittwer: Er sprach niemals über Architektur — war aber ein feinfühliger und bemerkenswerter Architekt. Mies: Weniger ist mehr.

LES MAITRES DU BAUHAUS

Gropius: Architecte signifie "Maître des arts", un homme qui transforme des déserts en jardins. Kandinsky: le dessin analytique est une initiation à l'art de l'observation et du rendu précis des éléments constructionnels d'un objet, de ses formes et de ses tensions. Klee: On peut faire beaucoup — mais pas tout — sans intuition. En premier lieu, nous sommes préoccupés par les fonctions; puis nous apprenons à chercher ce qui se cache derrière la façade, à fouiller, déceler, analyser. Moholy: Le dessin spatial est un réseau de formes illustrant le jeu alternant des tensions et des forces. Albers: L'étude des matériaux nous apprend à saisir ce qui fait leurs qualités: harmonie de l'équilibre, rythme libre ou mesuré, importance de l'élément central ou périphérique. Maîtres et disciples apprennent continuellement les uns des autres; lorsqu'il en est autrement, l'enseignement est un pain moisi. Breuer: La maison ne devrait que refléter la personnalité de son propriétaire. L'architecte ne crée que la moitié de la maison; l'homme qui y vit en modèle la seconde moitié. Hannes Meyer: L'architecte doit être épaulé par le savant, le sociologue et le psychologue. L'architecture ne consiste pas en la démarche émotive d'un artiste: la construction est une oeuvre collective. Hans Wittwer: Il ne "discutait" jamais architecture — il n'en était pas moins un artiste subtil et un architecte remarquable. Mies: Moins signifie plus.

Albers   Schepper   Muche   Moholy   Bayer   Schmidt   Gropius   Breuer   Kandinsky   Klee   Feininger   Gunda Stölzl   Schlemmer

34

The Bauhaus School was famed for its teachers rather than its students. The Bauhaus School teachers as they appear in Aryeh Sharon's book *Kibbutz+Bauhaus*, (from left): Albers, Schepper, Muche, Moholy-Nagy, Bayer, Schmidt, Gropius, Breuer, Kandinsky, Klee, Feininger, Gunta Stölzl, Schlemmer. None of them ever set foot in the Holy Land, of course.

Aryeh Sharon's student card at the Bauhaus School. In all of Israel, only four architects had such a card. From Aryeh Sharon's *Kibbutz+Bauhaus*.

Aryeh Sharon, worker's housing developments in Frug Street, Tel Aviv, 1935.
Aryeh Sharon's *Kibbutz+Bauhaus*.

Staunchly loyal to the school's philosophy, Sharon tellingly chose to title his autobiography *Kibbutz + Bauhaus*. He confirmed his opinions on the subject in an interview with the artist Yigal Tumarkin, published in *Kav* magazine in 1981.

Tumarkin began by asking: 'What is the Bauhaus in Tel Aviv? I mean the Bauhaus architecture that you brought as a style, say the "workers' housing" or the buildings on Rupin Street. I refer the question to you as the chief spokesman of the Bauhaus in Tel Aviv.' The 'chief spokesman of the Bauhaus in Tel Aviv' was admirably direct in his answer: 'The definition may need changing. Why? Because Bauhaus is neither a concept, nor a uniform institution.'[18] In what may be the cleanest demonstration of the difference between the way in which the Bauhaus is perceived and the way in which Aryeh Sharon himself and other Bauhaus graduates remembered it, the architect did not refer to the institution in the accepted manner by adding the prefix 'the' to its name ('the Bauhaus', 'the Bauhaus Style'), but rather used it as a proper noun.

Following their return from Germany, Bernstein, Weinraub-Gitai, Mestechkin and Sharon never formed an association, they never worked as a group and they never promoted themselves as a collective, despite the identical (and respected) stamp they shared on their diplomas. The appreciation of their contribution to Israeli architecture was made upon the work of each of them separately.

Moreover, according to the White City's historiography, the times of the Bauhaus Style ended in the late 1930s with the onset of World War II and a downturn in the economy in Palestine. However, the majority of works produced by these architects were completed *after* the war and in the years that followed the founding of the State of Israel, and were unconnected with the Bauhaus school or what Tel Avivians have come to associate with the aesthetics of the Bauhaus Style. The only architect who pledged a personal connection to Bauhaus was Aryeh Sharon, but he associated it more with a philosophical way of life which tied in with his experiences of communal living on a kibbutz. Indeed, to stress some kind of iron bond between Bauhaus the architectural philosophy and Tel Aviv the city seems rash, not least because it means culling 50 per cent of those Bauhaus graduates working in Israel in the 1930s from the White City story.

Round Corners

The jump then, from the biographies and professional résumés of these four Israeli Bauhaus graduates to the widely accepted theorem linking Tel Aviv with a Bauhaus Style, was a necessarily gargantuan one. But how, and why, was it made at all? Of the many architectural philosophies and design influences prevalent throughout Tel Aviv, why was Bauhaus exclusively chosen to brand the city?

Although the Bauhaus legend spread slowly as a rumour from the 1950s (largely due to the relevancy and popularity of Aryeh Sharon), the White City and the Bauhaus style mythologies should be seen, above all else, as a reflection of the time and place in which they were conceived: the cultural and political constellation of the State of Israel in the 1980s.

The story started to force its way onto the cultural agenda in the wake of the 1977 elections. With the country's leadership changing hands for the first time since the birth of the state, Israel's Labour elite suddenly found themselves usurped from their historical role as administrators of the Zionist project. Menachem Begin's new right-wing Likud government and the legitimization of the societal periphery were perceived by the veteran ruling elite as an increasing cultural and moral threat.

Mirroring the radical changes that Prime Minister Begin made to Israel's foreign policy upon taking office – peace with Egypt and, later, war with Lebanon – the new government's domestic policies were similarly characterized by a desire to turn the old order on its head. This onslaught began almost immediately with a dramatic course of economic liberalization, reshaping the country in one fell swoop and crippling the centralized economy of the Histadrut, the workers' union. But Begin also turned his attention to the organization of Israeli space which, up until that point, had been sculpted according to the needs and values of the Labour movement in power.

Presenting a new spatial manifesto for the radical-right, which stood in absolute opposition to positions promoted under previous governments, Begin directed settlement efforts away from the Jezreel and Jordan Valleys (both traditional Labour outposts) and towards the mountains.[19] On a smaller, though no less relevant, scale he encouraged two conspicuous building schemes – first, the rehabilitation of housing projects erected during the first three decades of the State of Israel, and second, the introduction of the 'Build Your Own House' programme, which enabled ordinary citizens to construct their own houses on new plots of land. The 'Neighbourhood Rehabilitation' and the 'Build Your Own House' projects were actually first floated by the Labour government in the early 1970s, but became central tenets of Begin's housing and development policy. While the Neighbourhood Rehabilitation project looked to repair damaged or worn-out existing public housing projects with added ornamentation and by painting the exposed concrete façades with shiny happy colours, the other programme proved a real lever for agrarian revolution. The Build Your Own House project enabled any citizen to lease land in order to build a private house according to one's own taste and means. Until then, the land regime and the real estate market had been strictly regulated by those centralized structures and organizations associated with Labour governments. Such a division of power had necessarily created a social system whereby one's link to the land was dependent on one's affinity with the ruling party. The distribution of land for housing (which in most cases meant land which had been confiscated from its original Palestinian owners during the war of 1948–49, and 'legally' transferred into state ownership via the Absentees' Property Law of 1950) had traditionally gone to high-ranking military officers and senior civilian staff. The Build Your Own House project enabled first-time access to the land for those populations who had, until this point, been confined to apartment blocks in massive multi-storey public housing projects and had been excluded from the land system. Unsurprisingly, the first Build Your Own House suburban projects which started to emerge at the beginning of the

1980s inaugurated new standards of bad taste and were characterized by an architectural cacophony, a mishmash of styles, a baroque of oriental images and Mediterranean colours.

It was in this social and cultural context that in 1980, four years before the *White City* exhibition, the Tel Aviv Museum of Art held an exhibition dedicated to the Bauhaus school, exploring the institution's departments and showcasing their designs and methodologies. The exhibition name-checked the few Jewish students educated there (beside the four Israeli architects already noted) but was appreciative of the fact that the establishment was exceptional for its teaching staff, none of whom were Jewish or had set foot in the Promised Land.

One immediate consequence of this exhibition was a return to vogue for 'Chaim', a particular font which had been created in 1925 by the designer Jan (Yacov Chaim) LeWitt.[20] After being (re)featuring in this display, its popularity soared and Chaim became the most widely used typeface in Israeli print and design throughout the 1980s – it became known in the 1980s mainly for its use in the logo of the Peace Now movement by one of Israel's leading graphic artists of the younger generation, David Tartakover. This revival also prompted a retrospective show curated by Tartakover at the Tel Aviv Museum of Art for Frantz Kraus, another modernist graphic artist brought back from the 1930s.

Beside any general interest in European Jewish modernist nostalgia for the 1930s, the pertinence of these two exhibitions – the Bauhaus and the Kraus – was that they implicitly provided a rhetorical infrastructure, a sentimental atmosphere and a historical background for the *White City* exposition to come. They were notable for alluding to a new narrative – one which tapped into a local Israeli identity specific to the 1930s, whose roots were firmly set in European progressive modernism. The sudden urgency for this retroactive process of identity construction arose directly because, at least until the rise to power of Menachem Begin and his right-wing Likud Party in 1977, Israeli identity had been taken for granted. Begin's legitimization of the 'Other Israel' – that particular section of Jewish-Israeli society which had always been seen, and treated, as secondary – challenged the white, European monopoly. There was a feeling that the old Labour elite had to recreate itself again socially and culturally as a response to these political transformations. This led the old guard to seek refuge in the drama of Dessau's 'missed utopia', investing in it as an allegory of the Zionist dream they believed had gone awry since Likud had come to power.[21]

In this sense, gazing west towards Dessau actually provided some form of solace; it enabled those who had always dominated Israeli society, but who now felt disinherited of their Israeliness, the opportunity to console themselves in the warm embrace of a familiar white, European identity. In opposition to 'Golden Jerusalem', the preordained capital of Begin's new traditionalist and faith-driven Greater Israel, the White City became the elected headquarters of 'Good Old Eretz Israel' (Good Old Land of Israel). Among members of this latter collective, the stoic purity of the Bauhaus Style was seen as representative and an extension of the values of order and rationality they preached, and a rebuke to the amorphous black chaos inherent in the non-canonical baroque style of the Neighbourhood Rehabilitation and Build Your Own House projects, as promoted by Begin.

That it was Dessau of Germany, specifically, which became a central reference point in the political sparring between 'whites' and 'blacks', between the European centre and the North African periphery, was not entirely surprising. It reflected the commonplace faith put in Ashkenazi social hierarchies and the status of Yekkes (German Jews) at the top of the ladder.[22] This particular nationality of Jews had always been given the stamp of cultural noblesse in Israel – not solely because the Jewish region of Ashkenaz in Germany had been the historical and geographical origin of all Ashkenazi Jews, but because of a desire to paint Israeli Ashkenazim as a continuation of the modern, intellectual and secular tradition of German Jewry, synonymous with the age of Enlightenment. This was considered a much worthier heritage to have than, for example, one which linked Israelis back to the poverty, traditionalism and religious fervour of Polish Jewry.[23] This phenomenon of projecting the cultural and moral balance of power within the European marketplace of identities had been set down in Israeli-Ashkenazi folklore, in which staple characters included the Polish aunt as a German 'wannabe' and the Romanian masquerading as a Russian.

The elasticity of these diasporan Jewish identities stems from the complexity of the European frontiers, but also from the movement and migration of Jews between these territories. The preference for Central European ancestry (German or Austrian) among emancipated members of the Jewish elite, rather than an Eastern European identity, can be seen as a reflection of the region's perceived cultural hegemony. Accordingly, members of Israel's cultural elite formed their identities and lifestyles around the cultural norms of Central Europe and North America. The affinity to Central Europe also had real historical roots, since in many cases Jews based in Eastern Europe were agents and representatives of Central European culture and economy. This age-old 'diversion' of identities, from Eastern to Central Europe, accompanied the

Zionist movement from the days of Herzl himself, who, despite being raised in Budapest until the age of eighteen, was educated in German and rejected with contempt any sign of his Hungarian identity or language.[24]

Just as these pseudo-geographical references have crept into, and manipulated, Israeli social and cultural mores, so too did they shape the narrative Tel Aviv wrote for itself in the 1980s about its 1930s architecture. Bauhaus Style structures were presented as strictly Central European in comparison with the eclectic, Orientalist architecture of the 1920s, which commentators like Nitza Szmuk depicted as Eastern European.[25] This, despite the fact that Orientalism by definition is an occidental term routed in the West European colonial heritage, that nowhere else in the world was there an example of Eastern European colonial architecture to refer to, and that it was indisputable that the central figures in the eclectic oriental architecture of the 1920s (Alexander Brewald, for example) were of German origin.

Eastern European elements in Tel Aviv's architecture of the 1920s were introduced in a similar way to Oriental influences: as something of a parody. The poet David Shimonovitz tapped into this distaste, scornfully describing Tel Aviv in its first decade as 'a mixture between Berdichev and Baghdad'.[26] The city's modern architecture, on the other hand, was sold as distinctly, unequivocally Central European. With this in mind, it is worth noting that

'A mixture of Berdichev and Baghdad' wrote the poet David Shimonovitz. The small Tel Aviv as a Mediterranean *shtetl*. From the exhibition catalogue for *Tel Aviv in Photographs: The First Decade*, curated by Ziva Sochovolsky and Batya Carmiel. Eretz Israel Museum, Tel Aviv, 1990.

even *after* the rediscovery of Eastern European modern architecture in the wake of the dissolution of the Eastern European bloc, there were no attempts to associate the International Style of architecture in Tel Aviv with the Eastern European style of Modernist architecture.

It is also important to remember that this same Eurocentric hierarchy – which placed Europe in the centre, and the centre of Europe in the centre of this centre – was not confined to Jewish architects in Palestine, and later Israel; the same concentration on Central Europe and dual disregard of other countries and continents was apparent in New York at the Museum of Modern Art's *The International Style* exhibition in 1932. However, as far as we are concerned with the establishment of a Eurocentric and Germanophile hegemony, in Israel this received double justification – on one hand as part of the balance of power between Jewish diasporas in Central and Eastern Europe, and on the other hand, as part of the balance of power between diasporas of modern architecture in Europe and America.

Theoretically, according to this stress on a Central European orientation, it would have been possible to tie Tel Aviv's local International Style with the Berlin architect Erich Mendelsohn. Active in Palestine on and off between 1924 and 1939, Mendelsohn also worked with architects like Karl Rubin and Paul Engelman, who both collaborated with him in his Berlin office before moving to Palestine. His influence on local Tel Avivian architecture was therefore both direct and indirect, and the dynamic forms and round corners which have come to characterize the city's local International Style are arguably more likely to have stemmed from his Expressionist approach than any other potential modernist influences, Bauhaus included.

And yet, despite the importance of his projects in Palestine and the fact that of all the architects active in the country during the 1930s he was the only one to gain international recognition, Mendelsohn and his contribution have been considerably downplayed. Michael Levin's *White City* catalogue was good enough to admit that he was a source of influence on the International Style of architecture in Israel but more widely he has been considered neither a visionary nor a champion of its production. There are three main reasons for Mendelsohn's relative absence from Israeli historiography of its International Style. First, he was the Schoken family architect in both Europe and Palestine, and maybe more than any other European designer of his generation was identified with capital rather than progressive, social-change programmes. This necessarily meant that neither Mendelsohn nor his architecture could ever be lauded or mobilized for Zionism's communal agenda in quite the same way that the Bauhaus and its ideology

Erich Mendelsohn: Schocken Department Store, Chemnitz, Germany. 1928–1930
STARTLING RIBBON WINDOWS MADE POSSIBLE BY CANTILEVER CONSTRUCTION. WALL
SURFACED WITH STONE PLAQUES. THE SET-BACKS REQUIRED BY BUILDING LAWS GIVE
AN UNFORTUNATE STEPPED EFFECT, AS IN NEW YORK SKYSCRAPERS.

Of all the architects to work in Israel in the 1960s, Erich Mendelsohn
was the only one who had gained international recognition at the time.
Erich Mendelsohn, Schocken Department Store, Chemnitz, Germany, 1928–1930.
From the exhibition catalogue for *The International Style*, curated by Henry-Russell
Hitchcock and Philip Johnson. Museum of Modern Art, New York, 1932.

could, and was. Second, he was not really active in Tel Aviv and the authorship
of the only project attributed to him, the Max Fine Technical School, is still
contested today. Third and most important was that even though he was
present in Palestine throughout the 1930s, he chose to leave the moment
work dried up, immigrating first to Britain and then to the United States.
In 1980s Israel, that was more than enough to disqualify him. During this
latter period, former prime minister Yitzhak Rabin's expression 'waste of
weaklings' (used to designate those Israelis who had emigrated *from* Israel)
was still raw in the Israeli psyche, and it was inconceivable at the time that a
yored (descender) would also be cast as a national hero.[27]

Another historiographic pathway left unexplored was the French
architectural connection to the city, which is no less relevant to Tel Aviv
than German or Austrian influences. It is a long-standing association,
nourished by Jewish architects like Dov Karmi and Benjamin Ankstein, who
practised in Palestine after graduating from Belgian academies, and Zeev

Rechter[28] and Sam Barkai,[29] who moved between their work in Palestine and studies in France, where they developed strong relationships with Paris and Le Corbusier respectively. It was none other than elected Bauhaus patron and graduate Aryeh Sharon who argued that the greatest influence on Tel Aviv has always been Le Corbusier, pointing specifically to numerous structures built '*sur pilotis*'[30] and entitling the chapter on Tel Aviv in his professional autobiography 'A Town on Pilotis'.[31]

Beside the many stylistic similarities between works produced by local architects such as Rechter, Barkai and Karmi, and Le Corbusier himself, the French International Style was also heavily influenced by Mediterranean and North African sources, and one can detect an underlying resemblance between Tel Aviv and Algiers. Both were attempts to found new, modern

From the *White City* catalogue: Sam Barkai, Katz House, Megido Street, Tel Aviv, 1935. (Demolished).

68-67 Shmuel (Sam) Barkai. Home of Bat Sheva and Itzhak Katz, Megido Street, Tel Aviv, 1935 (demolished).
68 Entrance Hall
69 Living Room
70 Plan

European cities overlooking or beside what were perceived as ancient, crumbling Arab dwellings. Both were exercises in settler colonialism and both were called White Cities. It seems likely that these ties were neglected in light of the unpopularity of France since Charles de Gaulle placed an embargo on military supplies to Israel in 1967, just before the Six Day War.[32] This sense of disapprobation then turned into veritable Francophobia with the pro-Arab presidencies of Pompidou, Giscard d'Estaing, and Mitterrand which followed.

To these omissions in Tel Aviv's architectural narrative, one might add the distinct lack of reference made to the modern *Palestinian* architecture produced during the 1930s or, stranger still within this context, the absence of certain local *Jewish* constructors. Among others, these include Haim Casdan, who was born in Jaffa in the first decade of the twentieth century; he studied architecture in Brussels and worked across the Middle East, predominately in Egypt and Lebanon. The most notable absentee however, is the otherwise legendary Yosef Eliyahu Chelouche; born and bred in Jaffa, he performed a series of industrial espionage operations across Egyptian borders in order to bring back to Palestine the secrets of silicate bricking and Egyptian Freemasonry.[33]

These omissions are odd in light of the official historiography and its tendency to brand Tel Aviv's International Style as expressly 'local' – as an extension of its European roots but still an unprecedented first chapter in the *Israeli* architectural tradition. While there may be some truth to this claim, there is also a strong argument to suggest that Jewish settlement in the territories of Israel/Palestine over the last century has spawned not one but two architectural traditions: *Eretz-Israeli Architecture* and *Israeli Adrichalut*.[34] *Eretz-Israeli Architecture* refers to architecture created by European Jews in Palestine *before* the declaration of the State of Israel; *Israeli Adrichalut* refers to architecture created by Hebrew-speaking Jews in the same territory *after* the declaration of the State of Israel. The distinction between these two traditions is chronological and political, but also clearly linguistic: the evolution from a foreign language to another demanded a swift shift from a European architectural culture to a fresh and fledgling Hebrew model. While the European-born or trained *architect* was supposed to be, as Adolf Loos noted, a 'builder who learned Latin', the Israeli-born or Technion-trained *adrichal* not only has never heard a word of Latin, but also, in most cases, has never opened a book. In this sense, the claim that the Bauhaus Style is a first chapter of an *Israeli Adrichalut* might be seemed as an appropriation of a foreign tradition, very often created by people who did not speak Hebrew at all.

Indeed, references to the White City and its association with Tel Aviv did not first appear in the 1930s at the time when the localized International Style buildings were being erected. Nor did the phrase unexpectedly break through into the Israeli lexicon when the same buildings were rediscovered by Michael Levin in the 1980s. The White City theme had previously appeared in various forms in Tel Aviv's early literature *prior* to the arrival of the International Style buildings – it can be found in Aharon Kabak's *The Riddle of the Land* (1915), Aaron Reuveni's *The Last Ships* (1923) and Yaacov Pichmann's *Tel Aviv* (1927).[36] After a brief lull, the theme resurfaced again during the war years in Aharon Ever-Hadani's *War Cycle* (1938) and Asher Barash's *Like a Besieged City* (1945).[37]

But it took music to really plant the imagery of the White City in the Tel Avivian subconscious. In 1960, twenty-four years before Levin's exhibition, the acclaimed Israeli songwriter Naomi Shemer released a song called 'White City'.[38] The song was included in Arik Einstein's first solo mini-album.[39]

White City

From the froth of a wave and a cloud
I built myself a white city
Stormy, fluid, beautiful

As a clean morning comes, a window opens
And you, girl, are looking at it
Just like a dove before its flight

Because the dawn and the light have come
And my city is out to commerce
And it is loaded
Heavily

Here is my city, big as the light
And you are a grey grain of dust
A grain of dust attached
To its scarf

From the froth of a wave and a cloud

I built myself a white city
Stormy, fluid, beautiful

As a soft evening comes, a window opens
And you, girl, are looking at it
Just like a queen waiting for her champion

Because the black night has come
And my city is illuminated all around
And its lights are a necklace
On your neck

Here is my big city at night
And it is a dark and huge palace
And my girl reigns in it
Until tomorrow.

Naomi Shemer[40]

Coinciding with Michael Levin's exhibition *White City*, the song resurfaced in 1984 when Arik Einstein re-released it on his LP *Nostalgia*,[41] the fifth album of his 'Good Old Eretz Israel' series, in which he crooned various Israeli oldies and classics. This version of the song quickly became Tel Aviv's unofficial anthem and the soundtrack to all municipal events – not least at each and every White City celebration from the 1980s up until the presesnt day.[42] The fortunate timing of the song's re-emergence, in almost perfect tandem with the *White City* show, just demonstrated the strong ties between those two images: the Good Old Eretz Israel and the White City. The encounter between these two nostalgias, one a yearning for the White City and the European modernist avant-garde, and the other a harking back to Good Old Eretz Israel and the glory years of the national Zionist Project under successive Labour leaderships, is of considerable significance because it reunites two cultures which were allegedly, theoretically opposite: Israel's official culture and Israeli counter-culture.

One of the best expressions of this wider union, with all its various overlapping tensions and contradictions, can be found in the duality which has come to define Arik Einstein's own career. As a military entertainment veteran, Einstein continued to promote the values of Good Old Eretz Israel, those official cultural maxims extolled by the reigning establishment in the decades immediately following the creation of the State of Israel. At the same time, however, he harnessed a reputation as a Tel Avivian counter-cultural icon through his work as a leading member of the 'Lul' (Chicken-Coop) ensemble – a collective of young Tel Avivian artists, cinematographers and musicians active throughout the 1970s.[43] Such was his effortless movement between establishment and 'fringe', Einstein sandwiched his first album in the 'Good Old Eretz Israel' series between a leading role in Uri Zohar's innovative film *Peeping Toms* and his heavy punk-rock album, *Drive Slowly*. Far from being alone in straddling these two worlds, much the same could be said of other heroes of Israeli popular culture, such as Dan Ben-Amotz and Haim Hefer – both of whom have been assigned prominent populist and patriotic roles in 1948 military folklore but who have also adopted counter-cultural, non-conformist lifestyles.

This remains one of the most extraordinary features of Israeli culture. In other societies, counter-cultural revolution is characterized, by definition, as dialectic aspirations to not only transgress the official culture, but to negate it. In Israel, the two paradoxically co-exist in harmony. It would be wrong to see this as indicative of a state of indecision or simply as a lazy case of 'sitting on the fence' (the title of Einstein's 1982 album). More accurately, this encapsulates simultaneous action in both fields – it is nearer 'one foot here, one foot there', than 'neither here nor there'. No one describes this modality better than Einstein himself who, in another album produced during the 1980s (*Fragile*, 1983), explains how in Israel 'one hand does it all'.

This inherent complicity between official and counter-cultures has enabled the mobilization of particular phenomena, personalities and ideas that would have undoubtedly been forced to the social and cultural margins of other Western societies. Early examples of this pattern can be found in Max Brod's cultural activity as a Zionist *politruk* during the 1940s or the establishment of an artists' colony on the remains of the Palestinian village of Ein Hod, an exercise initiated by the architect and painter Marcel Janco, one of the founders of the Dada Movement.[44] Indeed, Zionism has often systematically utilized the most contemporary and radical doctrines of the day to shape its living environment – it employed the International Style of architecture to settle Tel Aviv and its surrounding areas, manipulated the town models of Le Corbusier as a means of dispersing fresh immigration in the 1950s and 1960s, and utilized postmodernist doctrines in the 1970s in order to entrench a Jewish majority in the Old City of Jerusalem.

A simple explanation for this outstanding feature in both popular and high Israeli culture lies, like so many answers to questions regarding Israeli society, in the country's militaristic roots. Both those official, 'establishment' heroes – politicians and generals such as Moshe Dayan, Yitzhak Rabin and Ariel Sharon – and their counter-cultural and 'alternative' equivalents – the likes of writer Dan Ben-Amotz,[45] or the poet Haim Hefer[46] – served together during their formative years in the Palmach, the elite unit of the Haganah, Israel's pre-state paramilitary organization. From the country's conception then these two strands of Israeli culture have lived side-by-side, nurturing and nourishing each other, following after each other like the months in a calendar year; Dan Ben-Amotz's non-conformism can be seen as a natural extension of Yitzhak Sadeh's own sense of mischievousness,[47] the latter having been the former's commander in the Palmach; Arik Einstein's and Uri Zohar's successful alternative careers can be seen as a continuation of their service in the Nahal[48] military entertainment company where they learnt and crafted their trade, and where Dani Karavan who later became one of the White City's main spokespersons started as a set designer. If not a brotherhood of arms, the links between them are often built on simple blood relations – like those between Shmuel Dayan, his son Moshe Dayan, and other prominent family members Assi Dayan, and Yehonatan and Aviv Gefen – but the common denominator is an identity defined by biography, class and ethnicity.[49] Both sets of national luminaries share the same language and speak in the same flat, 'accentless' tones of the Israeli natives.

It may well be that this harmony between those two cultures is an essential primordial condition for any cultural activity in Israel, as its very existence is structured under a sovereignty that by definition is exclusively Jewish, in its use of the Hebrew language and by the mere fact that it is taking place within the State of Israel.[50] It may well be that this very fact dissolves any possibility of a true, independent, critical or radical discourse in the State of Israel.

In the encounter between the two nostalgias, it would be interesting to see how the nostalgia for Good Old Eretz Israel dismantles the avant-garde radicalism and neutralizes it, and kidnaps it for the sake of the Zionist left. The more profound aspect of these relationships displays the construction not only of Israeli culture but also that of Israeli identity. The ramifications of this interaction have not only shaped Israeli culture but have also had a profound effect on the construction of Israeli identity. Long before the White City was seen as European, avant-garde and radical, and had developed its 'ties' to the International Style or Bauhaus school at Dessau, there was Naomi Shemer and Arik Einstein's 'White City'. And for the national hymn writer and the counter-cultural hero, the White City was the capital of Good Old Eretz Israel.

The fact that Good Old Eretz Israel has never really existed and could never legitimately represent the country as a whole was immaterial. Conjured up in (and specifically for) the 1970s and 1980s, this dreamy, idyllic re-imagining of the nation endorsed a selective relationship with the past and mapped it out onto the country's geography accordingly. With the White City at its epicentre, the imagined landscape of Good Old Eretz Israel system-atically ignored all of the nineteenth-century colonies created by the Baron de Rothschild; [51] it circumnavigated the immigrant villages founded half a century later, completely omitted Jerusalem from its purview and skipped fancifully over sites of Palestinian urbanism as if they had never been there.

Instead, this illusory panorama celebrated the Labour settler movement's mythological frontier, promoted the agricultural regions of the Galilee and Jezreel Valley, and honoured *kibbutzim* and *moshavim* (collective villages) like Beit Alfa, Nahalal, Ein Gedi and Beit HaArava. Drawing on the poetry of Nathan Alterman and Alexander Penn, this allegorical never-never land was littered with physical remnants from a classic European literary tradi-tion – the 'local inn' and the 'country road' – as well as a background cast of engaging fictional characters to accompany the fighters and *kibbutzniks* (kibbutz workers) busy building the country – 'the sailor', 'the wanderer' and 'the bandit'. The degree to which this image of the past has penetrated Israeli public consciousness is really quite astounding. As Aviad Kleinberg noted in his obituary for Naomi Shemer in the daily newspaper *Haaretz* in 2004, very few people themselves experienced anything remotely similar to the Good Old Eretz Israel which had been projected for them; most were fed Shemer's personally embellished equivalent and internalized it as their own.[52]

Real or imagined, by 1984 the White City was for Tel Aviv what the Good Old Eretz Israel was for the State of Israel. In the 1980s it was Tel Aviv's counter-culture to embrace the old official culture of Good Old Eretz Israel that was carried over from one election to the next (in fact, since the ascension of the Likud to power in 1977, each time the Labour Party was in the opposition, it was embraced by the counter-culture). Except for the ordinary agents of the public sing-alongs (such as youth movements and regional councils) those who promoted that kind of practice in the 1970s and the 1980s were the agents of the counter-culture: long-haired guitar players and the youth of the Peace Now movement. With every election campaign loss, the songs of Good Old Eretz Israel became the soundtrack of the ritual lamentation.

Those repeated defeats of the Labour party were clear evidence of the growing chasm between Good Old Eretz Israel's concocted utopianism and the day-to-day reality of modern Israel. The Good Old Eretz Israel was another place, and its time was another time. Just as the geography of this imaginary country, whose seashore is sometimes a 'longing for a river',[53] was (in the terms of Michel Foucault) 'heterotopic', so its history was heterochronic – Good Old Eretz Israel was doomed to remain always 'old' (that was what made it so 'good'), but not so old as to encourage its inhabitants to actually investigate the period which preceded Labour settlement, as this had already been declared ancient and antique. In any case, history should have been left far enough in the past that it would not interfere with today's reality, and therefore its time was never the present:[54] 'May it be already tomorrow', wrote Haim Hefer in his poem 'May It Be' – a musical adaptation of which appeared on Arik Einstein's first album in the 'Good Old Eretz Israel' collection. But, as ever, no one summed up the wistfully romantic mood better than Einstein himself who, in 'Old Sad Days', the final track on his *Nostalgia* album dedicated to the White City, ended with the simple, doleful plea: 'Come back good days.'

Whiter than White City

Michael Levin may have put the White City on the cultural agenda and Nitza Szmuk certainly forced it onto a municipal platform, but Israeli artist Dani Karavan must take considerable credit for transforming the White City as a *theme* into a well-ordered *ideology*. Acting as the unofficial chief spokesperson for the 'movement' (as opposed to Szmuk's official moniker), Karavan used the preface in Szmuk's *Dwelling on the Dunes* to set down a manifesto. According to this text, the ideological significance of the White City was being overlooked – it was much bigger than local and contemporary debates over beauty versus vulgarity, Left versus Right, and Good Old Eretz Israel versus Begin's Other Israel. It formed the foundation for a whole system of national justifications – it was Tel Aviv's international passport, its character reference.

Karavan (born in Tel Aviv, 1930) is a well-known Israeli artist who has been practising within a field that was developed in the 1960s under banners such as 'environmental art', 'land art', 'landscape architecture', etc. The difficulties of working in this particular field usually stem from the inevitable tension between the establishment and the independence of the artist and their project. Realizing such large works often requires hefty budgets and considerable resources, and therefore is largely dependent on whether the artist has developed positive relations with commissioning or influential parties, such as governments, politicians and corporations. In the United States, artists such as Robert Smithson, Walter De Maria, Michael Heizer and Gordon Matta-Clark have all succeeded in maintaining a relative degree of independence while developing such pieces – perhaps in light of the financial structure in place in the American art world, or simply due to the sheer expanse of land available – but in Europe and Israel, art of this scale has always demanded the heavy involvement of governments, municipalities or corporations. Subsequently, within this particular field there has always been a fine line between free-spirited and committed art on the one hand, and commissioned and directed pieces on the other.

Since making his breakthrough as an illustrator and set designer in the cultural department of the Nahal in 1952, Karavan's success has stemmed from his ability to collaborate with commissioners, patrons and institutions.[55] He has developed a knack for supplying these influential bodies with a visual expression for their programmes. These have included, among other works, a mural for the passenger liner *Shalom* in 1963, a stone bas-relief for the Knesset assembly hall in 1966, a monument to the Negev Brigade near Beer Sheva in 1968, another bas-relief for the Bank Leumi's central offices in Tel Aviv in 1970, and yet another for their New York branch in 1980.

Karavan knew how to formulate the commissioned appearance of his work in a most effective way by systematically choosing not to acknowledge the commission's circumstances and by refusing 'artistically' to directly respond to the commission's programme (hence, for example, he chose not to display dead soldiers in his Negev Brigade Memorial Monument near Beer Sheva). This type of sculpture offers ceremonial and 'meditative' compositions of 'architectural' sculpture and 'sculptural' architecture loaded with archetypical forms (spheres, cubes and pyramids), walking axes, images, materials and associations. Karavan's idealized compositions are characterized by flowery abstraction and meaningful elegance, they outline ceremonial trajectories and majestic axes, offer meditative places, display archetypical forms such as cones, cubes and pyramids, and utilize basic materials like sand and water, sometimes with special laser effects.

It is to his credit that he has accepted all his commissions openly and wholeheartedly. He has approached each and every project without any hesitation or complexes. Karavan knows how to speak with authorities, politicians and donors, and above all is capable of providing them with images and visuals that *work*, that are usable and easy to live with. His early bas-relief for the Knesset assembly hall is a good example of this undisturbing decorative quality: it is always there, behind the Speaker and the Chairman's podium, but no one can remember exactly what it looks like.

Over the years, Karavan's work has systematically grown in scale. He has gradually moved from relatively small pieces within existing environments, like the bas-relief he added to the Regional Court building in Tel Aviv, to an architectural scale of production, overhauling total environments in his *Negev Monument* piece in Beer Sheva and *White Square* installation in Tel Aviv, or even to an urban and territorial scale like *An Environment for Peace* in Florence (1978) and *The Axis* in Cergy-Pontoise near Paris (1980). Naturally, as the scale of his work has increased, so too has his dependence on the authorities that fund, approve and regulate. Incidentally or not, Karavan moved the weight of his career to Europe after his Venice Biennial pavilion in 1976 and the Likud ascension to power in 1977. When he returned to Israel in 1982 for the Tel Aviv Museum of Art exhibition *Makom* (Place), he was already a well-known international artist whose projects expressed an incredibly huge amount of political power, by their technological means – a laser beam at Florence, or by scale – the urban axis at Cergy-Pontoise.

More than any effect or story, the main significance of Karavan's work resides in the means of its production; but unlike his colleague the environmental artist Christo, who treats the bureaucratic and production process as a part of the artwork, Karavan prefers to show only the final results. There is no doubt that in order to realize large-scale projects like the *Axis* of Cergy-Pontoise or the laser beam *Environment for Peace* in Florence, he had to sustain close relationships with high-ranking politicians and statespeople.[56]

In 1989 he inaugurated his *White Square* project: a sculpted environmental monument made of white concrete and a personal homage to what he called 'the people who built Tel Aviv, also known as the White City.'[57] Situated in a park in the east of the city, on a hill once belonging to the Palestinian village of Salame, the piece is presented as an 'environment' composed with sculptural platonic objects (a tower, a dome, a pyramid and a staircase) and visual clichés (an olive tree). It is a composition loosely based on the idea of an architectural observatory, inspired by works like the Jantar Mantar in Jaipur. In the *White Square*, Karavan designed the gaze over Tel Aviv's White City as a longing, stylized gaze towards the sea, towards the West. In actuality, *White Square* could be regarded as a conceptual model of the White City according to Karavan: The city as a work of 'environmental' art.

In the introduction he penned a few years later for Szmuk's book, the White City looks exactly like a piece by Dani Karavan and vice versa: 'They employed basic forms and materials: the cube, the sphere, the cone and the triangle; sand, gravel, water, cement and concrete.'[58]

In the 1930s the construction of convex surfaces like spheres was still quite rare, and even cones had not appeared in Tel Aviv before the 1950s, with the influence of Le Corbusier's post-war 'grey period'. Nevertheless, the idea was clear – either geometrical or material, these were the essentials and the roots which proved the White City's builders' originality and purity; they did not take anything from anyone, and they created the city out of nothing other than what god had given them – sand, gravel, water and cement:

> here, on the distant white dunes, former students of medicine, law
> and philosophy were mixing sand with gravel, water and cement
> and pouring the mixture into wood and metal moulds to form brick
> and grey building blocks, which they then loaded and transported
> to the building sites. They laid them, row upon row, in straight lines,
> angles and curves, attached iron and wood frames to them, clad them
> in plaster, a mixture of lime with sand, and rendered the simple forms
> white – making poetry out of plain materials to shape an urban expanse.[59]

The decision to specify those 'students of medicine, law and philosophy' who, far from home, had got down on their knees to mix the concrete of a new nation is revealing in itself. It demonstrates another attempt to present Tel Aviv's history as separate from the wider historiography of the region while exposing popular Zionist virtues of manual work and autarky. This point has always been crucial for the apologetics of the Zionist Project and its position vis-à-vis Europe: Zionism distinguished itself from European colonialism by claiming its intention had always been to colonize the territory, not the population.[60] And yet, despite the pronounced virtues of Hebrew labour, it is very likely that beside those students, the construction sites in the 1930s were packed with real labourers, in most cases Arabs or Yemenite Jews.[61] One might cross-check this with the claim of Haim Hefer, who played a similar role to that of Karavan but in the field of writing. In his musical *Little Tel Aviv* (1958), Tel Aviv's construction was shown as reliant on foreign toil: 'we are two builders / we came from Cairo / Just give us some bread and a bit of onion / and we will build for you Ahuzat Bayit / here we put some bricks / we earned two Egyptian Piasters / and in one day / you will wake up and find a city'.[62]

In the rest of his text, Karavan dutifully listed and reaffirmed all the standard components which make up the White City myth – he noted the Bauhaus legend, the purity, the utopianism, the innocent landscape of dunes which were the city's foundations. But he also emphasized other aspects of the fable which, up until that point, have not been explicitly vocalized, but reveal a far-reaching rhetoric:

> And here, on the sand dunes, alongside the small eclectic buildings, alongside the Orientalism and the heavy layers of history – the stark, the white forms took shape against the blue backdrop of sea and sky. Here, this style, the International Style, the Bauhaus Style, looks perfectly adapted to its new setting, as if born here, in Tel Aviv, a city in the making. It is as if this style tells the story of the people who wanted to build a new society here – pure, simple, frugal – the antithesis of ostentation and extravagance.
> […] All those young architects who had studied in Berlin, Amsterdam, Paris – under different historical circumstances, in conditions of peace and prosperity, some of them might not have come here at all. Instead, they would design there, in Europe, buildings that integrate with the culture there, buildings that strive to bring about a change, a declaration and the desired revolution. […] But they did come here – some of them in fact were expelled from there on the dual charge of being Jewish and of carrying the germs of intellectual and cultural progress. And they remained here, far from war, far from there.[63]

Wilfully acknowledging this dual charge of being Jewish and of carrying the germs of intellectual and cultural progress, Karavan repeated this narrative again and again. Ten years later, during the 2004 White City celebrations, Karavan went even further. In an interview with Army Radio, he ticked off all the usual tropes – the personal dimension, the dunes, the Jewish architects who came from Europe – but with one rather notable difference: he claimed that the White City transformed Jewish sacrifice and victimization at the hands of the Nazis into no less than a straight victory over their one-time oppressors:

> I was born many years ago, when Tel Aviv was still in dunes. My whole being is totally within this city, within this wonderful past, with all those special houses built by architects who came from Europe. In fact, today I can see that my art has been influenced by what I perceived in the streets. Today I know that this White City is one of Zionism's most wonderful creations. No one can deny it, and no one can dismiss it. Today I know too that a style survived here, a style that the Nazis wanted to exterminate, exactly like they wanted

> to exterminate other forms of civilization. Tel Aviv survived,
> so in fact, it overcame Nazism.[64]

This sentimental kitsch – philosophy students who became builders, the White City bravely standing in front of Orientalism, or the celebration of Tel Aviv's victory over Nazism – has finally became the rhetoric and apologetics of the city: Tel Aviv is not only beautiful, but just; it is not white, it is whiter than white.

Built on Dunes

One of the greatest deceits of Tel Aviv's urban legend has been that the White City was built on the dunes. In reality, the city was not really built *on* the dunes at all, but *instead* of them: unlike the local traditional Palestinian sandstone constructions which cling to the soft, spongy layer of sandstone typical of this region, in order to build modern Tel Avivian buildings with concrete foundations, one needed to remove the sand and the sandstone layer. In many places in the southern parts of Tel Aviv, where the historical borders between Tel Aviv and Jaffa or between Jewish and Palestinian properties were located, one may notice the topographic difference between the two cities. Tel Aviv's level is lower by a metre or two. In fact, Tel Aviv 'shaved' the natural topography of the region in order to carve its own place, not *on* the dunes but *in lieu* of the dunes. Today, it is still possible to see sections of these calcareous layers around Tel Aviv, each a testament to how the city has 'shaved' its topography.[65]

Besides remaining a vital, albeit diminishing, resource for the country's construction industry, sand continues to play a starring role in shoring up Israeli history and politics. It has been the main protagonist in the city's narrative ever since April 11, 1909, when sixty-six families are supposed to have gathered on a virginal dune outside Jaffa to participate in a seashell lottery to divide plots for Ahuzat Bayit, the neighbourhood officially believed to have spawned Tel Aviv. And yet, while this story has been in circulation much longer that the White City theme, as time has passed the two urban legends – the White City and the maidenly dunes – have become increasingly knotted.

These ties were officially welded together in 1994 after the 'Bauhaus in Tel Aviv Festival' and a bumper range of cultural paraphernalia – including Szmuk's book *Dwelling on the Dunes* and Noa Karavan's film *Air, Light and Utopia*[66] – which married the two narratives into one. Only a decade later,

UNESCO presented them to the world as part and parcel of the same meta-historical storyboard – one which told the tale of pretty, innocent white houses emerging on the dunes. It is a mesh of fables dependent on Avraham Soskin's famous photograph of the plot lottery, which has been given canonical status for immortalizing Tel Aviv's 'founding moment'.[67]

Like an innocent dream of a child who builds castles in the sand, the White City was born from the sand like Aphrodite was born from the waves. Naomi Shemer added a froth of wave and a cloud, Szmuk and Karavan sprinkled it with some light, air and utopia. The white sand represented Tel Aviv's origin and place, but also its raw material. It may have also provided a visual explanation for Tel Aviv's 'white' colour – the sand was supposedly the city's main construction material and therefore the city was white – but their real paramount status has nothing to do with the aesthetic or visual dots they link up.[68] The importance of the dunes in Tel Aviv's narrative does not only stem from its aesthetic or visual dimension. Above all else, the sand dunes are crucially associated with the ideal of *tabula rasa* – dear to both Zionism and Modernist architecture.[69]

These sandy dunes have played a major role in the establishment of the moral alibi of the White City, in the wording of its historical case: while an invisible but not unperceived shadow of illegitimacy or at least disagreement has been cast over other areas of the country due to the manner in which these lands were obtained (notably, during the war of 1948 which led to the founding of the State of Israel), the moral legitimacy of a White City which had emerged *ex nihilo* from the sand and had been built on an ethos of progressive socialism must not be challenged.

Ongoing processes of colonization and dispossession across the Occupied Territories and Southern Lebanon have only encouraged the city's self-importance and inflated sentiments of virtue and integrity. This sense of righteousness has proved the moral foundation for the city's self-imposed separation from the rest of the country and a cultivating force behind its reputation for escapism and detachment.

According to the common doctrine of the Zionist Left then, the legitimacy of Jewish settlement in Tel Aviv is incontestable in comparison with territories occupied in 1967 or annexed by Begin via the Jerusalem Law of 1980 and Golan Heights Law of 1981. This defence of Tel Aviv defines the boundaries of the State of Israel by its 'undisputed' borders, as opposed to any map which might include, for example, those regions which have been added through '*milhemet breira*' (wars of choice), beyond international frontiers. This separatist attitude is best demonstrated by the poet Meir

בתים מן החול

Houses from the Sand, title page with the
photograph of the plots lottery of Ahuzat Bait in 1909.

Wieseltier, who famously declared in a television programme during the
war in Lebanon in 1982 that 'he would only take arms when the enemy
reaches the Yarkon River.'[70] Even for those Israelis willing to 'concede
everything' in the name of peace, Tel Aviv often still remains non-
negotiable. The contradictions of this stance were highlighted (justly)
in the late 1990s by the YESHA Council[71] of right-wing Jewish settlers
campaigning against disengagement from the Occupied Territories, hanging
billboards across Tel Aviv with the slogan 'YESHA Ze Kan! ('Judea-

Samaria-Gaza, it is Here!'): The 'Here' was Tel Aviv and the 'There' could have been defined only by Tel Aviv's own separatism.

Szmuk (re)presented the case for the city built on the dunes in her book *Houses from the Sand* in 1994 and again in her exhibition, *Dwelling on the Dunes* in 2004. In a conference held at the Tel Aviv Museum in honour of the exhibition's opening, Peera Goldman, the architect elected to replace Szmuk in her municipal post, argued that 'the city had developed on the dunes because, first and foremost, these plots were the cheapest.'

The facts, however, are slightly different. Historical evidence shows that not only was the majority of Tel Aviv built on land that was *not* of the 'virginal sandy dune' variety, but that there were also other cheaper lands available as well. In her study of Jaffa, the historian Ruth Kark compares a map of land use in Jaffa drawn by the German Templar architect Theodor Sandel in 1879, and a British map from 1917. Both indicate conclusively that by the end of the nineteenth century, and come the beginning of the twentieth century, most of the lands occupied by modern-day Tel Aviv were cultivated.[72] In her pioneering book, *Dionysus in the Centre*, Tamar Berger analysed the ownerships and the description of the plots in the maps annexed to *The Book of Tel Aviv* edited by Alter Droyanov in 1936, and showed that the lands were made up of vineyards, vegetable gardens and orchards and that most of the dunes were concentrated in the Muslim neighbourhood of Manshieh.[73]

The majority of the plots which, by 1948, constituted Tel Aviv's municipal territory had been purchased in the 1920s. On the one hand, this was an inevitable consequence of the mass return of Jewish citizens from Jaffa and Tel Aviv who had been exiled from their homes by the Ottoman authorities at the end of World War I – this tide of remigration created a severe shortage of housing in the Jewish sector. On the other hand, the eruption on May 1, 1921 of anti-Jewish violent riots in Jaffa, had served to reinforce separatist tendencies among the Jewish community and coax its sprawl from south to north, from Jaffa to Tel Aviv. According to Droyanov's 'Map of Tel Aviv before the Building of the City' there were four categories of land available for construction: dunes, dunes mixed with vineyards, vineyards and orchards. By superimposing this map onto another published in *The Book of Tel Aviv* – 'Map of the Establishment of Tel Aviv's Neighbourhoods According to the Year of their Land's Salvation' – it is clear that most of the city's new districts were built on agricultural land. These included, among others, the southern neighbour-hoods of Neve Sha'anan, Yehuda, the German Vineyard, Ramat Hasharon, Chlenov, Commercial and Grocery Center, Saad Orchard, Shapira, Little

Orchard and Rishon LeZion Hill. On the northern side of the Jaffa railway, which today still acts as a kind of 'natural' border between Tel Aviv and the former Arab capital, new neighbourhoods, such as Nordia and Marmorek, were developed on top of Palestinian vineyards and orchards.

In many cases, the devaluation of the land was caused by the war as orchards were either neglected in light of reduced exports, or destroyed by the Ottoman army in order to provide fuel for the railways. Evidence of this can be found, for example, in a memorandum sent by members of Neve Sha'anan to the delegates of the XII Zionist Congress in 1921:

> On the border of Tel Aviv we succeeded in purchasing two hundred and sixty two Dunams[74] of orchard land (the trees had been cut down or harmed in the war) in thirty thousands Pounds, one hundred and fifteen Pounds per Dunam. The price is not high, if we take into consideration its location and the quality of soil, which is suitable for all sorts of agriculture.[75]

Insistence that the city's narrative be *rooted* in the dunes is also misplaced because, in any case, as long as Palestine was under British governance

A white city and a black city. German aerial photograph dating from 1918.
Taken from *Tel Aviv in Photographs: The First Decade, 1909–1918*.
Eretz Israel Museum, Tel Aviv

(from 1920–1948) all land-property transactions had to pass stringent legal procedures and were rarely obtained illegitimately. Even during the 1930s, in the very midst of the 'Wall and Tower' settlement operations,[76] lands owned by Arabs were purchased legally by the Jewish National Fund. The Big Land Theft only occurred *after* the establishment of the State of Israel and the passing of the Absentees' Property Law in 1950, which enabled the confiscation of Palestinian properties and 93 percent of all land across the country.

Nonetheless, the theme of the dunes has served other purposes. It continues, for example, to play a decisive role in framing the past, present and future of Tel Aviv simply by virtue of its association with the city's birthday. On May 21, 1910, the members of the Ahuzat Bayit Neighbourhood Association were called to a general assembly to vote on whether to alter the neighbourhood's name to 'Tel Aviv'. And yet, despite this definitive moment, the official date for the city's founding was fixed at April 11, 1909 – the date of Ahuzat Bayit's plots lottery. It is even more remarkable that this particular date has stuck when one considers the other options available to city chroniclers. They could have picked July 6, 1906, for example, the official founding day of the Ahuzat Bayit itself, but this was neglected. They could have plumped for any one of the founding dates of other Jewish neighbourhoods built *before* Ahuzat Bayit, such as Neve Tzedek in 1887, Neve Shalom in 1890, Mahane Yehuda in 1896, Mahane Yosef in 1904, or Mahane Israel in 1904, but they did not. These latter neighbourhoods were all annexed to Tel Aviv in 1921 once the city had been granted its own autonomous municipal status separate from Jaffa, but each had played integral roles as part of the outer swarm of Jewish settlements on Jaffa's northern boundary.

While there is a legitimate argument that suggests Ahuzat Bayit differed from these Jewish neighbourhoods because it stood on the *other* side of this boundary line, it was by no means the only Jewish neighbourhood to do so. Indeed, perhaps one of the most perplexing and unsettling truths to emerge when unpicking Tel Aviv's historical narrative has been the organized forgetting of Mahane Israel. Known today as Kerem Hateimanim, this environ was built a whole five years earlier than Ahuzat Bayit and was located much further north than the recognized 'first neighbourhood of Tel Aviv'. Perhaps tellingly, it was constructed by Yemenite immigrants and was, at least at first, seen as a suburb within the Arab neighbourhood of Manshieh. Despite being predominately Yemenite, its demographic make-up was a natural continuation of Manshieh's own vibrant ethnic mosaic, which included immigrants from all over the Muslim world – from Egypt and North Africa to as far afield as Afghanistan.[77] Still, as the first (and most distant) Jewish neighbourhood from Jaffa, there is no doubt that Mahane Israel should hold Ahuzat Bayit's adopted title as 'The First Neighbourhood'.

Clearly what April 9, 1909, and the Ahuzat Bayit plot lottery could offer which other dates could not was black and white photographic documentation of an event which supported both Tel Avivian and wider Zionist narratives – namely, that the Jewish people had returned to a barren, backward wasteland after thousands of years of persecution in exile and, with hard Hebrew labour, had 'made the desert bloom'. Interestingly, at the time very few of those Jewish settlers hoping for the best plot in this lucky-dip exercise considered the event itself as something to be remembered. It is of note, for instance, that none of the Jewish intellectuals living in Jaffa during this period bothered to assist in the lottery or pass commentary on its outcome.[78]

Just like other examples of mythological Zionist photography – such as Theodor Herzl's meeting with the German Emperor, Wilhelm II, at the Mikve Israel agricultural school in 1898 – the photograph was retouched.[79] In Soskin's original photograph, there had been a lonely figure standing in front of the members of Ahuzat Bayit. In the official version however, published in the booklet *Tel Aviv* and distributed thereafter, this figure was erased. There has been much speculation as to who this figure may have been, with Yaacov Shavit and Gideon Bigger convinced that the deleted was none other than Akiva Weiss, one of the group's leaders and a bitter opponent of Meir Dizengoff, Tel Aviv's first mayor. They have argued that his removal was a political manoeuvre and part of Dizengoff's electoral campaign. Shavit and Bigger also detail popular speculation at the time, which suggested that the removed individual was none other than 'the son of the converted Shlomo Feingold'. Having said this, it is worth noting that Feingold had neither converted (he was only married to a non-Jewish woman) nor had a son. Feingold was one of the entrepreneurs who operated out of Yefe Nof (Bella Vista), a Jewish enclave built on the beach of the Arab neighbourhood of Manshieh.[80] According to popular legend, Feingold or his (unborn) son conveniently cried out to the assembly a disbelieving 'you are crazy, there is no water here.' But according to the writer and Tel Aviv historian Shlomo Shva, the assembly did not lack any water since one of the figures he identified on the right side of the photograph wearing a turban and shifting a tin can was Yosef, the Yemenite water-carrier from Mahane Israel.

While alterations to the photograph have been crucial for the establishment of Tel Aviv's moral alibi, it is the huge amount of work that has gone into maintaining an emphasis on the purity of these sands which is much more disconcerting; it reveals motive, heavy conscience and a readiness to conceal truths. It exposes a desire to provide an *image* of Tel Aviv's legitimacy, which trumps any inclination to factually prove it. According to Soskin's image – Tel Aviv's image of itself – not only is the White City the most unproblematic part of the Zionist project but it stands as its ideological and moral core. If Zionism's central objective has always been the normalization of the Jewish people, it is Tel Aviv, and not Jerusalem, that should be crowned as the real Zion. Born from a lottery on untouched dunes, there was nothing there before it; it was at no one's expense; all it did was to turn wilderness into bloom.

All those artefacts – the photograph of the Ahuzat Bayit lottery, the White City on the dunes – illustrated the famous Zionist formula of 'a land without people for a people without a land', which has structured the whole nation's working rhetoric.

In order to understand the consequences of this formula, one must go further back, beyond Szmuk and Karavan, to the man who turned it into theory and then put it into practice. Speaking at the Jewish National Fund Conference in 1943, David Ben-Gurion outlined the Zionist movement's two central tasks: the first was the 'Ingathering of the Exiles', a collection of all those Jews dispersed around the world, and the second was 'to rebuild the rubble of a ruined, abandoned country ... that has remained in its desolation for two thousand years.'[81] According to this second maxim, there was a duty to 'repair' the damages made to the country by all those who had occupied the land while the Jewish people had been in exile. Treading the thinnest of all possible fine lines, between desperately trying to ignore the fact that there were inhabitants living in this 'land without a people' and necessarily looking for someone to blame for its supposed 'ill-repair', Ben-Gurion used another speech to blame the Arabs – 'who transformed not a few flowering countries to deserts.'[82] Thus, before it could be harnessed to support the narrative of Tel Aviv the city, the sand was used to counter Palestinian claims of entitlement. This was what Ben-Gurion referred to in 1943, five years prior to Israel's 'War of Independence', as 'The Disinheritance Libel':

> *There is a settlement here that claims for itself possession of the land for one thousand, three hundred years, and based on this claim, they want to dispossess us from the only hope that the Jewish people have been preserving for all those hundreds of years, since they have been banished from their country – the hope of a return to Zion. We may ask: what is it those conquerors and occupiers did for this land? The answer, in four words: they turned Eden into a desert.*[83]

It is not necessary to be a contemporary radical post-Zionist in order to take umbrage with such rhetoric. Writing in 1929 in the conclusion to his memoir, *Reminiscences of My Life*, Yosef Eliyahu Chelouche inadvertently addressed Ben-Gurion, his ilk and the contradictions they espoused. An Arabic-speaking Jew, who was born in Jaffa and went on to become one of Tel Aviv's most influential leaders and constructors, Chelouche knew the two communities well and dedicated much of his life to bridging the gap between them.

> And those who are familiar with the history of our settlement from
> its very beginning, know that the question of closeness to our neighbours
> and a life of peace with them, was the first duty of the natives of this
> place, and that we tried our best to fulfil. And if we succeeded in our
> work, it was mainly because we had respected and took into consideration
> our neighbours, next to whom we had to build. But – and here we have
> to spell the bitter and terrible truth – the truth is that our leaders, and
> many of the builders of the Yishuv (settlement) who came from the
> diaspora in order to direct us, have not at all understood the important
> value of neighbours' relationship, of this simple and elementary
> principle. Either they did not understand or they did not want to keep it,
> and by not keeping this principle, this issue had been complicated and
> became the most painful question of our settlement. And it was already
> said publicly and written, that since the appearance of Herzl and the
> idea of political Zionism, the Zionist propaganda in all countries and
> in all languages described the country in which we are to build our
> national settlement as a wasted, ruined, desolate country with no
> inhabitants. And after such an oral and written description of the
> country, as only a virgin land, they put up all the Zionist methods to
> rebuild the land, which included everything except taking into
> consideration those inhabitants that had been living there.[84]

As early as 1913, Chelouche strongly advised Dizengoff to purchase all available dunes right up to the Yarkon River. While he was undoubtedly a shrewd businessman and knew the price of land was cheap for what it was, he also foresaw what political Zionism never did nor ever wanted to: the inevitable impracticalities of pitting this one set of inhabitants against their new neighbours. His rich background – Jewish and Arab, Zionist and Palestinian, citizen of Jaffa and Tel Aviv – perhaps meant he had a greater understanding of the intricacies involved but he also passionately believed that Zionism could prove beneficial for everyone, including the local population. He did not, however, take into consideration the fact there could never be such a thing as 'non-political Zionism', that Zionism would always be political by default. Moreover, he sacrificed his own place in Tel Aviv's history when he failed to acknowledge there was nothing political Zionism opposed more than the human bridge he was trying to be between the two communities.

In the end, the sand, the dunes and the wilderness are only literary decorations within a wider story. A story which, in essence, is really no different from the 'Bauhaus Style' or 'White City' fables. Each of these wonderfully idealistic yarns is brimming with heroics, each spells out a lesson in noble sacrifice, each proclaims passionately 'if you will it, this shall not be legend'. And yet, their similarity also lies in what is missing from each narrative, what is glaringly absent and what has been subtly pushed from the story's frame. None mention the 'important value of a neighbours relationship'; there is no reference to the necessity of 'taking into consideration those inhabitants who had been living there' or, in the words of the UNESCO declaration itself, pursuing 'integration with local traditions'.

All traditional communities – Christian, Muslim and Jewish alike – centre around concepts of good behaviour, with the aim of translating a basic ethos of righteousness and respect into practical interactions with the Other. And this is precisely where the White City narrative, as an extension of Political Zionism and architectural Modernity (both of which are strongly opposed to notions of tradition), is different. It is also where, as we shall see, all the human and universal promises made under banners of Political Zionism and architectural Modernity are ruthlessly dashed. If there is something anthropomorphic in any piece of architecture and if any building is also a fable of the human beings that built it, then the story of Tel Aviv's White City reveals clearly how, in the sharp words of Toni Morrison, the Jews became white.[85]

In this respect, the story of the White City is only beginning. Now it is time to see who turned Eden into a desert.

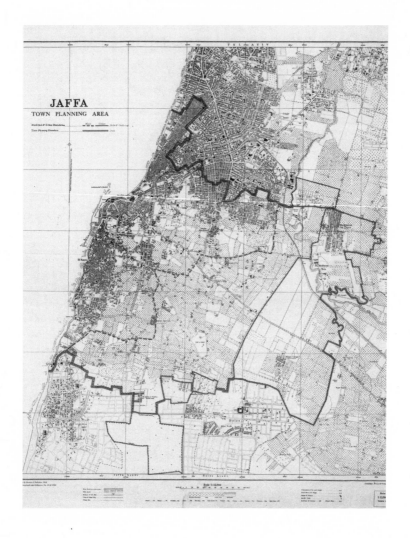

JAFFA
TOWN PLANNING AREA

Part II

BLACK
CITY

Architecture: there are only four architectural orders.
Of course, that is if one does not count the Egyptian, the Cyclopean,
the Assyrian, the Indian, the Chinese, the Gothic, the Roman, etc.
Gustave Flaubert, 'Architecture', *Dictionary of Received Ideas*

Hey guys, we have been discovered
(An Indian, observing Christopher Columbus)
Georges Perec, *Species of Spaces*

Whether it starts in Siberia or in Hollywood with a 'Hava Nagilla',
At the end of every sentence that you say in Hebrew,
there is an Arab guy sitting with a narghilla.
Meir Ariel, *Pain Song*

Opposite: Map of the Jaffa region, 1945.
Yad Avner Geographical Database, Department of Geography, Tel Aviv University.

The White City narrative does not disintegrate because of analytical inaccuracies or misplaced minutiae; it falls apart because of its fundamental flaws. If we adopt Flaubert's definition of Architecture, these stem from an arbitrary process which determines what makes it into the final edit of a story and what is left out. It means that the whole perspective of this entire narrative is constructed from the blind spot of the obvious, from the story outside the story.

In this sense, the most interesting chapters in Tel Aviv's account of itself are, without doubt, the ones which have been left out. Recovered, they spin an altogether very different account of the city: one less about construction and creation, and one more about effacement, and the effacement of the effacement.

The White City narrative's first bungle was to impose a correspondence between its supposed historical and geographical borders in an attempt to anchor Tel Aviv's architectural narrative in the exact moment when these boundaries were determined (in the 1930s) and across the precise perimeters of their territory (in this case, across the sand dunes). In architectural terms, there is no real justification for these geographical borders of the White City. As we have already observed, the Montefiore, Neve Sha'anan and Jaffan neighbourhoods all contain numerous examples of International Style buildings, constructed *before* the 1930s and *outside* the official boundaries of the White City. Jaffa is of particular note given that it was more of an international city than Tel Aviv has ever been and still boasts a multitude of different international styles to prove just *how* international it once was. These include, it should be noted, structures built within the *Jewish* neighbourhoods of Jaffa, such as Chlenov and Shapira.

As it happens, the geographical borders of the White City coincide precisely with other economic, social and geopolitical borders – and this doubling-up is no accident. In fact, the perimeters of the White City are the borders of Tel Aviv before 1948 – the very same mental iron curtain which has divided the city into north and south ever since the 1930s. Today, it is a partition marked in an infinite number of ways: from prohibiting north-bound traffic from Jaffa Road into Neve Tzedek to determining the flight path for planes landing at Ben Gurion Airport; from the amount the city municipality invests in infrastructure, landscaping, and sanitation on either side of the border to the mapping of pizza delivery routes.

The correlation between these different kinds of boundaries is evidence of Tel Aviv's bottled homogeneity, every aspect of which is constructed and administered to reinforce the idea that it is historically, geographically and

Even today, the 1931 city map excluding Jaffa, the south of Tel Aviv and the Hebrew neighbourhoods around it is the cognitive map for most Tel Avivians. Nitza Szmuk, *Houses from the Sand* (Tel Aviv: Tel Aviv Development Foundation and Ministry of Defense Publications, 1994).

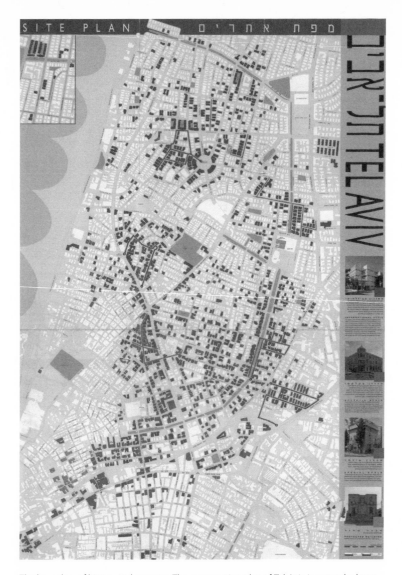

The boundary of history and memory. The conservation plan of Tel Aviv is cut at the heart of the city. Even though Jaffa and the Hebrew neighbourhoods have been under the jurisdiction of Tel Aviv for decades, it is still customary to print maps of the city excluding many of its southern parts and Jaffa.

ethnically distinct. As a Hebrew city, it is unlike Arab Jaffa; as an Israeli city, it is dissimilar from the Jewish diaspora; as a modern city, it is at odds with the ancient urban history of Europe and the Middle East. In this same spirit of uniformity, Tel Aviv defines everything outside the imagined walls of the White City as its opposite – what is outside the history of the White City maps perfectly onto what is outside Tel Aviv's geographical borders, and what is outside the 'historical city' is outside both the city of Tel Aviv as a whole and its history. Consequently, the streets, squares, sidewalks and structures that do *not* appear in the city's history books are eventually, inevitably, expunged from the civic map as well. An increasing number of residents, who live in neighbourhoods and districts with equal, if not richer, histories than the White City chronicle, are finding themselves deleted from Tel Aviv's annals. In some cases, as with Jaffa, they have even been forcibly stripped of their own narratives. While unforgivable, it is perhaps not so surprising when we acknowledge the first commandment of historical record: namely, that pushing something beyond the pale, nudging it beyond the reach of a community or extracting it from the pages of a school textbook, all necessarily mean it can be re-defined – an alternative identity can be prescribed based on a new history.

The second flaw in the White City fable is the borders of reality which frame it. When it becomes impossible to provide political solutions for an existing urban reality and therefore architectural solutions are utilized instead, discourse on that architecture and that city inevitably become political. In the case of the White City, the narrative appears desperate to confine itself to the architectural, and is heavily reliant on the modernist tradition of the autonomy of artistic discourse as a means of neutralizing the political. And yet, under closer inspection, Tel Aviv's history gives itself away by the tendentious manner in which it cherry-picks certain political facts while excluding others.

To begin with, it is a story framed solely within the context of international and Israeli architecture. Its plot is laced with the names of countless architects, peppered with references to architectural movements and key architectural sites, and saturated with architectural debates which have been ongoing for centuries among Western and European commentators. On the whole, the architects of 1930s Tel Aviv had been passive listeners rather than active participants in moulding the Modernist movement's ideology, and yet, out of nowhere, theoretical discussions of autonomous architecture's form and function, its very envelope and structure, suddenly became the central theme in Tel Aviv's historical narrative. It was almost as if the city had not been born out of the orchards of Jaffa at all, but had been fertilized in the cracked pavements of the Weimar Republic. No one has questioned the organized forgetting of vital information from the city's story which might actually have shed some light on what was going on much closer to home, in Ahuzat Bayit, in Tel Aviv itself. In fact, save for those pointers provided on European history, such as the closure of the Bauhaus school and the emigration of Jews after World War II, the story of the White City makes no reference whatsoever to formal history as we know it – to History with a capital 'H', complete with its 'big axe'.[86]

This lack of historical perspective appears to be a result of the fact that the majority of International Style buildings constructed in 1930s were erected in Jaffa, the Arab capital of Palestine, and not in Tel Aviv. The White City story appears determined to ignore this fact. Indeed, with the single exception of Dani Karavan's defiant repudiation of 'Orientalism', there are no Arabs (or even Arab architects for that matter) in this whole architectural history. This, despite the fact that the story itself is supposedly a celebration of an *International* Style. Hardly all-inclusive as it turns out, the only architects lucky enough to feature in this fable are either European Jews or Germans.

Instead of dwelling on these omissions, Tel Aviv's story bounded unhindered down the sequestered roads of academic and professional architectural discourse, gaining momentum every step of the way. Ultimately, it was afforded recognition and entered the international canon, returning victorious from UNESCO in Paris to the reality of the Middle East crowned in laurels. Again, it made its way in through the back door of the museum, only this time it was cloaked in the language of national apologetics: 'these buildings are not just attractive', it proclaimed, 'they are also righteous and moral'. If I may be allowed to tweak Ludwig Wittgenstein's famous formula, Tel Aviv has not only justified itself aesthetically, but also ethically: because the city is white, because the city was built on virgin dunes.

The manner in which this architectural story has unfolded was equally problematic. It was the municipality of Tel Aviv-Jaffa which approached UNESCO on behalf of the city, preparing and submitting its application for world heritage status. Needless to say, one is not expected to pass judgement on oneself, nor is it the job of the municipality to write history – either the history of the city or the history of its architecture. Especially when that history suspiciously slots with great ease into an existing state system in which *other* tracts of history, geography, archaeology and architecture are all recruited for the ideological education of the population and its army.

The commingling of these disciplines has created a thick military, educational and political complex which is deployed in different frameworks – 'Moledet' (homeland) and civic lessons in elementary education, 'Land Knowledge' (Geography) and 'Battle Legacy' in the army, 'Eretz Israel Studies' in the universities, or simple 'Hasbara' in politics.

Whether in educational, cultural, military, political or academic contexts, all participating disciplines of this complex share the same ideological horizon, that Zionism and the protection and projection of Zionist interest take precedence. As a result, the writing of history and geography in Israel sits awkwardly on a seam between the army, governmental organs, public bodies, academic entities and cultural institutions. A prominent manifestation of this phenomenon has been the regular involvement of military leaders (such as Yigael Yadin, Moshe Dayan and Rehavam Zeevi, for example) in instances of local archaeology and public museology. Similarly, governmental committees have been charged with the task of penning the State of Israel's 'official' histories.

Finally, it is clear that discussions over architecture cannot relate solely to Le Corbusier's 'magnificent play of volumes in light'.[87] Since construction and destruction are the primary expressions of the division of power in Israel, we cannot help but attribute political value to virtually every undertaking of the sort, particularly when political benefit appears to be gained at the very same time political motive is denied. Paradoxically, as soon as there is political advantage to be derived from the idea of autonomous art the idea itself, one of the basic principles of modernism, becomes meaningless, as does the ensuing argument over whether or not art and culture carry political weight. In this case, the discourse surrounding the White City has had, as we have seen, obvious political implications for the story of Tel Aviv and its founding. The desire to confine the discussion to the purely autonomous realms of traditional architectural debate has served transparent political interests, with little effort made to actually disguise them. It is no accident, for example, that the Israeli Architects Association, who wholeheartedly supported the municipality's 'White City' campaign, happen to have their offices based in an old Palestinian building situated in the middle of Jaffa.

After all the pomp and fanfare of the UNESCO celebrations, which were attended by just as many politicians and heads of state as architects and academic commentators, it became clear that the White City story extended beyond any regular discourse on modern architecture and the architecture of Tel Aviv itself. Soon enough, it became part of Tel Aviv's 'official' political history and was deemed crucial for understanding the place and purpose of the city within Zionism's wider narrative; it told the legend of those warrior

Aerial photograph from 1917. The 'Black City' is located exactly on the black stain marking the orchards of Jaffa. Even though the colours and uses have changed, the borderline has barely been moved. The black stain is now quarters 6, 7, 8 and 9 on Tel Aviv's map. This partition corresponds with other partitions, such as the one between the two police sub-districts in Tel Aviv. Naturally, the definitions of north and south derive from these partitions, but also the characterization of certain areas and populations as 'dangerous quarters' and 'dangerous classes'.
From the exhibition catalogue for *Tel Aviv in Photographs: The First Decade*.

ideologues who had rebuilt both the Land of Israel *and* Israeli identity in one fell swoop. As a result, the White City became intrinsically enwrapped in the apologetics of Zionist endeavour on a much grander, State level.

We have an obligation to cross-examine the story of Tel Aviv, to move beyond the prescribed perimeters of the White City and to try to unpick the architectural discourse which surrounds it. As soon as we do so, details which were previously expunged, suddenly re-emerge and it becomes clear that the Pandora's Box of Tel Aviv contains more than just the White City. For there, in among the utopian blueprints, the rejuvenation over disaster and the ethical pioneering, there is another story of war, destruction and suppression. Just as the historical and cultural construction of Tel Aviv is allied with its physical, concrete construction, the glaring gaps in this narrative dovetail with the physical removal of sites and landscapes which once made up the region's geography. It is worth noting that these processes are not new, nor did they begin with Tel Aviv; construction and destruction have been entangled since the dawn of time. With this in mind, the

Frenchman Baron Haussmann, perhaps the first modern urban planner, had good reason to describe himself as an 'artiste demolisseur' (demolition artist).

But like it or not, these stories of war, destruction and suppression will all eventually find their way back into Tel Aviv's narrative. Who is cast as hero and who is cast as villain in this rewrite remains subject for debate but there is no question that there are winners and losers. And if the title of the winners' story has already been claimed as the 'White City', it is only natural that the losers' story be called the 'Black City'.

The Black Patch

Photographs can have a prophetic quality. To get a better idea of the Black City and its historical borders, we have to go back and examine old aerial shots of the region from 1917–1918. The Black City appears as a sprawling dark patch in the photograph, covering everything outside Ahuzat Bayit and the white patch of sands. It represents the city of Jaffa and its environs, the district considered Greater Jaffa before the establishment of the State of Israel, meaning the Arab and Jewish neighbourhoods of the city and the surrounding area of orchards and villages.

On the one hand, it represents the built-up sections of Jaffa proper, including both its Old City and the densely populated Palestinian neighbourhoods of Manshieh and Ajami. On the other, it encompasses Greater Jaffa and those Arab and Jewish environs which were located outside the city's walls but which still fell under the city's jurisdiction prior to 1948. The largest swath of darkness, however, denotes the sea of orchards which spread out from the city's centre, hugging the roads to Ramla and Lydda and encircling Palestinian villages like Abu Kabir, Salama, Yazur and Hiriya.

If the white of Tel Aviv is not really white, then a closer look at these old photographs reveals that the black is not really black either. The varying shades tell us something about the condition of the orchards after World War I, with the lighter areas indicating those plantations which had been damaged, cut down, desiccated or abandoned.[88] Such instances of deterioration had far-reaching consequences because when their Palestinian owners could not economically justify maintaining such unsustainable terrain, Jewish land-agents were on hand to pluck these plots at bargain prices: when the black patches turned white, they also turned Jewish.

Within less than a decade, the lighter areas in these photographs were transformed into Jaffa's new Jewish neighbourhoods: Neve Sha'anan, Shapira,

Chlenov and Florentine. Not much later, additional orchards were scrapped to make way for what would become the neighbourhoods of Ezra, Hatikva and HaArgazim. All this took place in the 1920s, a whole decade prior to the closure of the Bauhaus School and the construction of the White City, and it took place atop the farms and orchards of Jaffa, not the barren sands of the Mediterranean coastline. To this day the Black City can still be easily identified on any map of the Tel Aviv-Jaffa municipality, and is immediately distinguishable by looking at any statistical data on the region. It remains the same shaded mass of land, trapped within almost exactly the same borders ninety years on, and is clearly indicated in all official documents, graphs, and maps as Quarters 7, 8 and 9.

The blatant disregard reserved for Jaffa and the Black City, as implied by their omission from Tel Aviv's own official narrative, is translated in the municipality's priorities and its unequal distribution of resources. Such are the disparities between North and South, one can't help but feel that it is more than just an issue of neglect; the southern areas of the city have been systematically encouraged to collapse and continue to be deliberate targets of decay. Everything unwanted in the White City is relegated to the Black City: all the inconveniences of metropolitan infrastructure, such as garbage dumps, sewage pipes, high voltage transformers, towing lots and overcrowded central bus stations; noise and air polluting factories and small industries; illegal establishments like brothels, casinos and sex shops; unwelcoming and intimidating public institutions such as the police headquarters, jails, pathological institutes and methadone clinics; and finally, a complete ragtag cast of municipal outcasts and social pariahs – new immigrants, foreign workers, drug addicts and the homeless.

While a re-read of the municipality's history might suggest that there has been a concerted effort to paint the South black in the most literal sense – be it traders who turned profit selling tar-paper covered shacks to Florentine in the 1920s or developers who dumped the asphalt and soot monstrosity that is the New Central Bus Station in Neve Sha'anan in the 1980s – in reality, the Black City is not black because of its physical colouring or because of the colour of its residents. It may well be true that, as the dumping ground for all those industries the White City considers too dangerous to be near its elite population, these southern neighbourhoods have become home to a large concentration of different kinds of 'blacks' – those minorities who are distinguishable from mainstream Israeli society because of their religion, nationality or skin colour. But paradoxically, this has actually ensured that the Black City is the most colourful, heterogeneous and cosmopolitan city space

Parking zones
of Tel Aviv.
From Tel Aviv's GIS.

The sectors of Yarkon
and Yiftach police
subdivisions.
From Tel Aviv's GIS.

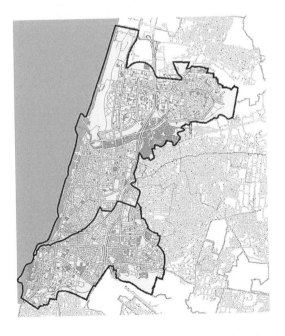

in the whole of Israel. Ethnically, culturally and architecturally diverse, its vibrant multiculturalism means that it is actually the only urban space within the municipality which gives the impression that Tel Aviv might actually be the global city it advertises itself to be.

Much more than a physical location boxed in by calcified geographical frontiers, the Black City is a condition. And it is a condition which exists only in relation to the White City. Without it, the Black City is invisible; it is everything hidden by the long, dark shadow of the White City, everything Tel Aviv does not see and everything it does not want to see – it is the pictures left behind in the dark room never to make it into the museum display, the stories and events slashed from the history books, the street names deleted from the map and the houses ripped from their foundations. In this sense, the Black City can be found wherever the White City is not. It has been necessarily conceived as its direct opposite; as Tel Aviv and the White City's absolute Other. It is the black background without which Tel Aviv cannot continue to appear white.

But that is not all; in many ways, it is also the black flag flying over Tel Aviv.

War

The story of the war between Tel Aviv and Jaffa began in earnest long before the creation of Jewish neighbourhoods in the 1880s or the founding of Ahuzat Bayit in 1909. Its origins are rooted in the late eighteenth century and stem from a particularly violent episode, considered by many as the moment in which modern Zionism was born out of the colonial delirium.

On the March 4, 1799, Napoleon Bonaparte brought his army from Egypt to Palestine and laid siege to Jaffa, the 'Bride of the Sea'. It is said that of the ten Jewish families which inhabited the city at the time, only one remained – the family of Don Aharon Azriel stayed behind to watch over their grain stores. Offered the post of Napoleon's personal translator, Don Azriel willingly agreed.[89]

During this same period, Napoleon was in the process of granting emancipation to the Jews of France. One day he asked Don Azriel to translate the following letter:

General Headquarters, Jerusalem
To the rightful heirs of Palestine

*Israelites, unique nation, whom, in thousands of years, have been
able to be deprived of their ancestral lands, but not of name and
national existence!*

...

*Arise then with gladness, ye exiled! A war unexampled in the
annals of history, waged in self-defence by a nation whose hereditary
lands were regarded by its enemies as plunder to be divided,
arbitrarily and at their convenience ... and while time and
circumstances would seem to be least favourable to a restatement
of your claims or even to their expression ... it offers to you at this
very time, and contrary to all expectations, Israel's patrimony!
Rightful heirs of Palestine!*
*The great nation which does not trade in men and countries as
did those who sold your ancestors unto all people (Joel 4, 6)
herewith calls on you not indeed to conquer your patrimony;
nay only to take over that which has been conquered.*

...

*Hasten! Now is the moment which may not return for thousands
of years, to claim the restoration of civic rights ... which had
been shamefully withheld from you for thousands of years, your
political existence as a nation among the nations, and the
unlimited natural right to worship Jehovah in accordance
with your faith publicly and most probably forever (Joel 4, 20).*[90]

This proclamation was published on April 20, roughly a month after Jaffa had fallen. In his history of Jaffa, Shmuel Tolkovsky offers an account of events in the city as described by one of Napoleon's army doctors. After marching into Jaffa on March 6, the French army conducted 'a horrific massacre unlike anything seen before in a city under siege.' The brutal rape and murder of the citizens went on for over thirty hours:

*The soldiers cut down men and women, old and young, Christians
and Turks; anyone created in human form was a victim of their rage.
The riot of slaughter, the shattered doors, the houses collapsing from
the report of guns and the slashing of swords, the women's screams,
a father and son piled up one atop the other, a defiled daughter on
the corpse of her mother, the smoke of the dead smouldering in their
clothes, the smell of blood, the moans of the wounded, the shouts of
the victors fighting over the spoils of a dying victim, the raging*

soldiers responding with ferocity and sharper blows to the cries of
despair, and finally people falling helplessly, intoxicated by blood
and sated with gold, onto the heaps of the dead – that was the scene
that the wretched city revealed until night fell.[91]

When he learnt of the rampage, Napoleon sent two officers to try and dampen the hellfire and negotiate a Turkish surrender. Once the Turkish forces had surrendered in exchange for their lives, Napoleon realized he had no idea what to do with them and no place to send them. After mulling over his alternatives for two days, he proceeded to renege on the pardoning, ordering the mass public execution of all 4,000 Turkish prisoners on March 10 on Jaffa's main beach.[92]

The Turks were not the only ones let down by one of Napoleon's broken promises; Azriel, the translator who had been assured that sovereignty of Jaffa would pass to the Jews, also had his hopes dashed. The day after the city was captured, a plague broke out and Napoleon's army made arrangements for a speedy exit and, on March 24, they headed north for Acre. In their wake, they left a city in ruin, still bleeding from the French onslaught and brought to its knees by a plague, which affected every family in the city. With the soldiers gone, the remaining citizens attempted, unsuccessfully, to repair the breaches to the city walls. They needn't have bothered because the French returned to Jaffa two months later, promptly tore down any renovations and deposited their ill and wounded across the city's quarters. Richardot noted that the beach was still littered with the bleached skeletons of the Turkish soldiers.

According to some historians, before leaving Jaffa for the second time, Napoleon ordered his doctor to kill all ailing soldiers with a swift administration of opium, but the medic in charge refused. Perhaps in order to stifle this rumour, other accounts, detailing Napoleon's regular solicitous visits to the plague-stricken men, were disseminated. The French army finally left Jaffa, and Palestine as a whole, on March 27.[93] Azriel and the rest of the Jewish community in Palestine would have to wait another century before Herzl came to visit and his book, *Altneuland*, replaced Napoleon's letter as Zionism's cardinal text, along with the declaration of another colonial power, Great Britain.

As Jaffa entered the nineteenth century, it began to recover from its brutal rape at the hands of Napoleon's army, and slowly but surely, brick by brick, begun to flourish again, establishing itself as the foremost city in Palestine. Ironically however, these very same processes of rehabilitation and prosperity proved instrumental in facilitating the creation of Tel Aviv

– the city which promised to be everything Jaffa was not and which would eventually swallow the Arab capital whole. Jaffa's burgeoning reputation as a bustling international port meant that by the 1840s she was already attracting a steady flow of Jewish economic migrants from North Africa. Settling in Jaffa upon their arrival, these communities soon began to establish a strong Jewish base there. As more and more docked in the famous trading harbour, the city became known as 'Sha'ar Zion' – the 'Gate of Zion'.

Fleeing Jaffa

If we try for a moment to put aside the idea of separation – the beating heart of the White City narrative – and study Tel Aviv and Jaffa together, their relationship is best defined using a term coined by the Israeli geographer Yuval Portugali to describe wider Palestinian and Israeli interactions: one of 'implicate relations'.[94] Adopting Portugali's hypothesis, it is impossible to separate these two cities as each one contains the other, defines the other and, in a sense, creates the other.

With this in mind, it is important to remember that Tel Aviv was not born from the dunes at all, but from, in and on top of its Arab neighbour. Perhaps because of this, Tel Aviv's attitude towards Jaffa has always been reminiscent of Christianity's relationship with Judaism; it is one which naturally hinges on a combination of contradictory and violent elements, encompassing birth and matricide, continuity and separation, heritage and appropriation, guilt and justification. Since the birth of Neve Tzedek, delivered from Jaffa's womb in the 1880s, Tel Aviv has been perpetually locked into two simultaneous struggles, each at odds with the other. On the one hand, it has desperately tried to escape Jaffa, and on the other, it has desperately tried to chase it down. The White City's pitched battle over the symbolic and historical space of the metropolis is a natural continuation of this, Tel Aviv's uneasy relationship with Jaffa and its stepchildren.

It conquered and subjugated Jaffa, emptied it of its population, liquidated whole neighbourhoods and expunged public edifices. One city turned the other upside down. And in doing so, Tel Aviv also laid war on Jaffa's memory. This is a war which did not cease with the requisition of Jaffa or the exile of its Arab population in May 1948; it is one which continues unabated to this day. Yaakov Sharet and Yosef Milo may have referred to Jaffa as a dead city in their well-known song, 'Nama Yafo' (Jaffa is Asleep), but Tel Aviv is clearly not done abusing the corpse.[95]

Regrettably, this complex and ambiguous relationship with Jaffa is Tel Aviv's true story. Since its establishment as a separate city, Tel Aviv has constructed itself culturally, ethnically and historically according to Jaffa – as its split, as its dialectical negation. For Jaffa, this symbiotic relationship has proved fatal: as Tel Aviv built, wrote and rewrote itself, it also demolished and erased the Arab capital, recasting the city as an inverted reflection of its supposed self: a nocturnal, criminal, dirty space – a black city. In doing so, Tel Aviv actually projected an image of Jaffa which dovetailed perfectly with Theodore Herzl's original observations of the Arab capital during his historical visit in 1898.

Herzl's first impressions of the Promised Land, as noted in his diary, were at odds with the accustomed Zionist practice of expressing one's unadulterated 'Love of the Land'.[96] Herzl seemingly had no qualms demonstrating his revulsion at the state of Palestine's two main cities, Jaffa and Jerusalem. Jaffa's port was naturally his first stop and after having debarked on October 27, 1898, he cynically chimed: 'Well, here we are in Jaffa! Again, poverty, suffering and heat in cheerful colours. Confusion in the streets and no carriage for hire.'[97] During his first two days in the country, Herzl used Jaffa as a base for short excursions, travelling to Jewish agricultural colonies, like Rishon LeZion and Rehovot. However, these expeditions clearly did not take him far enough and, still utterly miserable about 'the terrible heat' in Jaffa,

Herzl did not like Jaffa and despised Jerusalem. At the end of his visit to Israel he was even willing to wait for a few days on a shoddy ship at the Jaffa port, in order not to spend a few more days in the sweaty streets of the city. To judge by his novel *Altneuland*, Herzl believed in Haifa.

Herzl boarded the train to Jerusalem on October 29. Here, he soon fell ill and, disgusted by the 'ugly miserable and cunning beggary' near the Wailing Wall, remarked that, 'If I ever will remember you, Jerusalem, I would not be delighted with this memory. A dirty residue of thousands of years full of nothingness, religious fanaticism and dirt resides in your stinking streets.'[98]

Herzl returned to Jaffa on November 4, determined to leave Palestine as soon as possible. Unfortunately, he missed his connecting boat to Alexandria and was forced to re-evaluate the situation. With his will to leave as strong as ever, he announced his intention to board a vessel travelling in the opposite direction:

> I wished to take a boat to Beirut and from there to return [to Alexandria – S.R.] with a Lloyd ship in order that I will not have to stay here any more. But it was impossible, since the boat was already steaming, our luggage was still at the terminal, and there was no guaranty that we would find a boat to return from Beirut.[99]

Finally, the only options left were to either take a Turkish boat to Constantinople, squeeze onto another ship heading for Beirut, board a Russian cargo carrier to Alexandria (due to depart in four days), or persuade an American journalist called Gordon Bennett to let him make use of his yacht. Herzl sent a note to Bennett, practically begging him to take him and his friends to Alexandria but the American did not respond and Herzl was forced to remain, for the time being, in Jaffa.

This did not please the Zionist visionary, who focused his disdain on the old Arab capital in particular: 'The last day in Jaffa was unbearably unpleasant, with many beggars and spies that kept on coming to hustle us.'[100] On 5 November, Herzl went 'sans crier gare' to the port of Jaffa and managed to fight his way onto the *Dandy*, a small British cargo ship carrying oranges to Alexandria:

> When I saw that we could find five places, even bad ones, I made a reservation and sent Wolfson to the land in order that he would bring the luggage. For myself, I stayed on the ship […] only on this wreck, my ship, that as we assumed, would be dancing in the open sea, I could feel safe.[101]

All Herzl's companions were opposed to the idea of taking a vessel so small and plainly unsafe, but given Herzl's desperation to leave, everyone begrudgingly took their seats. As expected, the trip was arduous, the heat in the cabins was intolerable, the sea was agitated and three members of the delegation fell ill. The party decided to stay on the deck all the way to Alexandria, where, in Herzl's words, they went to sleep '*à la belle étoile*'.[102]

In *Altneuland*, Herzl had plotted an imaginary European utopia built by the Jews of Palestine, which would modernize the country and Westernize the Orient. Adamant in his repugnance for Jaffa (the political, cultural and economic capital of the country), and perfectly open about his aversions to Jerusalem (alias-Zion), he chose instead to set his new, modern, 'White City' as far away as possible from both: in Haifa, in the northern reaches of the country. Herzl could not have dreamt, of course, that one day Jaffa would be marginalized by Jewish settlement from outside its own city walls but over a century later, Jewish Tel Aviv is still following the path beaten by Herzl in his desperation to flee Jaffa – both mentally and geographically, the city streams northwards. It is not such a great leap then from Herzl's personal abhorrence for the Orient to Dani Karavan's celebration of the White City as a righteous, European bulwark in the face of what he considered to be Jaffa's backwards, primitive Orientalism.

But this antipathy has never been a simple question of identity and taste. Indeed, for many inhabitants of the region it was a question of life and death.

Bypassing Manshieh

The war between Tel Aviv and Jaffa, which would end with mortars and machine gun fire, began with leases and landscaping as Neve Tzedek and Neve Shalom, the first Jewish neighbourhoods of Jaffa, vied for spatial dominance with the Muslim neighbourhood of Manshieh.[103] All three were located in the northern quarter of the ancient city, adjacent to Jaffa Road and the railway lines which led off towards the Holy City of Jerusalem. Charting the physical development of these neighbourhoods, from makeshift shacks to bloated modern suburbs, is a revealing process; it is like watching the unfolding of an Olympic 800 metres final or a game of *Go*, in which each competitor tries to block, flank or cut up his opponent in a bid to reach the finishing line first – in this case, the sea.

Neve Tzedek was established in 1887 as a joint initiative between the Ezrat Israel Company, belonging to brothers Shimon and Eliezer Rokah, and the aforementioned Yosef Eliyahu Chelouche. The latter owned land north of Jaffa and agreed to sell lots to the siblings for low prices on the condition that

A postcard from the 1930s shows the proximity between Ahuzat Bayit and Manshieh.

construction would commence within a year.[104] Soon after its inauguration, other neighbourhoods sprouted up nearby and in 1890 Neve Tzedek was joined by Neve Shalom, and in 1896, by Mahane Yehuda. Forming a Jewish continuum which branched out of Jaffa and spread north, running parallel to the coastline, this swarm of settlements was appended to Ahuzat Bayit in 1909. Crudely stapled together, they formed Tel Aviv.

But the neighbourhood of Manshieh still held a significant topographical advantage over this collection of neighbourhoods which would form the basis for the 'first Hebrew city'. Preceding these early Jewish environs, Manshieh had been constructed *on* the coastline itself. With foundations laid by a small group of Egyptian agricultural labourers who had immigrated to Palestine in the 1830s, the Arab neighbourhood swelled in the 1870s as migrants flocked from around the world to Jaffa's international port.[105] By the twentieth century, it had ballooned to the extent that the borderlines which had separated it from surrounding Jewish enclaves had become increasingly frayed sites of meeting on the one hand, and friction on the other. Right up until the Arab Revolt of 1936–1939, Manshieh had the potential to bridge the animosity bubbling between these two cities but advances drew suspicion on both sides. On Tel Aviv's part, cuddling up to Manshieh was not an option; not only did the Arab neighbourhood represent a threat to Tel Aviv's security, but it also simply blocked Tel Avivians' access to the beach.

While the lion's share of Manshieh was razed to the ground between April and May 1948 during Israel's War of Independence, organized processes for its destruction had been put in place much, much earlier. Either as an apocalyptic prophecy which would later fulfil itself, or just as an exercise in wishful thinking, it was systematically erased from the drawings of Nachum Gutman, the quasi-official 'painter of Tel Aviv'.[106]

Repeating the same image throughout his life's work, Gutman depicted the 'Little Tel Aviv' of his childhood, framed during World War I, with the area emptied of its Jewish population after they had been forced into exile by the Ottoman authorities. Cast in complete isolation, it floats alone among the barren, endless dunes. In this doctored panoramic, there is nothing to separate Tel Aviv from the sea – neither the Arab neighbourhood of Manshieh, nor the Jewish-Yemenite neighbourhood of Kerem Hateimanim. Gutman would often alternate the orientation of Herzl's Street axis and rotate the whole city westwards to the sea, thus showing that nothing separates the Herzliya Gymnasium from the beach. In his drawings, Little Tel Aviv has been depicted from various viewpoints, but, other than the vague silhouette of the Church of St. Peter perched on Jaffa's hilltop in the distance behind the white dunes, the Hebrew city always stood in perfect solitude.[107]

This same drawing was retraced again and again throughout Gutman's career; from his first sketches, *Shmuel Hagar fights the dunes* and *The first street lamp* in 1936, when it was inconceivable to imagine the complete destruction of Manshieh, right up until the latter stages of his life, when Manshieh had already been deleted from the map. The image was reproduced again in 1959 for the cover of Gutman's seminal book, *A Small City with Few People in It*, and enlarged on a much grander scale as a mosaic base to the fountain erected at Bialik Square, the quad outside Tel Aviv's historic municipality headquarters.[108]

How, in 1936, could Gutman have predicted that Manshieh would eventually be cleared from the map? Did the city consciously or subconsciously seek to realize the familiar vision they had always been presented by one of their most celebrated sons? Either way, once again, reality followed the fable, structural form followed elaborated fiction. Tel Aviv had never wanted Manshieh as one of its environs; it was considered an Arab smudge on what was supposed to be a beautiful white, Jewish utopia. In the immediate years after the city's emergence, Tel Aviv did not even want Kerem Hateimanim or those other Jewish neighbourhoods still considered part of Jaffa to be annexed to Tel Aviv, so keen were its leaders to divorce the new, modern Hebrew City from the venerable old Arab metropolis. After 1948, Manshieh – the hyphen which had moored Tel Aviv to Jaffa up until this point – was ruthlessly demolished. Even the passage between the two cities was blocked

From where did Manshieh disappear? Sketches of Ahuzat Bayit on the sands that Nachum Gutman drew in 1936 and 1959, before and after the neighbourhood was torn down. From the book *Nachum Gutman's Tel Aviv, Tel Aviv's Nachum Gutman*.

off by the architectural equivalent of a land-fill – the strange structure of the Dolphinarium, later recycled as a nightclub, which would be the site of a suicide bombing in 2001, several overbearing landscape installations, vast parking lots and an elaborate system of breakwaters that prevent possible communication between the two cities along the beach and the waterline.

Manshieh had always been a Muslim stronghold, but Jewish families had also lived there in the first few decades of the neighbourhood's existence. The region's first Jewish hospital had been built within its borders and, in 1887, a small Jewish compound named Yefe Nof (known locally as Bella Vista) was developed on its western fringes. And in 1904, the entrepreneur Shlomo Feingold – the very same father whose imaginary son is supposed to have ridiculed the plot-lottery – constructed his very own Jewish pocket within Manshieh called the 'Feingold Houses'.

Under different circumstances, it may have been possible for these mini Muslim, Christian and Jewish colonies to have continued growing in size, structurally overlapping and coalescing in harmony as they leaked out of the 'Bride of the Sea'. Those Jewish neighbourhoods built around Manshieh in the late nineteenth century – Neve Tzedek, Neve Shalom and Mahane Yehuda – had been originally designed as continuations of Jaffa anyway, not as suburbs. The construction of Ahuzat Bayit as a separate Jewish entity however, cast Manshieh in a new role; from the Great Arab Revolt in 1936 right up until the proclamation of the State of Israel in 1948, it emerged as the main site of antagonism between Arabs and Jews and *the* battlefield for open, violent confrontation between Jaffa and Tel Aviv.

Under the Ottoman authorities, who refused to grant the small Jewish settlement autonomous municipal status, and even deported the Jewish population of the Jaffa region during World War I, Manshieh had gained a large advantage over Tel Aviv and succeeded to sprawl northbound. The result of this preliminary strategic negotiation between the two communities could be seen clearly in Ahuzat Bayit's initial scheme and the special location of the Herzliya Gymnasium, the first Hebrew school and the neighbourhood's most important public building. Symbolically positioned at the end of Herzl Street, at the very mouth of Ahuzat Bayit, it reiterated the relevancy of education as a spearhead for what would be the first Jewish city in Palestine. Facing south, this façade forced passers-by to turn their backs on Jaffa in order to take in the full-scale of its imposing Oriental design. But practically, its positioning was also an act of resignation in light of Manshieh's location which blocked off any hopes of expanding north-west towards the sea. In this sense, the Herzliya Gymnasium marked the city's frontier; it was

The first bypass road in the country: Allenby Street (Sea Street) bypasses Manshieh and slopes towards the sea. Section along the beach near St. Remo Hotel and the Casino (1932). Matson (G. Eric and Edith) Photograph Collection.

TEL-AVIV. Allenby St.   תל־אביב, רחוב אלנבי

A postcard from the mid twenties showing Allenby street going to the sea. Photo: Eliyahu Brothers.

The dedication of Allenby Street: 'We, the inhabitants of Tel Aviv, having met today, Thursday the 17 of Kislev 5679 (November 21, 1918), at a general and special meeting, have resolved to erect a perpetual souvenir in honour of the Commander-in-Chief of H.B.M. Forces, General Sir Edmund Henry Hynman Allenby. Conqueror and victor, in order that his name may be repeated by us and future generations. We have, therefore, this day and forever named the long and wide road of the Township of Tel Aviv, situated North-East of the Railway and leading to the seashore, by the honoured name of "Allenby" which shall henceforth be called "Allenby Road". May this be our perpetual token of our gratitude, veneration, and deep respect towards the General Commander for the regard in our hearts and the hearts of all Jewry for the happy deliverance that the brave British Forces have brought us having freed us from the yokes of tyranny allowing us to enjoy the light of justice and right, and hastened the fulfilment of our historic aspiration, the hope of Israel as prophesied by the prophets of truth and justice.'

the cork that stopped Herzl Street from going into Manshieh and what was essentially, at the time, enemy territory, defining Tel Aviv's historical main street as a cul-de-sac.[109]

Only many years later, once Jaffa had been plundered and Manshieh had been extirpated, was there any justification for picking Herzl Street up again and stretching it to reach the Mediterranean. This necessarily also involved demolishing the Gymnasium (as the acting stopper) and in 1962 the municipality moved the school to another site in Tel Aviv to make way for a clean path to the beach.

Since its conception, Tel Aviv has always searched for different paths to the sea. In fact, its early physical development was almost wholly defined by this insatiable desire to reach the Mediterranean. This necessarily meant bypassing and flanking Manshieh in order to prevent Jaffa sprawling to the north, thus guaranteeing Jewish territorial continuity along the region's coastline.

During Tel Aviv's early years, the only possible means of reaching the beach had been to take a side-path *east* of Ahuzat Bayit which connected the neighbourhood to Kerem Hateimanim but practically, paradoxically, encouraged the Tel Avivians to go to the beach by getting farther away from it. This beaten groove led north to the Yemenite enclave, bypassed Manshieh in its entirety, then turned west back on itself towards the sea. The 'Manshieh Bypass Road' would actually be the first of its kind in the region, although today replicas of this original model can be found criss-crossing the West Bank.[110]

Up until the British occupation, this route was simply nicknamed the 'Sea Street' and it was only after the British assumed control that the Tel Aviv's residents decided in a special gathering, as a token gesture, to rename it Allenby Street after Edmund Hillary Allenby, the general who had led the British Egyptian Expeditionary Force in their conquest of Palestine.

Only a few years later Allenby Street had assumed Herzl Street's role as Tel Aviv's main road. Still blocked from emigrating north by the cul-de-sac created by the Gymnasium and barred from heading south by Jaffa's thick barrier of orchards, Herzl Street no longer led anywhere and became increasingly irrelevant. Allenby Street, on the other hand, became the central thoroughfare leading on to all other streets and on to all other places and at long last, to the beach. Up until 1948, the whole city had been organized according to Allenby Street to bypass the neighbourhood of Manshieh and to prevent its further sprawl. Without Allenby Street and Kerem Hateimanim, Tel Aviv would never have succeeded in fleeing Jaffa.

Spatial Contradiction

One glance at Tel Aviv's linear structure and it is clear the city is distinctly at odds with the traditional littoral planning found in other coastal Mediterranean cities, Jaffa included. This is because however important it was to beat a path to the sea, this goal was always secondary to the flight from Jaffa. This, more than anything, has shaped (and continues to shape) Tel Aviv's spatial order.

The familiar complaint espoused by Tel Avivian inhabitants, that their city is not 'open' enough to the shore, is rooted in this determination to emigrate as far up the coastline as possible. In fact, from the moment Allenby Street actually reached the beach, the city quickly lost interest and energy and resources were redirected once more towards the sprawling push northwards. Right up until the mid-1960s, when the municipality of Tel Aviv initiated the construction of several hotels fronting the beach, there was no difference between the 'first row' of buildings abutting the dunes and those located further inland. With the emphasis firmly on stitching up the western hem of the city, wealth and industry were dragged out with the tide and this littoral edge became the most integral part of the city's street network. Today, this interminable, century-long advance northwards designates Tel Aviv's main traffic routes, it orders essential institutions of the city and defines the urban class system; like some kind of physical income barometer, the statistically poorest municipal inhabitants live in the south, while the richest can be found in the leafy northernmost residential neighbourhoods of Afeka and Ramat Aviv. This vector defines the trajectory of the municipality's public investment, educational levels and real-estate prices.

The flight from Jaffa shaped the spatial order of the metropolitan region and in many ways, that of the whole country. This same gap between north and south may be found in the differences between rich northern residential suburbs like Ramat Hasharon, Raanana or Herzliya and the poorer southern suburbs like Holon, Bat Yam and Rishon LeZion.

The French sociologist Henri Lefebvre argued that social and political conflict could be explained through processes of 'spatial contradiction'. If we adopt this thesis, it is clear that for over a century Jaffa and Tel Aviv have been locked in perpetual spatial combat which bore a geometrical character.[111] Prior to 1948, it had been the vortex of several important routes heading east; as the national centre, Jaffa was the point of departure to destinations in the inland, like Lydda, Ramla, Salama and Jerusalem, respectively, thus organizing the whole region according to a triangular geometry.

While the remains of this triangular structure are still discernible today – at the untitled Jaffa junction, for example, which connects with the old Salama Route (now Shalma Road) and old Lydda Route (now Kibbutz Galuyot Road), or further away to the city centre, at the historical Jaffa Clock Tower Square which connects with the Old Petah-Tikvah Route as well – the force of Tel Aviv's post-1948 metropolitan command has blown this traditional geometry away. Long gone are the days when Jaffa, as a cultural, political and economic centre, framed the region's spatial logic. In its place has emerged a new ruling order: a Jewish network which connects Tel Aviv with the southern towns of Holon, Bat Yam and Rishon LeZion, shaped according to the Jewish exodus from Jaffa, as a new centreless orthogonal system.[112]

'Those Polish of the Orient'

Like most other Arab cities in Palestine during the nineteenth century, Jaffa housed a tiny Arab-Jewish minority, who lived in relative harmony beside much larger Arab-Muslim and Arab-Christian communities. Even though the establishment of Neve Tzedek in 1887 and Ahuzat Bayit in 1909 proved critical in encouraging separatist aspirations and calls for a Jewish nation, coexistence between Arabs and Jews had continued beside, and in spite of, these fledgling Zionist settlements.

Any sense of tranquillity was promptly shattered, however, with the British conquest of Palestine in 1917 and the signing of the Balfour Declaration on November 2 that same year. In one fell swoop, this act of betrothal dramatically altered the political horizons for the Jewish population living in the region and for the burgeoning Zionist movement at large. The appointment of Herbert Samuel (a Jewish diplomat and an ardent Zionist) to the position of High Commissioner in 1920, practically assured that governance of Palestine would eventually pass to the Jewish minority. The Arab population of Jaffa, still psychologically scarred from the bloodshed which had accompanied Napoleon's declaration of Jewish solidarity in 1799, had just reason to be suspicious. From this moment on, fear spread among the native population and the potential for the peaceful cohabitation of Arab and Jewish communities was dealt a severe blow. As an unhealthy cocktail of anxiety and belligerence brewed, a mental, as well as a physical, chasm between Jaffa and Tel Aviv developed; relations between the two cities from 1917–1938 were so fractious, the author Chaim Lazar branded this period the 'Thirty Years' War'.[113]

Tel Aviv's final, and somewhat inevitable, separation from Jaffa was facilitated by the incoming British authorities, who not only made a handful of concessions to Jewish institutions but decisively annulled the Ottoman limitations put on Jews purchasing land. While many of the Jews in Palestine shared a European heritage with their new masters, the affinity which developed between the two essentially derived from the similarities and common interests which tied their respective colonial projects; the push to shore up the British Empire on the one hand, and the Zionist drive for a Jewish state on the other. Paradoxically, at least for the first few decades, these two designs dovetailed nicely. While the British made full use of their special status in Palestine under a League of Nations mandate as a smokescreen for adding this strategic outpost to their colonial network, the Jewish population saw the benefits of assisting their new governors. Although almost all Jews considered themselves as separate from the British imperial project at hand, and some were openly hostile to the British occupation of what they considered to be Jewish land by divine decree, it became clear that acquiescence would be beneficial in the long term. This relationship of convenience could be compared to the bond forged between the *pieds-noirs* settlers in Algeria and the ruling, imperialist French government, in which the interests of each party sometimes differed but the advantages of political and military assistance largely outweighed any negatives.

As it turns out, the Zionist movement would benefit most from this unlikely dalliance; leaning on the British colonial machine, they were able to lay down a foundational infrastructure for the future State of Israel and prepare logistically for the war in 1948 which would guarantee their independence. For Tel Aviv, this meant the construction of airports, power stations, railways and ports and, in 1925, invaluable instruction in urban planning from the famous Scottish architect and engineer, Sir Patrick Geddes, who, on his way to the British Indian colonies, made a stop in Palestine in order to prepare Tel Aviv's urban building scheme.

From the outset, the British misjudged relations between the Jewish and Arab populations. Predicting a lively but largely harmonious marriage between the two, commanders thought a garrison force of only a few hundred would be enough to govern the country. But they had not calculated in several unforeseen factors which, together, conspired to greatly aggravate the situation.

Firstly, within the Jewish population, memory of their forced exile from Tel Aviv during World War I was still raw. The return had not proved any easier since many of the apartments in Jaffa had been destroyed in their absence or requisitioned by new Arab tenants. Secondly, floods of Jewish immigrants arriving from Eastern Europe after World War I (an immigration wave known as the 'Third Aliya') had only increased what was fast becoming a serious housing crisis.[114] In the short period between September 1920 and May 1921 alone, 10,000 Jewish immigrants entered through the 'Gates of

A view from the Abu Kabir cemetery of Brenner House, the building of the national leadership of the 'HaNoar HaOved VeHaLomed' (Working and Studying Youth), built in 1978 where the Yatzkar House once stood. The latter was designed by Bauhaus graduate Shmuel Mestechkin.

Zion' (or infested the 'Bride of the Sea', depending on one's ethno-religious allegiance).[115] Lastly, and most importantly however, was the ideological make-up of this latest batch; having survived their infancy in among the pales and pogroms of Tsarist Russia and their adolescence absorbing the revolutionary fervour of 1917, these immigrants were considerably more radical than previous influxes. With them they brought an activist Zionist-Socialist ideology which imbued the Zionist movement in Palestine with a new steely intransigence, and a whole classroom of personalities who would go on to lead the movement over the following decades.

As this fresh mob of politically lean Jewish nationalists swarmed Jaffa and its environs, they inevitably rubbed up against the local Arab population. Tensions between these two groups began to mount and in the spring of 1921, they reached a fever pitch.

On hand to document this most irascible of atmospheres was Yosef Haim Brenner, a pioneer of Modern Hebrew literature and a highly respected teacher at the Herzliya Gymnasium.[116] Only a few months earlier, Brenner had moved in with the Yatzkars, a Jewish family who rented an isolated mansion on the outskirts of Jaffa, located in the Arab village of Abu Kabir.[117] In April 1921, in one of the last notes Brenner ever penned, the author described a stroll through the dusty paths of Jaffa's citrus orchards, documenting two chance encounters with different Arab inhabitants he passed along the way. Unable to converse with these individuals due to his lack of Arabic, these fortuitous meetings were characterized (much to Brenner's regret) by misunderstanding and an overwhelming sense of disappointment.

First, Brenner encountered a young, elegant Arab landowner who, sitting in front of his Bayara house-gate, demonstratively refused to return his greeting.[118] Clearly offended, the author noted sarcastically that 'even among the local *fellahs* [farmers] one can find a resemblance to Israel's diasporas [...] one better bump into a Lithuanian from Kaunas than one of those Polish of the Orient.' His second encounter was with a thirteen-year-old boy who worked as an agricultural labourer for this same landowner. Reading like a dialogue of the deaf, Brenner's record of the conversation seems to drift between the real and the imagined. The author asked the boy if he came from Salama, a large Palestinian village east of Jaffa, to which the boy shook his head. With prompting, the youth went on to explain the story of his life, how he had lost his parents in the war and what the working conditions were like under his current employer. Brenner enquired as to boy's salary and began to preach socialist ethics, before reprimanding himself: 'No, not politics now, but rather contact between the souls, from now and for generations, with no purpose, no intention except brotherhood and friendship.'[119]

To understand the relevancy of Brenner's commentary, one must appreciate Zionist understanding of Arab-Palestinian society during this period, especially the popular theory that the Arab *Fellahs* were of Jewish origin. Brenner was almost certainly influenced in this regard by his good friend David Ben-Gurion, who wrote at least three essays on this subject between 1917 and 1920. In the first of these, entitled *Clarification of the* Fellahs' *Origin* and published as a chapter in his 1931 book, *Me and Our Neighbours*, Ben-Gurion argued that the Arab population of Palestine could be divided into three groups. These included 'Arabs', who he described as Bedouins deriving from the Arab Peninsula or Syria, and who could be easily identified by 'their only clothing, a rough dress that covers their sun-tanned flesh'; 'Urbanites', who were 'a multi-coloured and speckled population, a rabble of races, nations and languages that one does not find even in the world's largest cities [...] natives of Egypt and Algeria, Tunisia and Morocco, Zanzibar and Madagascar [...] and among them there is a large number of "Arabized Negros"'; and lastly the '*Fellahs*', of whom he claimed 'there is no doubt that there is a lot of Jewish blood that flows in their veins – they are the ignorant

Jewish farmers that in hard times, had chosen to alienate themselves from their own religion, their only purpose not to be uprooted from their land.'[120]

In the run up to the violence of 1921, Ben-Gurion had argued passionately for a pact between the Zionists on the one hand, and the *Fellah*s and working-class elements of Arab society on the other. He believed that such an alliance would split any united Arab front, forcing the upper classes into isolation and drawing the lower, working classes into a joint struggle with the Jewish people in order to 'lead the Near Eastern nations in their struggle for liberation and revival.' Looking to canvas support for this idea, Ben-Gurion used the Ahdut Ha'avoda (Unity of Labour) convention in 1921 to propose the following resolution be adjoined to the party's manifesto:[121]

> *Setting friendly relations between the Hebrew workers and the masses of Arab laborers, based on a mutual economic, political and cultural action – is a necessary condition for our salvation as a free nation and for the liberation of the working Arab from the enslavement forced upon him by his oppressors – the landowners and proprietors in power.*[122]

Without questioning the durability of this unlikely combination of socialist ideology and racial-genetics, such a pact would undoubtedly have had far-reaching consequences for both the Jewish settlement project and the country's agrarian economy given that all lands purchased from Arab landowners were cultivated by the *Fellah*s. In *The Fellah and his Land*, which Ben-Gurion wrote in 1920, the future Prime Minister went even further, suggesting that with any transaction of land, a certain portion would go to the *Fellah*s. If this were not possible, he noted, they would be given a different tract in an alternative location.[123]

It is difficult to ascertain how many Palestinians, if any, were familiar with Ben-Gurion's essays but if we can deduce anything from Brenner's conversation with the youth in the orchard, it is that such ideas, if expressed by Arabic-speaking Jews such as Yitzhak Ben Zvi who shared this idea about the *Fellah*s' origin, could be disseminated fairly easily among the *Fellah*s. Moreover, it would have been relatively easy to measure the influence of Ben-Gurion's propositions within local Arab society, especially in an area like Jaffa where the flourishing citrus trade meant there were very clear-cut class distinctions. Among the rich, upper echelons the response would no doubt have been unequivocal; any attempt by left-wing Zionist parties to encourage the *Fellah*s to rise up in a Socialist revolution would have been perceived as a serious threat to their lifestyle and security.

Which political vehicle would Brenner have sacrificed: the Zionist politics of colonization or the socialist politics of an agrarian revolution? We will never know. But from his interesting description of the Arab landowner as 'one of those Polish from the Orient' and the frustration he expressed at not being able to communicate, man to man with his Arab neighbour, we can assume such a decision would have been disorienting. Regrettably, a much more tragic expression of this kind of confusion took physical form only a few days after Brenner's chance encounters. On the eve of May 1, 1921 – coincidentally both the date of the annual Workers' Day parade *and*, on this particular year, also the last day of celebrations for the Jewish festival of Passover – an Arab woman knocked on the Yatzkar family's Red House, desperately searching for a lost child. Brenner opened the door to her. As was later reported, he was deeply disturbed by her distress and a foreboding sense of dread swept over him. Somehow associating the lost child with the explosive combination of the Passover frivolities and the May Day demonstrations to come, Brenner begged his friends to stay clear of the parade and to avoid the fracas he forecasted.

The next day, a quarrel broke out between two factions of the Jewish Socialist marchers at the May Day demonstration in Jaffa. Very quickly, this altercation developed into an all-out brawl. Given the anxiety and tension which had enveloped the city in recent years, it did not take long for the situation to erupt as Arab bystanders, misunderstanding the melée for a Jewish attack, perpetuated a pogrom on what they supposed were their assailants. Some testimonies of this confrontation accuse the local police of inflaming what was already an electric atmosphere by opening fire on the Jewish protestors.[124] True or not, the violence spread quickly to a nearby immigrant hostel run by the Zionist Congress and then, like a bushfire, into other parts of the city. The following day, the riots left the city walls and fanned out across its outskirts. Before long, the flames of discontent had reached Abu Kabir where, upon finding the lost child's body, the funeral march to the village cemetery ended with a massacre at the Red House.[125] Attempts to rescue the inhabitants were only partially successful and only women and children could be evacuated to Tel Aviv in time. Yosef Haim Brenner, Yehuda Yatzkar and his son Avraham, Zvi Gugig, Yosef Luidor, Zvi Shatz, and two Jewish farmers from Nes Ziona were all slaughtered. According to the interim report submitted by the British authorities to the League of Nations, they made up some of the eighty-eight fatalities recorded over this two-day period, which also left 238 injured and much of Jaffa in a state of disrepair.[126]

The Massacre of May 1921: a photograph of the murdered Yosef Haim Brenner from his 'Selected Reminiscences', edited by his friend Mordechai Kushnir.

Yosef Eliyahu Chelouche. Image courtesy of Lea Aleksandrowicz (Chelouche) Collection

While the extremity of the Arab violence sent shockwaves of fear through the Jewish community in Palestine, there was, as ever, a background to these events. As noted, in the immediate years following World War I, Jaffa had been flooded with Jewish immigrants. The majority of these newcomers had not come in family units or arrived in their dotage but were made up of a very narrow demographic of young males, following each other as if it were some kind of summer trend. They were through with the troubles in Russia and Eastern Europe, so they came to find new ones in Palestine. Ten thousand of these disgruntled, idealistic, energetic adolescents arrived in Jaffa in the space of a year, forming one quarter of the city's new population and instantly altering its visual, social and political landscape. With or without vodka from the continent, they were enough to unsettle the locals and provoke the established order. Even today, it would not be too difficult to imagine the impact – just take one enormous rave festival and place it bang in the centre of Gaza. Rock the Casbah.

This link between the riots in Jaffa and the radical spirit of the Third Aliyah immigrants was reiterated again in the autobiographical account of Yosef Eliyahu Chelouche – a man who refused to spare criticism for either Jewish or Arab communities. When he heard about the violence, Chelouche walked all the way from Tel Aviv to Jaffa, whereupon he was attacked by an Arab mob, only to be rescued by another Arab man who reprimanded the rabble for abusing a native of the country, just like them. Chelouche went to Jaffa's municipality and met with three of the leaders. After admonishing them for encouraging the riots, they answered: 'But whose fault is this if not that of those Bolsheviks that you have been bringing from Moscow?' Chelouche acknowledged the impact of the influx of Eastern European immigrants but was adamant in his response: 'My new brothers came from abroad to build the country and not to destroy it, but you have not understood it yet!'

In the end, all agreed to gather the heads of the three religions and, meeting in the presence of General Deedes,[127] an understanding was reached that sermons of peace would be delivered in all the mosques, churches and synagogues across the region.[128]

Separation

The 1921 riots proved a pivotal moment in Tel Aviv's history, serving as the main catalyst for what would be an exceptional growth spurt over the next decade. For Jaffa, the consequences were disastrous; cut from its periphery, it was left completely isolated and suffocated by Jewish settlements.

After the 1921 events, it became clear that the Zionist movement could not and did not wish to sign a pact with parts of the Arab population, as Ben-Gurion had hoped. On the contrary, the Jewish national movement with its two main projects, immigration and settlement, created a double threat that had unified every class of the Arab population against it, and in fact it helped establish the basis of the Palestinian national identity. The ethnic and political polarization of the two populations, and their consolidation around their respective national projects, made it impossible to maintain a mixed urban environment. It was no longer possible to try to keep a mixed, double or in-between identity, like that of Yosef Eliyahu Chelouche. Jews had nothing to look for in Jaffa, and the city had been transformed from a cosmopolitan city into an Arab one. Jewish enclaves within Jaffa, such as the Feingold Houses in Manshieh, had gradually deteriorated, atrophied and been abandoned. The housing crisis in the region initially caused by the waves of immigrants from Europe had worsened due to the massive departure of the Jewish population from Jaffa, and soon, the whole region of Tel Aviv and Jaffa was swamped in tent encampments.[129]

As a result, Tel Aviv's population in the 1920s multiplied twenty-fold, from 2,084 inhabitants at the beginning of the decade, to 42,000 at its end.[130] Mass overcrowding encouraged more land acquisitions and the majority of deals for plots in what is today considered part of Tel Aviv were conducted during this period. Consuming abandoned agricultural proper-ties (vineyards and orchards) at a rate of knots, Jewish settlement started to sprawl east and north of Ahuzat Bayit, leading to the establishment of new neighbourhoods like Merkaz Baalei Melacha, Geula, Trumpeldor, Tel Nordau and Nordia. But the city also stretched south, beyond the railway line which had demarked Tel Aviv's unofficial border, and a large number of land transactions completed during the 1920s were made in those grey zones within the 'black patch' of Jaffan orchards, as seen in the 1917–1918 aerial photographs. These were largely properties which had been damaged during World War I and discarded by their owners who had decided to leave the faltering citrus business and agricultural work in order to make the most of the booming real-estate economy.

The first of these Jewish settlement-drives southwards occurred immediately after the troubles in 1921 and led to the creation of Neve Sha'anan. Over the next few years new neighbourhoods were added and Neve Sha'anan A was joined by Neve Sha'anan B, Chlenov A, Chlenov B, Florentine and Shapira. Apart from the Neve Sha'anan, most of these southern Jewish neighbourhoods did not fall under Tel Aviv's jurisdiction. But they were also not really considered part of Jaffa either. Their inhabitants paid their taxes to the Jaffa municipality through Jewish '*Mukhtars*' (tax collectors) who acted as intermediaries, but their children went to school in Tel Aviv (mostly to the Bialik School in Neve Sha'anan). Neither city claimed responsibility for infrastructural issues in this buffer zone and residents were forced to solve problems locally, constructing makeshift wells and drilling ad hoc cesspits whenever necessary.

Despite the intensity of the 1921 clashes and the proximity of these southern Jewish neighbourhoods to sites of Arab-Palestinian dwellings, until the next clash between the populations, in the 1936 Great Arab Revolt, these braided areas were not necessarily zones of hostility. According to many testimonies, this zone of frontier was also a place of encounter and co-habitation. This was inevitable because of the complexity of the seam: the separation between the two cities did not fully correspond with the separation between Jews and Arabs. The borderline was complicated and winding, since it was drawn according to land ownerships, which, at the time, were still defined by the real-estate market. In practice, life in these zones created complex situations, like that along Salame Road, where in addition to the traditional role of an Arab commercial strip, a Jewish centre of small industry gradually developed; or like the Shapira neighbourhood, which surrounded an Arab orchard that Meir Getzel Shapira, the neighbourhood developer, had not been able to purchase in 1924. Its proprietor, a farmer from Abu Kabir, continued to cultivate it even after the outburst of the 1936 revolt, until the complete halt of citrus export from the Jaffa port in World War II.[131] According to veteran inhabitants' testimonies, summer folklore of daily encounters and interactions developed in those years around the remaining active orchards, and especially at the Biyara houses' irrigation pool. In the wake of the 1948 war, the grey zones were transferred over to the Tel Aviv municipality, which begrudgingly embraced these poor, largely Mizrahi, neighbourhoods. The orchards were promptly recycled into industrial areas, public housing projects and metropolitan and urban infrastructures.

Map of Jaffa region, 1945. Hatikva, Ezra and Haargazim neighbourhoods keep Salame village away from Jaffa. The location of the Hebrew neighbourhoods of southern Tel Aviv along strategic roads while isolating the Arab villages was one of the main factors in Tel Aviv's victory over Jaffa.
Yad Avner Geographical Database, Department of Geography, Tel Aviv University.

Historically then, they went from being Jaffa's stepchildren to Tel Aviv's, with neither parent particularly thrilled with the responsibility of custody. And yet, strategically, they played an absolutely integral role in determining Jaffa's capitulation and guaranteeing Tel Aviv's dominance across the region for decades to come. In much the same way that the poor, Yemenite neighbourhood of Kerem Hateimanim had protected Ahuzat Bayit's passage to the sea two decades earlier, in the 1920s and 1930s these southern neighbourhoods acted as a vital buffer, protecting the White City of Tel Aviv from the perceived threat of a lurking, Palestinian-nationalist Jaffa. Even more decisively, they linked up with other Jewish settlements, like the Hatikva neighbourhood for example, thereby cutting the territorial continuity between Jaffa and *its* Eastern satellites – Abu Kabir, Salama and Yazur. Similar patterns of expansion had been repeated across other parts of the country on countless occasions, but this was the first time that Jewish settlement had succeeded in smothering a whole region so effectively. Jaffa was doomed. For the first time in its history, it was cut off from its rural hinterland, from its trade routes and from the rest of the country as a whole. The surrounding Hebrew neighbourhoods transformed it into an enclave. This solitary status would be recognized and reinforced in the United Nations Division Plan of 1947 (which designated it as an Arab enclave within the future Jewish state) but even this judgement was rendered irrelevant after the city's bloody defeat and surrender in 1948. In the intermediate years however, these Hebrew neighbourhoods served as important bases for underground military organizations like the Etzel[132] and the Lehi,[133] for terrorist activities against the British, but mainly against Jaffa's population and civilian institutions. From 1921, and until the establishment of the State of Israel in 1948, Tel Aviv's flight from Jaffa gradually became a chase.

British 1930s

Popular and architectural histories of Tel Aviv associate construction during the 1930s with particular Central European aesthetic and architectural qualities, but in reality the city's expansion was much more of a grand exercise in British urban planning. The Bauhaus creations which have come to characterize the era were only a fraction of the total mass of buildings erected, most of which formed part of a British programme to modernize Jewish settlements in Palestine. Over the course of the Mandate, the British revolutionized the country; they built power stations, airports, ports, railway lines and trains stations, roads, pipelines, hospitals, schools, government buildings and army barracks, all in and around the emerging Jewish settlements. It was an unprecedented project and one which has not been replicated on a similar scale since; in less than three decades (with the majority of construction completed in the first half of the British occupation, before World War II broke out), the ruling British government did more for the country's infrastructure than the State of Israel has done in all its years of existence. In many ways, then, building the State of Israel was actually more of a British project than an 'Israeli Project'.[134] Even today, substantial parts of modern Israel's infrastructure – from its prisons and ports to its police and power stations – are British hand-me-downs. After centuries of Muslim governance, the British also established a new infrastructure of modern and liberal governmental traditions, administration, civil and public service, and set the basis of Israeli law and legislation.

Other British influences have also prevailed: a first colonial exhibition was held at the Zionist club in Rothschild Boulevard. In 1925 the municipality of Tel Aviv allocated an area in the southern neighbourhood of Neve Sha'anan for colonial exhibitions: in 1925, 1926 and on the occasion of the 20th anniversary of Tel Aviv – a 'Jubilee Fair' in 1929. In 1932 Tel Aviv celebrated the 'Orient Fair', a gigantic international exhibition that covered the entire Yarkon Peninsula in the northern part of Tel Aviv. It was a temporal modernist white city that could have even turned Daniel Burnham, the architect of Chicago's 1893 World Columbian Exhibition, green with envy. In the same year, Tel Aviv organized the First Maccabiah Games. Both venues enabled the arrival of a new generation of young, relatively wealthy and sporty generation of immigrants.[135]

The separation of Tel Aviv from Jaffa, its quick transformation from a cluster of scattered Jewish neighbourhoods into one Hebrew City, was made possible only under the British Mandate government and with its encouragement: in July 1920, a few days after his appointment, Sir Herbert Louis Samuel, the first High Commissioner for Palestine and Transjordan, visited Tel Aviv and heard the inhabitants' claim for separation. On May 11, 1921, he signed the 'Order of Tel Aviv Township', granting it with an independent status and providing it with a borderline which separated it from Jaffa. In 1925 the British provided the city with a new urban scheme designed by the Scottish town planner, Sir Patrick Geddes.

The strategic significance of the Jewish construction during the 1930s overshadows its aesthetic qualities. Apart from the White City, which, by itself, represented not only an architectural achievement but also a crucial strategic factor for the whole region, there were other Jewish construction projects such as the 'Settlement Offensive' of the 'Wall and Tower' (Homa Umigdal) settlements throughout the whole country during the Great Arab Revolt between 1936–1939. The revolt broke out in April 1936 with the assassination of four Jewish immigrants in Tul Karem, anti-Jewish riots, lynchings and attacks in Jaffa and a general strike that was declared all over the country; it was directed against the Jewish population and against the British Administration which was judged to be pro-Jewish. The Settlement Offensive was the first time in the region's history that architecture was used as a military tool. The idea was to establish, in the shortest period of time, a network of new settlements that would create a Jewish contiguity and define the future borderline of the State of Israel. This continuum took the form of the letter 'N' superimposed on the valleys that cross the country – from the northern point of the Jordan Valley to Beit Shean Valley, to the Yizrael Valley, and throughout the Littoral plain, to the Negev desert. To realize the Settlement Offensive strategy, the main tactical tool was Homa Umigdal – the Wall and Tower Settlement.

Wall and Tower was a system of settlement, seemingly defensive but essentially of offensive form, invented in 1936 by the members of Kibbutz Tel-Amal (today Kibbutz Nir-David) in Beit-Shean Valley. The invention was attributed to the Kibbutz member Shlomo Gur[136] and was developed and encouraged by the architect Yohanan Ratner.[137]

From the start, the objective of this communal and fortified type of settlement was to seize control of land that had been officially purchased by the Keren Kayemeth LeIsrael (Jewish National Fund)[138] but could not be settled upon.

The system was based on the hasty construction of a wall made of pre-fabricated wooden moulds filled with gravel and surrounded by a barbed wire fence. All in all, the enclosed space formed a 35m by 35m yard. Within this enclosure were set up a pre-fabricated wooden tower that commanded the view of the surrounding area and four shacks that were to house a 'conquering troop' of forty people. Between the years 1936–1939, some fifty-seven such outposts were set up throughout the country and rapidly developed into permanent rural collective settlements established according the Zionist Labour movement's two main settling types: the kibbutz and the moshav. In many cases, they defined the State of Israel's borders in 1948.[139]

But Jewish settlements were not the only urban dwellings undergoing a significant revamp. Alongside their readiness to develop Tel Aviv, the British also took the liberty of implementing 'Project Anchor' in Jaffa, a most significant example, no less emblematic than the Wall and Tower settlement system, of things to come. Project Anchor was a strange mixture between a military operation and an urban project, in which the British tried to subdue the Great Arab Revolt that had spread to the Palestinian capital, to repress the dockworkers' strike taking place at the city port and to safeguard the army's access to Jaffa's harbour.

On June 16, 1936, the British army ordered the evacuation of the residents of the Old City of Jaffa, promising monetary compensation for any damage that might be caused to their houses as a result of the planned infrastructural improvements. Three days later, on June 19, 237 buildings were demolished in order to clear the route to the harbour. Once the dust had settled, Henry Kendall, the British Adviser for Town Planning, prepared a new plan for Old Jaffa following the 'remodelling'.[140] According to the plan, which was approved by the British in 1937, the rubble would be cleared to make way for a large square, with two adjoining roads which would divide the Old City into two smaller sections. 'It was probably the beginning of the evacuation of the central quarter in the heart of Old Jaffa, and the beginning of "The Big Zone"' – rightfully commented Dov Gavish in his essay on the suppression of the revolt in Jaffa, published in the journal of Israeli studies of the Ministry of Tourism, named *Kardom* (Hebrew for 'axe').[141]

But the events of 1936 would have much wider implications for the future of Jaffa. For most of the residents of the Jewish settlement in Tel Aviv, the Arab city became a 'forbidden city'. In turn, Palestinian residents of Jaffa became increasingly aware of their isolation, cut off from Jaffa's hinterland and surrounded by a growing number of Jewish settlements and neighbourhoods. An inevitable result of this physical and social disengagement was an economic detachment, as Tel Aviv sought to survive independently of the old trading metropolis. In this sense, the construction of the Tel Aviv port was a direct retaliation to the boycott of Jewish merchandise at Jaffa's port, while the perceived danger of shopping in Jaffa prompted the establishment of the HaCarmel Market in Kerem Hateimanim and a new wholesale market.[142]

Each of these substitutions bent the balance of power between the two cities that little bit more, strengthening Tel Aviv on the one hand and weakening Jaffa on the other. The moment when the Arab city would be completely at the mercy of the Hebrew one drew ever nearer.

The British 'Operation Anchor' in the historic city of Jaffa in 1936.
Matson (G. Eric and Edith) Photograph Collection.

Dubek cigarettes playing card dating from the beginning of the 1940s, showing settlers of tower and stockade settlements in Ein Hakore examining the model of their new settlement. Dubek.

Kendall and Shor's overall plan of Jaffa following 'Operation Anchor', 1937. *RAF Aerial Journal*, 48–49.

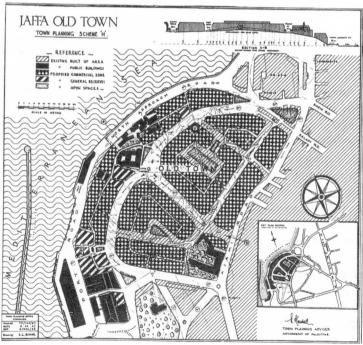

The British 'Operation Anchor' in the historic city of Jaffa in 1936: before and during.
RAF Aerial Journal, 48–49.

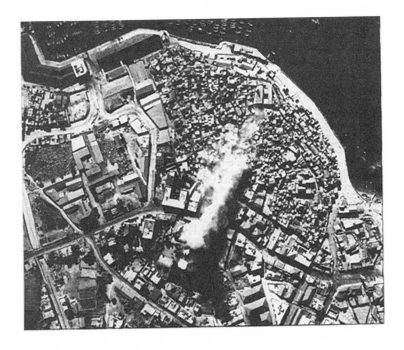

Just as Tel Aviv had come to symbolize the materialization of the Jewish national aspirations in a physical, urban form, so Jaffa came to represent the metropolitan embodiment of the Palestinian cause. For that same reason, many Jews (both in Tel Aviv and across the country as a whole) began to regard Jaffa's independent and autonomous status as something intolerable. Indeed, for figures like Menachem Begin, the leader of the Etzel paramilitary group, Jaffa was not only an obstacle that might later risk the very existence of the Jewish State, but also a possible base for an Arab landing and for an attack on Tel Aviv and the Jewish Settlement.

According to the United Nation's decision on November 29, 1947, which divided the country between Jews and Arabs, Jaffa would be granted the special status of an independent Palestinian enclave within a future Jewish State. But only five months later, on April 25, Jaffa was attacked and by the time it surrendered on May 13, the city had already been massively destroyed.

In the months between the United Nations ruling and the declaration of the State of Israel on May 15, 1948, the country was brought to a state of civil war, in which Jewish organized and un-organized paramilitary forces fought the civilian population. As for Jaffa, the historian Benny Morris argues that the common belief among Haganah forces during this period was that Jaffa did not actually pose a significant strategic threat to Tel Aviv – their assessment was that it was made up of a large, unarmed, civilian population and was surrounded by Jewish settlements.[143] But the Etzel and Lehi thought differently. Perhaps due to the fact that the Etzel's style of assault was more suited to large cities, or maybe because Tel Aviv was Begin's beloved hometown (when he was elected prime minister he decided to give up formal

Opposite: The Plan of Partition Between the Jewish and Arab states (Appendix A in UN Decision 181). Appendix B marked in general terms the partition borders in the Jerusalem region. It could have been expected that Appendix C would mark the division in the Jaffa and Tel Aviv region, and yet the only reference to the division of the region appears in the text itself, in the part discussing the Arab state: 'the area of the Jaffa enclave is located in the part of the Jaffa plan stretching to the west of the Jewish areas south of Tel Aviv, towards the continuation of Herzl Street up until the Jaffa-Jerusalem Road [today's Kibbutz Galuyot Road – S.R.] to the south-western part of the Jaffa-Jerusalem Road stretching south-east of this junction, westwards towards the Mikve Israel lands, to the north-western corner of the area of jurisdiction of the municipality of Holon, to the north-east corner of the area of jurisdiction of the municipality of Bat Yam. The question of the Carton neighbourhood will be determined by the border committee and would aspire to include the slightest number of Arabs in the domain of the Jewish State.'

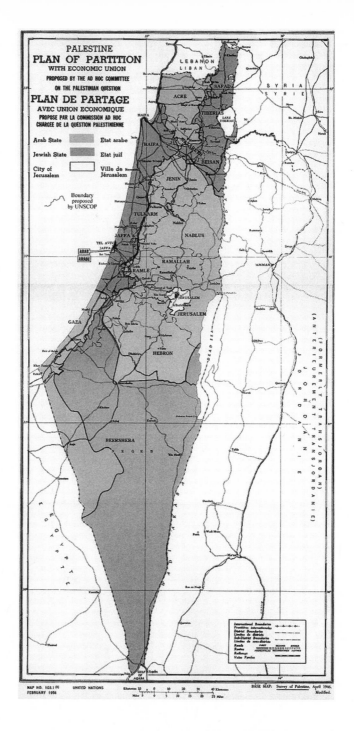

residence in Jerusalem in order to remain in his modest house in Tel Aviv); either way, Jaffa became the main site for the organization's activity.

The violence had started as early as December 2, 1947, and forced a massive departure of inhabitants of the middle and upper classes. With their exodus, the public and municipal services inside Jaffa collapsed and most of the businesses in the city came to a standstill.[144] The siege was not absolute – Jewish citrus farmers had insisted the port remain open for the export of their produce – but the net was closing in on Jaffa.[145]

According to both Jewish and Palestinian testimonies, the terror tactics used during these operatives ranged from the rolling of 'barrel bombs'[146] down the city's streets and snipers focused on the entrances of popular cafés, to the explosion of the New Seraya building, Jaffa's town hall built by Ottoman authorities, on January 4, 1948.[147]

Gathering confidence from these attacks, the Etzel leadership decided to forgo waiting for the British to pack up and leave as planned on May 14, 1948, and instead launched an early, full-scale attack on Jaffa on April 25. This began with a rain of mortars over the city, sustained right up until the old Arab capital fell. According to Palestinian accounts, the bombardments were coupled with radio broadcasts in Arabic in which the Etzel promised the civilian population that their fate would be similar to that of the inhabitants of the village of Deir Yassin, near Jerusalem, who had been massacred few days earlier, on April 9, by the Etzel and Lehi's fighters.[148] At the same time, the Haganah launched 'Operation Chametz' in the villages surrounding Jaffa: Salame, al-Hiriya and Yazur all fell before May, while Fedja and Sheikh Munis were forced to surrender even earlier, leaving Jaffa disconnected from its hinterland. Collectively, some 40,000 residents fled these villages and many followed those Jaffan refugees who had left their homes and headed for Lebanon or Jordan.[149] In the latter stages of the hostilities, however, Jaffa's ever-increasing isolation meant that the only viable means of escape was via the sea. The city's port stopped exporting oranges to the continent and started packing people in boats heading north to Beirut and south to Gaza. Despite the best efforts of British protection to facilitate these transfers, such was the sense of panic at the port, many died in their desperation to escape, drowning after being forced off overcrowded boats or from swimming out to reach them. Of all the numerous, unwarranted times the phrase 'push them into the sea' has been flippantly bandied around in the context of the Arab–Israeli conflict, this may well be the only instance in its history when the expression has literally taken form.

But those impelled to the port were not only seeking refuge from the

A postcard showing the New Seraya Building. From the book *Jaffa in the Mirror of Days* edited by former General Rehavam Ze'evi, later known as a right-wing politician.

Etzel's cannons, they were also fleeing the fierce battle raging in Jaffa's streets. Here, the Etzel commander Amichai 'Gidi' Faglin led his fighters in what is still considered to this day to be a landmark operation within the field of urban combat.[150] Developing (or more accurately, rediscovering) a technique based on the gradual reduction of the urban mass from the inside-out, in which fighters moved from house to house under the protection of façades, he sought to take advantage of the traditional fabric of the continuous city block. This 'mouse hole' technique was preceded by two sources. The first came from *La guerre des rues et des maisons* (The War of Streets and Houses), the book written almost exactly one hundred years earlier by Maréchal Bugeaud, the French military leader responsible for conquering Morocco and Algeria.[151] In this manuscript Bugeaud recommends a combination of engineering and fighting forces, working in tandem in order to bypass exposed routes which may be barricaded or are subject to fire from burning buildings. He advocates creating an alternative axis for engaging the enemy, by digging passageways from building to building and moving from apartment to apartment under the shelter of the built mass, thereby taking over whole streets via the flanks. A decade later, this modus operandi was reinvented by Louis-Auguste Blanqui in *Instructions pour une prise d'armes* (Manual for an Armed Insurrection).[152] Blanqui, one of the great rebels of nineteenth-century France, could not have been familiar with Bugeaud's book as *La guerre des rues et des maisons* had still not been published at this point and because, as of 1848, Blanqui would spend most of his remaining life in prison. Nonetheless, Blanqui details almost exactly the same 'mouse hole' technique as Bugeaud, only stressing the importance of adjoining barricades as a means of blocking opposition traffic.[153]

While it is unclear whether 'Gidi' Faglin was aware of these two manu-scripts, he certainly put some of their key ideas into practice and was the first to actually use 'mouse holes' in a military operation. Benjamin Runkle describes how Faglin dug out two parallel 'overground tunnels' from the built mass of Manshieh, through which he was able to outflank the Arab posts and reach the neighbourhood's extremities. Faglin then used the psychological effect of his forces' presence on either side to create a heightened sense of panic among those Arab inhabitants and resistance fighters trapped in the middle. Chaim Lazar notes how Faglin also adopted a similar tactic to the one championed by Blanqui, blocking major traffic axes with sandbags and rubble from ruined buildings.[154]

In the beginning of the twenty-first century, the Israeli Defense Forces have employed similar methods in the West Bank and Gaza. The interpret-ations offered by Buguead, Blanqui and Faglin have been reinvented again within the context of *modern* urban combat, and the 'mouse hole' technique

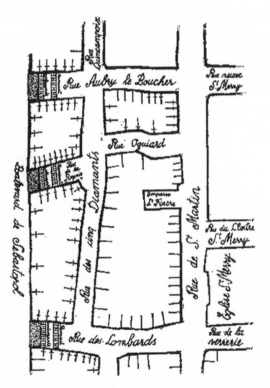

Passing through walls: a sketch showing a combination of barricades and 'mouse holes'. From Louis-Auguste Blanqui's *Manual for an Armed Insurrection*.

has morphed into a twenty-first century 'worm'. In Nadav Harel and Eyal Weizman's film, *War in the City*, Brigadier-General Aviv Kochavi, commander of the 98th Paratroopers Division, expanded on his adaptation of this methodology, recounting the theory he applied when leading the Israeli assault of the Balata refugee camp in Nablus, in April 2002:

> *The meaning of the territory no longer has any importance; there is no value anymore in declaring 'I won.' […] the reality and the space are subject to interpretation. We no longer wish to conform to the alleys, the streets, or the city. We do not want to conform to their interpretation as the architect or city planner who planned them envisaged them, we will interpret the space by the manner that suits us: if the alley is a place to walk through, then the alley will be a place where walking is forbidden, and door and window would become places one cannot pass through. […] Do not interpret the urban space in the classic manner but in a wholly new one. That is the reason we chose the method of passing through walls, like a worm chewing and ending up in a different place every time. The idea of passing through walls may not be new, but for the first time we took this tactic, this micro-tactic, and turned it into a method. […] This is what allows reinterpretation of the space. This is what we teach our soldiers – there is no more passage through alleys, through streets, through roofs. Movement is only through walls. […] The reality is the interpretation of the one who assaults and the one who defends. Someone could tell me one moment what does it mean? – a house is a house and an alley is an alley; but I say no way, those are just interpretations.*[155]

Kochavi's new, forced geography makes the urban space and the existing order irrelevant by decision, in exactly the same way one might make a conscious decision that something else, anything else, was no longer relevant. In a military context, it permits the assailant to reject threats and refrain from stepping into traps set out in the enemy's space by creating alternative routes on their own alternative map. For the defender, on the other hand, it cancels out the most basic component of the existing order within a city: the separation between the private and public space. In this sense, this new geography of the city turns the existing geography of the city (in a manner not devoid of irony) into some sort of artifice – into an illusion, a camouflage, a trick, a stunt, an installation. Both Faglin and Kochavi were interested in their respective enemies still believing that the house was a house, the alley an alley, and the city a city – both knew only too well that as soon as *their* shadow city was invented, that it would be the only city which mattered.

Since the British forces, still officially in charge, entered into the second phase of this fighting, the battle of Manshieh presented other military and urban aspects. After all, this was the first time during the Israeli War of Independence that the Etzel fighters faced direct confrontation with an established military force. They were victorious again on this occasion, just as they had been in driving out Jaffa's Palestinian inhabitants, thanks to Faglin's ability to re-imagine the urban reality. If in the first stage of the battle, the space of Manshieh had been redesigned and emptied of its content, then this second assault against British forces re-imagined the same neighbourhood as a weapon in its own right. Drawing on his experience as an explosives expert and his knowledge of the area's intricate network of streets, Faglin plotted detonation devices across the city – concealed in alleyways, in thorough-fares, in dilapidated buildings – and waited for British tanks to roll into the neighbourhood before exploding it on top of them. In doing so, he was able to recycle the city itself into a barricade, blocking off main traffic junctions and altering the battlefront to suit the Etzel's strengths and resources.

Throughout the conquest of Jaffa, Faglin displayed an acute understanding of both the malleability of urban form and the limitations of his enemies. Fully aware of the fact that the majority of British forces saw the battle for Jaffa as unnecessary – (as far as they were concerned, they were soon leaving Palestine and the Zionists would almost certainly take control of it once they had gone) – the commander decided on a dramatic finale. During negotiations with the British to reach some kind of détente, he held a press conference while simultaneously ordering the destruction of the police station in Manshieh, which was supposed to be under British governance up until the end of the Mandate. The echoes of the explosion which rang out across Jaffa were a chilling prompt for the British army to follow the city's residents and evacuate as soon as possible. On May 13, 1948, they duly did so.

On that date, following the British evacuation, the members of Jaffa's Arab Emergency Committee, Ahmed Abu-Laban, Salah Nazar, Amin Andreus and Ahmed Abdul Rahim, signed a surrender treaty.[156] Only a few thousand people remained in the city.[157] Some claim that even fewer stayed behind – about 2,500 inhabitants, most of whom were refugees from the nearby villages, Salame and Yazur. In his book *The Conquest of Jaffa*, Chaim Lazar of the Etzel claims that in the first census held in Jaffa 3,665 non-Jewish residents were counted, out of whom 2,047 were Muslim and 1,540 were

Christian, as well as some non-Arab Christians, including clergymen. Morris recounts that on May 18, Ben-Gurion visited Jaffa and wrote: 'I could not understand: how did the inhabitants of Jaffa leave this city?'[158]

The conquest of Jaffa is something of a unique case in the history of the 1948 war; it differs from the subjugation of other Arab cities or villages because the 'Bride of the Sea' had been granted special status under the United Nations Partition Plan of 1947. Beyond the military defeat of the city, and the humanitarian disaster of the mass departure of its inhabitants, the conquest of Jaffa was first of all a violation of an international decision.

The city's surrender on May 13, 1948, two days before the founding of the State of Israel, is politically relevant because it proves that 'Israel' (or least the Zionist forces that would soon come to represent Israel) breached

Passing through walls: plan of the advancement of Etzel forces in the battle of Manshieh. From Chaim Lazar-Litai's *The Conquest of Jaffa.*

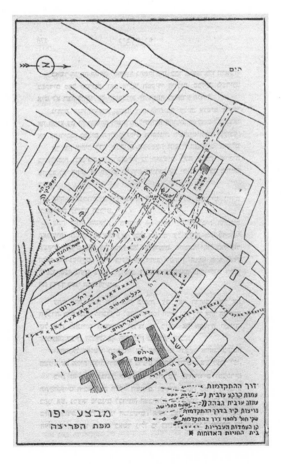

the strict terms of the United Nations partition agreement. This fact stands in direct contradiction to the State of Israel's formal rhetoric that casts the responsibility for the outbreak of the War of Independence on the Arab states, who did not accept the UN's decision and attacked the State of Israel following its declaration. While it is certainly true that external Arab armies did attack the State of Israel in the wake of Ben-Gurion's Declaration, Zionist forces had already wrapped up the war against the Palestinians by this point; the region's Arab population had been driven out and any local ramshackle resistance had been crushed long before the British had left, let alone before the new Israeli prime minister addressed the world. In the Declaration of Independence Ben-Gurion said:

> WE APPEAL – in the very midst of the onslaught launched against us now for months – to the Arab inhabitants of the State of Israel to preserve peace and participate in the upbuilding of the State on the basis of full and equal citizenship and due representation in all its provisional and permanent institutions.

But at those moments, only a few streets away from Rothschild Boulevard where the Declaration of Establishment of State of Israel took place, Jaffa and its neighbourhoods lay in ruin, trampled and mutilated, and spontaneous and organized looting had already begun.[159] These scenes were replicated across the area we know today as 'Gush Dan' (the official span of Tel Aviv, from Netanya in the north to Ashdod in the south) and in all those 'mixed cities' up and down the country – in Haifa, Acre and Ramla.

The almost complete disappearance of Jaffa's Palestinian community, which had constituted roughly 97 percent of the city's population as a whole even in late 1947, was just as unnerving as the city's physical destruction. According to Palestinian testimonies, during the Etzel bombardments the city's hotels had been turned into hospitals. It is unclear how all these hospitals were evacuated during the quick escape from Jaffa, when many of the city's inhabitants tried swimming to reach the boats docking outside the harbour. To this day it is unclear what happened to most of Jaffa's residents. According to Chaim Lazar, at the end of the battle on Manshieh the Etzel piled dozens of bodies of Arabs for the Red Cross in a field by the beach.[160]

Many of the residents who stayed in the city flew the flags of different countries, hoping to be saved. A literary testimony which alludes to the grisly fate of those inhabitants of Jaffa who fought and then surrendered can be found in *Swimming Competition*, a short story penned by Binyamin Tamuz:

the narrator, a Jewish Fighter from the Haganah, returns to a Bayara house in Tel-A-Reesh in the eastern outskirts of Jaffa where as a child he used to swim with Arab children. During the battle a Palestinian fighter, once the narrator's childhood friend and the boy who had beaten him in a swimming competition, is captured and later murdered. 'A western wind carried with it the smells of Jaffa', writes Tamuz as he describes the Haganah's revenge mission in Tel-A-Reesh, 'But at a later time, a back wind came in from the Holon's neighbourhoods and brought with it the scent of white houses.'[161]

Cleansing

Despite this outline, the full story of Jaffa's capture in 1948 has yet to be told. When it is delivered in its entirety, it would be appropriate if it relied on both Hebrew and Arab accounts.

Jaffa did not only lose its inhabitants in 1948. For the first time in 5,000 years, it ceased to exist as an urban and cultural entity. It was stripped bare of its heritage and left beaten, bruised and lifeless. The speed at which this transformation occurred, and its totality, was astounding. Cities like Hiroshima, Dresden and Berlin all suffered exorbitant damage during World War II but each emerged from the dust-clouds of conflict intact, even vibrant, urban

'Tel Aviv and its Sites':
Jaffa as a Tel Avivian site.
Cover of *Ariel Journal for Eretz-Israel Studies*, 48–49, 1987.

entities. The physical destruction of Jaffa was obviously on a much, much smaller scale than the pummelling meted out at Nagasaki, for example, and yet its annihilation was as total as the ancient eradications of Ai, Troy, Carthage and Pompeii.

The Palestinians of Jaffa had been forced into exile in much the same way Jewish communities throughout history had been repeatedly driven from *their* own homes and villages. And just as in these cases of Jewish expulsion, when the Palestinians of Jaffa were exiled, their culture, economy, government and history was thrown out with them. Within days the community had melted away, almost as if it had never existed in the first place. The sense of hollowed emptiness which enveloped Manshieh, Ajami and Tel-A-Reesh, the Palestinian neighbourhoods of Jaffa, spread across the region as a whole, as the satellite villages of Salama, Abu Kabir, Jammasin, Mas'udiyya, Summayl, Hiriya and Sheikh Munis all stood in ruins.

From any aspect – practical or symbolical – and from any point of view – Palestinian or Israeli – Jaffa's fall was an even more significant than the conquest of Jerusalem's old city nineteen years later. Whereas the fight for the Holy City would be about regaining possession of an important religious site, in 1948 Tel Aviv was concentrated on emptying Jaffa of its Palestinian population. The conquest of the city might have led to the annulment of its autonomous standing as a Palestinian enclave, as prescribed in the Partition Plan of 1947, but this was nothing in terms of political impact when compared with the blanket disappearance of anywhere between 100,000 and 140,000 Palestinian citizens from the Tel Aviv region.

Jaffa – Tel Aviv

On October 4, 1949, a government assembly met in order to discuss and determine the annexation of Jaffa to Tel Aviv. The minutes of this meeting ran as follows:[162]

> *Minister M. Shapira*: 'I have sent you a memo concerning the annexation of Jaffa to Tel Aviv. Within ten months we have created annexations – we have appropriated parts of Jaffa and added them to Tel Aviv twice [...]
> *Minister M. Sharett*: You've annexed annexations and deprived deprivations [...]
> *Minister M. Shapira*: [...] this remains to be clarified. The

territory annexed is of 9,000 dunams. There is still need to appropriate 7,000 more dunams. On the administrative, economic, and municipal levels, this territory already comprises part of Tel Aviv, with all it entails, and it is something not very, […] and also unnatural, to have a narrow street separating two cities. This brings me to the conclusion that Jaffa needs to be annexed to Tel Aviv. This is a pressing matter given the upcoming elections. I would like to fix the elections for the end of the year. As for the name, I suggest that this city be called 'Jaffa – Tel Aviv'. We cannot give up the name 'Tel Aviv' – a quarter million Jews will not be willing to cancel it completely, and we should not do so. Budapest is also a combination of two names – 'Buda' and 'Pest'. When the two names would be adjoined, they would create a beautiful name. I suggest Jaffa would come before Tel Aviv – it makes sense phonetically and historically. This is evident to all … that Jaffa is much older than Tel Aviv. It is possible that this merging may postpone the elections, due to the need to create the voter registry. I am doing everything I can in order for the preparation to be done as rapidly as possible, however, I believe this merging is so important, the elections could be postponed for a few weeks if necessary.

Minister D. Yossef: For the protocol, I would like to express my doubts concerning this matter. I fear that it is unhealthy to create such a big city, and it is preferable to have two smaller cities, one by the other.

Minister B. S. Shitrit: I do not understand this demand to annex Jaffa to Tel Aviv or Tel Aviv to Jaffa. Let Jaffa remain as it is, elect its own municipality, and Tel Aviv, which symbolizes resurrection and revival, will remain a separate city. Why slur over one city with another? I believe the historic Jaffa needs to remain as it is, and Tel Aviv as Tel Aviv. That way there will be another city in Israel, we will not cover up one city in another, and we will not minimize the country.

Minister M. Shapira: We are now adding cities over cities […]

Minister B. S. Shitrit: The mixture of neighbourhoods should not be seen as the final combination, and I would offer that Bostrus remain within Jaffa. […]

Prime Minister D. Ben-Gurion: While I appreciate Mr. Shitrit's logic, I see two important reasons to support the unification. Firstly, it is unhealthy to separate a city comprised of immigrants from a city that is built, rich, and wonderful. Jaffa will have only slight means for improvement if left on its own. Second, I hope that one day the name 'Tel Aviv' will be erased and only 'Jaffa' will exist. [...] Who is for the unification of Jaffa and Tel Aviv?

With a majority of 7:2 votes they decide to give the Minister of Interior Affairs the power to unify the two cities – Jaffa and Tel Aviv – into one metropolis.

> Prime Minister D. Ben-Gurion: As for the name, there is an offer to call the city Jaffa–Tel Aviv, and an offer to call it Jaffa.
> Minister M. Sharett: I would offer to introduce the writing of the name Tel Aviv as one word. [The proposal is not accepted]

With a majority of 7:5 votes the party decides that the unified city will be called Jaffa – Tel Aviv.

A joint committee composed of representatives of the Ministry of Interior and the mayors of Tel Aviv and its southern suburbs, Holon and Bat Yam, negotiated the borders of the new united city; Tel Aviv's mayor Israel Rokah insisted that the city shall be named 'Tel Aviv – Yaffo' and so it was published on June 18, 1950, in the State of Israel's official gazette.

An Occupied City

After the murder comes the inheritance.

In fact, Jaffa remains under military occupation to this day. After the city had been ransacked of its population, the IDF relocated some of its units there and took over various houses and estates, transforming Jaffa into a city of barracks. Over half a century following its 'liberation' and the army still hasn't released its grip on the former Arab capital. IDF bases and army headquarters still litter the cityscape – among others, the military radio station (Galey Tzahal), the Military Attorney's offices and the State of Israel's Military Courts can be all found in Jaffa. The city and its residents have been reinvented as a human shield in order to protect them.

The new State of Israel devoted its energies and resources to bulldozing ancient, Arab Jaffa. This involved both the physical overhauling of city spaces and the nullification of those symbols and images which had previously imbued them with charge. All Palestinian social, cultural and historical content was decanted and the empty shell was refilled with a triumphant Zionist mythology. A magic wand flitted above the city, turning the Kfar Kassem Intersection into the Kessem ('magic' in Hebrew) Intersection, Salama Road into Shalma Street, and the world-renowned Al-Hamra Cinema into the Alhambra Theatre. Nobody queried the origins of this beautiful building, constructed in an Art Deco style which had never existed in Tel Aviv, or looked to locate the architect who had designed it.

The new open areas and the remaining old buildings spread throughout the city, which had survived the Etzel's assault, provided a picturesque and exotic décor which, after a few years, began to gradually draw in tourists and artists. In time, Jaffa's old port and the Ajami neighbourhood would become the target of real-estate speculation and gentrification would threaten to wipe Palestinian Jaffa off the map once and for all.[163] Eventually, Jaffa's heritage was conquered as well.

A detailed account of the different urban planning policies employed in Jaffa and its satellite villages since May 1948 could quite easily fill a library. Today, the city stands as an encyclopaedia of ruins, a dictionary of destruction. The demolition of Jaffa became so blatant in the immediate aftermath of the 1948 War that no official explanation has ever been provided; and so it continued with the first case of demolition being used as justification for further demolition. Jaffa's physical decay may have begun in earnest with the Etzel's shelling in December 1947 but it has not ceased since.[164] Indeed, Jaffa's current state of dilapidation is so extensive that it is difficult to ascertain what was ruined during the war, what was ruined immediately after it, and what has been ruined more recently: there is so much decay in Jaffa, it is hard to make it out anymore.

A historical atlas is necessary to properly examine the changes which the city has undergone. Among the litany of urban transformations, the neighbourhood of Givat Aliyah was established on top of what was once the old Palestinian neighbourhood of Jabaliya, only to be re-branded Jabaliya again at a later date;[165] roughly 2,000 homes have been destroyed between 1948 and 1990, all in the Palestinian neighbourhoods of Ajami and Jabaliya.[166] In the beginning of the 1970s the government started the building of a major hospital named after its donor, the Israeli millionaire Shaul Eisenberg, on the site of an old Palestinian orchard on the city's eastern outskirts. But soon after the huge steel structure's erection the project was abandoned and the gigantic empty metal skeleton fell into disrepair, standing until its final disassembly and demolition in 2003. The village of Abu Kabir vanished off the face of the earth, to be replaced by the neighbourhood of Kiyrat Shalem and, at the initiative of the Jewish National Fund, a pine grove; Tel-A-Reesh mysteriously morphed into Tel Giborim overnight. The lands of the old Palestinian village of Salama were divided into various neighbourhoods shared between two municipalities: in one section, Kfar Shalem was founded, a Tel Avivian slum neighbourhood, which today is made up of a mixture of Palestinian gravel architecture, various public housing initiatives from the 1960s and 1970s and some 'build your own home' constructions from the 1980s. The rest of Salama was split into two neighbourhoods now considered part of Ramat Gan – the exclusive Ramat Chen, and the immigrant enclave of Ramat Hashikma (previously referred to by everyone as Salame Gimel after the new immigrants' transit camp that was once located there). Elsewhere, the ruins of Yazur became the new Israeli town of Azor, and both Jaffa's main beach and the old village of Hiriya were hidden from view by mountains of trash. The list of examples goes on and on and on.

Hebraized City

If in order to change the city, the city's story needs to be changed, then deciding the language which the new adaptation is told in is absolutely imperative. When Jaffa was annexed to Tel Aviv, and all of its properties were transferred into the hands of the government legal guardian by the Ministry of Justice following the Absentees' Property Law,[167] the first thing Jaffa lost was its language, its Arabic. There, straddled beside the first Hebrew city, a new Jaffa arose from the ashes of its destruction in 1948 – Israel's very first Hebraized city.

Jaffa's shift from Arabic to Hebrew was perhaps the Tel Aviv municipality's ultimate act of effacement. It didn't just mean the selective elimination of one particular event or of a singular historical recollection; it was the complete and utter obliteration of all stories, of all memories, of all acts of commemoration, of all aspects of formal, public and private documentation that had taken place there prior to 1948. All of Jaffa's texts were erased – from the love songs written about the 'Bride of the Sea' by the Palestinian equivalents of Naomi Shemer and Arik Einstein, to mundane, municipal paperwork; from columns in local newspapers to climacteric literary debates. While a considerable chunk of the city's official history had perished in the explosion of the Seraya town hall in January 1948, whatever was left was systematically binned: almost every record of its institutions, citizens, elected

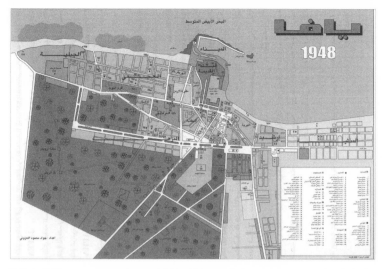

Yaffa in 1948, a reconstructed map of Jaffa with its original street names in Arabic drafted by Jawad Mahmoud Al-'Azuni. From the website Palestineremembered.com.

'The house of the loved ones is deserted / And Jaffa has been translated to its bones', Mahmoud Darwish, *Diary of a Palestinian Wound*, 1969.
A municipal street sign at the corner of Salame Road and Herzl Street, stating: 'Shalma Road – the street leading to Kfar Shalem ('Seleme') where Judah Maccabee had beat Nikanor (*First book of Maccabees*, 31)'.

'Jaffa and its sites': *Kardom* Magazine. Jaffa enters the 'Eretz Israel' studies discipline, 1981.

administrators, procedures, bills, letters – everything was deleted. Jaffa's story was over, and there was no one left to read or write it.

Jaffa's history was kidnapped by the historic-geographic complex composed by the new compulsory discipline of 'Land of Israel Studies' taught in every Israeli school, high school and university across the country, by the Ministry of Tourism and the various agencies and agents of the tourist industry, as well as by the army's education officers and *Politruks*. Here, it was weaved into a fresh historic-geographic narrative that .formed the basis of Land of Israel Studies, a compulsory subject taught in every Israeli school across the country. The city's rich, ancient history was exploited by archaeological bodies, like the Israel Antiquities Authority and the National Project of Single-Layered Archaeology, who also selectively picked and chose whatever tallied with Zionism's linear and homogenous interpretation of the past. All of Jaffa's former life has vanished.

As a result, modern Jaffa was born again in 1948, like a reformatted computer or a watch reset. The original street names were erased and re-inscribed. Bostrus Street became Merchav Shlomo, Jamal Facha Boulevard, which had already been altered during the British occupation to King George Boulevard, now became Jerusalem Boulevard. As a result, Jerusalem Boulevard in Tel Aviv changed its name to Mount Zion Boulevard, and Jerusalem Road in Jaffa became Yitzhak Ben Zvi Road.

At best, street names were changed into numbers (3021, 3025 etc.)[168] and at worst to Hebrew names: Israeli flora (Hasayfan [Gladiolus], Hadudaim [Mandrake]), fauna (Mazal Dagim [Pisces], Hadolphin), Polish rabbis (Rabbi of Kerlin), nationalist heroes (Marzuk and Azar), and other international figures (Michelangelo, Dante). Salame Road turned into Shlomo Road.

And yet, while the streets of Jaffa were adorned with freshly painted Hebrew names, the actual Hebrew being spoken *in* Jaffa was of a relatively poor quality: The deserted homes once occupied by the city's Palestinian inhabitants, who had since been forced to become refugees in foreign lands, had been quickly filled by tens of thousands of *other* refugees: Jewish refugees, arriving from North Africa and the Balkans (and Bulgaria in particular). Few of these new immigrants had prior knowledge of the new State's official language. This inevitably affected, and certainly continues to affect, the way Jaffa interacts with its past. It means Jaffa is a mute, deaf and amnesiac city, which no one really recognizes – least of all the people who live there. It exists today as a non-existent city, an invented city, a city whose past, present and future have all been sculpted and manipulated time and time again, until no one is really sure where the real city begins and the imagined one ends.

In the 1950s, Jaffa's story was amended again with the creation of 'The Big Zone' – a new title given to an area which had, for centuries up until this point, been Jaffa's Old City.

Chaim Lazar claims that as early as 1949, following the collapse of a building near the French hospital in Jaffa's Old City which subsequently caused the death of seventeen people, 'it was decided to demolish the entire old city. A few hundred houses were destroyed with explosives and bull-dozers, notwithstanding their historical value or picturesque beauty. This site, which had formed the centre of Jaffa since biblical times, was turned to ruins.'[169] In much the same way that the Mugrabi neighbourhood in the Old City of Jerusalem was expunged to make a piazza in front of the Western Wall in 1967, or the manner in which the IDF tends to go about its business in the Occupied Territories today, Jaffa's nucleus was razed to the ground. This new, vast open space added to the hole already created by 'Project Anchor', the clearing operation carried out by British forces in 1936, which now appeared positively benign in comparison. Only the outline of the Old City remained in the wake of this latest 'facelift', providing the illusion that something still existed within its walls.[170]

Today, 'The Big Zone' is officially known as 'Gan Hapisga' [Garden of the Peak] – perched atop of Jaffa's hill, it offers perfect panoramas of Tel Aviv and the White City below. But it was not always so. For more than two decades, this shaven area surrounded by the remaining ruins of the old city, hastily and densely populated with new immigrants from the Balkans and North Africa, has been rooted in popular Israeli culture as 'The Big Zone', and its name was not affiliated with picnic spots and sunset vistas but with the dark margins of the white metropolis, synonymous with degeneracy and criminal activity.

While it is difficult to trace the origins of the 'Big Zone' title, it is clear that this gross simplification served some useful purposes – namely, the name change nullified any historical or cultural heritage the area might have had.

In this sense, it was no less the subject of a cultural campaign than the advertising crusade which continues to promote the White City as a bastion of virtue and ethics. It was an exercise in slander which sought to associate Jaffa's 'Big Zone' with anything and everything at odds with the puritanical Zionism extolled by the ruling Avoda Party (Labour Party): night life, black market economy, crime, drugs, alcohol and orientalness. Those responsible for the transformation of the historic city to The Big Zone and its inclusion in popular culture in the 1950s and 1960s were the same Palmach

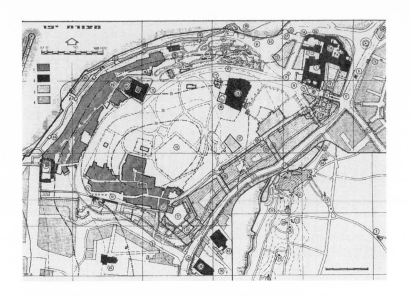

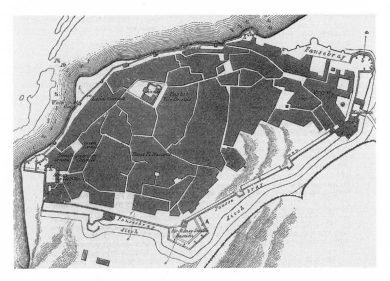

Before and after: the old city of Jaffa in the middle of the nineteenth century in a map drafted by British Military Engineering in 1842, and the old city a decade after the War of Independence, in the 'Antique Jaffa' project (the map's title is 'Jaffa Fortress').

Immigrants from Bulgaria, The Big Zone, 1949.
Zoltan Kluger, National Photo Collection.

The invention of 'The Big Zone': 'Jaffa slum section soon to be demolished'.
Teddy Brauner, 1949, National Photo Collection.

Demolition of buildings in The Big Zone, 1949.
Teddy Brauner, 1949, National Photo Collection.

generation figures that later promoted the White City's imagery; singers like Arik Einstein, screen-writers like Yigal Mosenzon (who wrote the screenplay for the film *Kazablan*), actors like Yehoram Gaon (who starred in *Kazablan*) and journalists like Menachem Talmi (who had a regular column in the *Maariv* newspaper entitled 'Jaffoite Pictures').[171]

Jaffa became the other, dark side of the White City. In opposition to the then provincial puritanism of Israeli culture, Jaffa had become a real rough-and-tumble port city brimming with bruising sailors, sexist slurs, debauched promiscuity, wild drinking, Levantine hedonism and Mediterranean life-styles. This was 'real life': a world of irresponsible impulsiveness, dominated by earthy values like the joy of living and the need to be streetwise. For Tel Aviv, whose cement had supposedly been mixed by students of medicine, law and philosophy, 'The Big Zone' provided the folklore it otherwise lacked:

This is what it's like in the world
There's no trust in human beings
What are we, after all, from The Big Zone
My dear let's drink beer
We'll each finish twenty
And check out Elvira's, what the friends are up to
We'll see Chico the driver, Moishe Thief the glazier

מִקְרָא:

כל אחד מהסמנים מתיחס לקבוצה של 4 משפחות

מאותה ארץ מוצא הגרות בדיור של 50 מ׳

■ — יוצאי   מרוקו

⊙ — ״ —   אירופה המזרחית

⌐ — ״ —   טריפול

⊥ — ״ —   ארצות אסיה

▲ — ״ —   בולגריה

'Old Jaffa, concentration of populations according land of origin': a map of Jaffa's old city (alias The Big Zone) figuring in the Ministry of Housing's survey, detailing the origins of the inhabitants. Each icon represents a concentration of four families. The origin lands mentioned are: Morocco, Eastern Europe, Tripoli (Lybia), Asian Countries and Bulgaria. Old Jaffa (The Big Zone). Economic-Social Survey, Ministry of Housing, 1962.

Along with the physical destruction of Jaffa, its reputation was tarnished. The Big Zone became the black hole of the Tel Aviv metropolis, where, at least according to the mythology created by figures such as Haim Hefer, Dan Ben-Amotz, or Menachem Talmi, all shady dealings took place together. Without doubt, this was a new interpretation of a tradition that had started as early as the 1920s, with Nachum Gutman's sketches of Jaffa's brothels.

Cover of Menachem Talmi's second tome of the book series 'Tmunot Yafoyiot' (Jaffa's Scenes), a collection of Damon Runyon style short crime stories located in Jaffa. Illustration: Shmuel Katz. Sifriat Maariv, 1982.

Eli Poker the gambler
And one flunky cop
There's nothing like Jaffa at night, nothing like Jaffa in the world
Let's go out with Lotta now, for a walk on the beach
      'Nothing like Jaffa at Night', Haim Hefer, composer unknown.

Listen to the Bouzouki warming the soul
We'll give you a glass of Arak to go down to your heart
And then you'll feel it in your bones
That once again you love, you love Jaffa,
      'Jaffa', Amos Etinger and Dov Seltzer

Here salt and smoke and the sound of guitar
drawn knife and backgammon games
Here someone's drunk, not from Arak
And it is hot, not for the 'steaks' on the fire [...]
And once again, girl, no 'why?' or 'what for?'
My hand holds your arms
There's something weird and unknown
There's something wonderful in this city.
      'This is Jaffa', Yossi Gamzu and Moshe Smilansky

And so, without a 'why?' or 'what for?' Jaffa's new mythology was accepted as a fact of nature – the city, and the 'The Big Zone' at its heart, were stigmatized as the municipality's corrupt backwaters. This in turn, provided the necessary alibi for the complete emptying of historic Jaffa and a wholesale takeover of its territory and assets. 'How else would the major social problems of The Big Zone be tackled?' the municipality asked. What was needed, they deduced, was a comprehensive cleaning operation to rid this unruly underground space of all the liquor, petty theft and lusty bawdiness which had seduced it. What was needed, they deduced, was something substantial.

Antique Jaffa

A little over a decade following the occupation of the city, it was decided that its social and architectural restoration would become a national project. Despite the fact that a 1950s social and economic survey of The Big Zone determined that the majority of its population were self-sufficient and not dependent on welfare services, the area was labelled a 'deprived neighbour-hood'.[172] In light of this, between 1959 and 1960, the municipality evacuated the few remaining inhabitants of Jaffa's Old City and moved them into new governmental housing projects built on the outskirts of the city.

In 1961 the Israeli government and the Tel Aviv municipality founded the Old Jaffa Development Corporation, 'Whose objective is to build and restore the area of Jaffa Mound (also known as 'The Big Zone'), a hothouse for crime, prostitution, and drugs.' The Corporation was founded as a joint project: half its shares owned by the Tel Aviv-Yaffo municipality, the other half by the state along with associated organizations (the Israel Lands Administration and the National Corporation of Tourism). The corporation is an independent legal entity classified as an economic corporation. In addition to the founding of the corporation the area of Old Jaffa was categorized as an Urban Building Scheme 606, as an architectural reservation, aiming to reconstruct and restore the buildings in the old city in keeping with their character and harmony with the landscape, in an attempt to attract a new population, and turn the area into a centre for tourism, leisure and art. Furthermore, the building scheme stipulated that only artists have the right to live in Old Jaffa.[173]

The development project for Old Jaffa aimed to transform Jaffa from The Big Zone to the 'Jaffa Mound' or 'Antique Jaffa'.[174] Each of these – The Big Zone, Jaffa Mound and Antique Jaffa – is an obliteration of Jaffa as an actual city and as an Arab city. The major sites that were preserved and highlighted were crusader and Christian elements like the fort and church, Andromeda's Rock (Ancient Greece), findings from the sparse Jewish presence in the city, the Napoleonic episode, and an unprecedented project of archaeological excavations intending to look for findings from Roman times and prior epochs, particularly Biblical times, which lasts to this day.

Sa'adia Mendel, Eliezer Frankel and Ora Yaar were selected as the team of architects responsible for planning and implementing the development and restoration of Old Jaffa. However, given that a large part of the area's urban design had already been decisively shaped during, and directly after, bouts of armed conflict, military personalities like 'Gidi' Faglin should probably also take some of the responsibility for the way 'Old Jaffa' was designed. In fact, the planning of Old Jaffa by architects following its destruction by military means is a repetition of the model of 1937, when the architects Shor and Kendall cooperated with the British army in the exact same place. Jaffa was presented with an architectural plan that implemented the new physical facts created after the War of Independence in 1948, embellished them, and expressed the desires and cultural values of the area's new landlords.

According to this plan The Big Zone became a park named Hapisga ('the peak'). After all, one of the goals of the Old Jaffa project was to turn the city into a brand. The built area became a sort of façade of Old Jaffa, which no longer exists. The remaining houses were given out exclusively to artists, artisans and architects, according to the law and the approved statutory plan.[175] Among the first to enjoy the new loot was Haim Hefer's good friend, the journalist and author Dan Ben-Amotz.

All that was left from the historic city of Jaffa was this small collection of choice remnants, the Church of St Petrus, Napoleon's cannon, and the Andromeda Rock in the sea. Jaffa has become everything but an Arab city. In its place the 'Fort of Jaffa' has broken out. Jaffa has become Old Jaffa, Ancient Jaffa, Antique Jaffa. In the middle of the twentieth century, Tel Aviv has built itself a European medieval crusader outpost.

Archaeological findings came to be among Jaffa's most prominent quarried materials. Archaeologists have dug up the city in order to erase evidence of one national apologetics, and to find evidence for another, and archaeology has become one of the tools used to uproot contemporary uses and erase the fresh memories.

Sa'adia Mendel, Eliezer Frankel, Ora and Yaacov Yaar and Hillel Omer: Proposal for the renovation of Old Jaffa, perspective view, early 1960s. Commissioned by The Old Jaffa Development Corporation, the Tel Aviv municipality, and the Office of the Prime Minister. Courtesy of the collection of Zvi Elhayani, Archive of Israeli Architecture.

Jaffa was just the beginning, the experiment. The experiment, which worked so well in its Old City, was repeated in almost all of the other Arab conurbations captured in 1948: in Acre, Tiberias, Safed, Nazareth, Caesarea, Ramla, Lod and Beer Sheva; new-'old' cities miraculously arose thanks to national-municipal corporations and government-funded development projects. The newfound 'antiquity' projected onto these urban centres bordered on the absurd, with Beer Sheva, for example, heralded as an ancient relic despite being built by the Turkish authorities in 1900, thirteen years after the foundation of Neve-Tzedek, nine years before the plots lottery of Ahuzat Bayit. Just as in Old Jaffa, in Ein Kerem on the Jerusalem Mountains, and Ein Hod on the Carmel Mountains too, Palestinian ruins became homes for Israeli bohemians. In all of these locations, culture has been enlisted for the mission of repopulating the Arab places, turning the deserted ruins into spaces of living and working, exhibitions and performances, recycling the dilapidated quarters and turning them into sites of classical music festivals and *other* theatre.

If there is any consolation to be found in Jaffa's transformation from a booming economic, cultural and political capital into a European crusader city, it was that it was spared another, potentially even worse, fate. By all accounts Ben-Gurion might have turned the city into a theme park, with the Old City playing the part of the pirate castle. When Ben-Gurion spoke with Jewish fishermen in Haifa in 1943, he claimed that Jaffa had been the centre for Jewish piracy since the time of the Second Temple:

> the Jewish seamen in Jaffa wrote one of the most wondrous chapters of bravery in the Jewish-Roman War. The Jewish historian Josephus Flavius did not especially like the Jewish warriors and called them pirates, but it was 'pirates' who set up the marine strength of England (and that of other nations as well). The Jewish 'pirates' in Jaffa, who according to Josephus, burgled Syria, Phoenicia, and Egypt, and cast terror on all seafarers around them, fought with anguished bravery against the legions of Vespasian, and would rather kill themselves than fall in the hands of the Romans, and the sea of Jaffa was red with Jewish blood.[176]

The Old City was by no means the only Palestinian site in Jaffa razed and 'renovated'. Manshieh was also privy to several consecutive waves of destruction and 'development'.

After their assault on the neighbourhood, the Etzel released the following statement to the press: 'On the 1st May, 1948, the Southern part of liberated Manshieh became a mound of ruins. The police of Manshieh no longer exists.'[177]

After its conquest by the Etzel, the neighbourhood has gone through consecutive stages of destruction:[178] in fact, the Tel Aviv municipality planned to demolish the neighbourhood once the battles ended. This however proved impossible in the immediate aftermath, because batches of new Jewish immigrants broke into the ruins in early June 1948, fashioning shelter out of the debris and refusing to move on.

Over the next two decades, this neighbourhood, one of the largest future real-estate deposits in Tel Aviv, became something of an experimentation site for Israeli, and to some degree also for international architecture and planning. At first, Tel Aviv municipality's new city engineer Aaron Horowitz, an American town planner and Cleveland's chief engineer, who was appointed in 1951 in order to conceive a new master plan for the city, suggested avoiding any commercial development in the neighbourhood and recommended the development of a large beach park. As very few of Horowitz's ideas were implemented, his Manshieh plan was shelved too.

In 1959, Yitzhak Perlstein, one of Israel's first commercial architects, who designed the Shalom Tower on the very site of the Herzliya Gymnasium, proposed a new scheme for Manshieh, imagining it as a business district. Mordechai Namir, Tel Aviv's new mayor elected in the same year, adopted the idea and appointed a team of thirty architects and engineers headed by the architect Aviah Hashimshoni in order to develop a new master plan for the city, this time focusing on the city's new areas beyond the Yarkon River, the seafront and the Manshieh business district.[179]

In November 1962 a governmental-municipal corporation, 'Ahuzat Hahof' (estates of the beach), was established. The first thing Ahuzat Hahof did was to initiate an international open-call competition for the design of the area – bounded by Allenby Street in the north-east, Eilat Street in the south-west and the coastline adjoining the two. The idea was to encourage planners to make full use of Manshieh's 2,400 dunams (by now considered state property) and include public and municipal buildings, shopping and commerce areas, office towers, hotels, thousands of new homes, centres of

The ruins of Manshieh.
Photograph by Rudi Weissenstein, December 1948. Photohouse Pri-Or.

leisure and entertainment, open public spaces, and a system of roundabouts to connect the city centre and the new neighbourhood to the sea. All this while also 'maximising exploitation of the beach for the public' and bridging Tel Aviv and Jaffa.[180]

Responsibility for this commission was eventually bequeathed to Amnon Niv, Rafi Reifer, Amnon Schwartz and Dani Schwartz. The task of designing a park within the same stretch was given to poet and landscape architect, Hillel Omer.

Just as Jaffa's Old City had been carved up in the 1950s under a banner of 'development', 'planning' is still offered today as a justification for the continued dismantling of Jaffa's remaining Palestinian neighbourhoods, Ajami and Jabaliya; Manshieh's final destruction was also couched in the language of 'renovation' and 'urban renewal'. As it happened, the project

Manshieh in the 1960s.
Courtesy of the Zvi
Elhayani Collection,
Archive of Israeli
Architecture.

outlined by Niv, Reifer, Schwartz and Schwartz, which promised extensive corporate development, did not take off. While elements of their blueprint were included in the final outline for the neighbourhood, most of the area was left in its flattened form, despite the dizzying investment and the high commercial expectations.

In practice, this final design was actually unnervingly familiar. It bore an uncanny resemblance to the vision of the region already mapped out by Tel Aviv's favourite son, Nachum Gutman. Manshieh had seemingly served its time as a decrepit, bombed-out site of ruins (a period in which it was regularly used as a movie set, not least for the production of *Kazablan*). Now it would be definitively gutted, hollowed out and cleared to make way for the vista the people's painter had always assigned for it: empty, open dunes.

Like many other plots of land confiscated by the state in 1948, Manshieh was given a treatment which ensured that the neighbourhood's Palestinian inhabitants would not be able to return or reclaim their properties. The old

ARCHITECTURE IN ISRAEL 1984 אדריכלות

Amnon Niv, Amnon
Schwartz and Dani
Schwartz, Manshieh
project. Cover of
Architecture in Israel
magazine, 1984.

street lines and lot divisions which had once demarcated and framed the neighbourhood were erased and new, completely different, markers were put down. The easiest (and subsequently most common) way of utilizing these new empty spaces was to landfill them with gardens and car parks, and Manshieh was no different.

Easy come, easy go; it was erased, and a new desert of asphalt and greenery was laid down where it had once been. The train tracks, which had been ferrying produce and pilgrims to Jerusalem since 1892, were scrapped to make way for a series of parking lots. The train station itself was transformed into an IDF museum. In the immediate space in front of the Hassan Bek mosque, Manshieh's most prominent landmark and a surprising survivor of the hostilities of 1948, the municipality built a park in memory of Jaffa's Jewish 'liberators' and flanked this commemorative knoll with some more car parks and a bus terminal. Other parts of the neighbourhood were designated as dumps for building waste or ironed out and left as plain, bare fields.

One righteous man in Sodom: Aba Elhanani, *Memorial for Manshieh*.
From *Tvai* 4, Winter 1976.

The cherry on top of this grisly exercise in pulverization was the establishment of the Sir Charles Clore Park, which would only be completed in the 1970s. Named after the British financier who had donated large sums to the new State of Israel and designed by Hillel Omer, the landscape architect, it was another layer on the flattened mound of what had once been the neighbourhood of Manshieh. Again, Zionism had made the desert bloom; only this time the grass was artificial and coloured green.

Raping the Bride of the Sea

This natural cycle of effacement, destruction, desertification and bloom demonstrated in the Manshieh development project was but a proper background to the true architectural allegory of Altneuland/Tel Aviv. In Manshieh the realization of Herzl's oxymoron came to life, displaying an indigenous, genuine, Tel Avivian interpretation of meshing the 'old' and the 'new'.

Three of the Manshieh project's architects – Amnon Niv, Amnon Schwartz and Dani Schwartz – were also responsible for the sole project completed in the neighbourhood which sought to retain some kind of association with its past. In 1978, they used the last standing remnant of Palestinian Manshieh (other than the Hassan Bek mosque) – three walls of a lone house which had

Etzel House commercial brochure.

otherwise been gutted – as a foundational frame for what would eventually become the Etzel Museum. Officially opening in 1983, Beit Gidi (House of Gidi), as it is also known, was dedicated to the memory of those Etzel fighters who died 'liberating' Jaffa in 1947–1948.[181] It charts the history of the paramilitary organization and gives their particularized account of the Etzel's involvement in certain, often contentious, historical episodes. Among other bloody instances, these include the massacre at Deir Yassin, the *Altalena* affair and, as a centrepiece, the conquest of Jaffa.[182]

Nailed to the ruins of what had once been a regular Jaffaite stone house, the Etzel Museum stands as a sort of localized version of Mies van der Rohe's universal glass box. Arguably even more of a modernist statement than Le Corbusier's white cube, which probably originated from Mediterranean architectures in Greece or in North Africa, the glass box was affiliated with the Bauhaus school and a German building tradition. Walter Gropius had explored the glass box as an architectural method when designing the Bauhaus School building in Dessau and it was a concept that the school's last director, Ludwig Mies van der Rohe, had developed while in Germany and then, later, during his time in America. Within the context of the Etzel Museum, the simplistic connection between the glass shell, with its Western, corporate façade, and the antiquated walls of this simple, oriental dwelling inevitably invite a barrage of age-old clichés and turns the museum into Tel

Aviv's own poor allegory of itself, in which the exterior phraseology of the architecture is integrated with the architects' verbal phraseology: 'from the shattered walls of the old building grow dark glass walls, [...] schematically completing the building to what it once was. [...] An attempt to freeze the special moment and time of the day when Jaffa was liberated.'[183]

Nonetheless, if the objective of the piece was to freeze the museum in time against the beautiful, restless background of the Mediterranean Sea, then the architects in question succeeded. The Etzel Museum has become one of the most emblematic architectural objects, not only in Israeli architecture, but maybe in universal architecture as well. This may be due to its simplified clichéd character, but the architects' clear and transparent identification with the structure's historic relevancy and a more general consciousness of time have also proved powerful factors.

And yet, there are unquestionable problems with this kind of architecture. One only need examine the work of Albert Speer, Adolf Hitler's head architect throughout the Nazi era, for an indication of the kinds of danger which may arise.

An exceptionally problematic example of consciousness of time can be

Walter Gropius, the workshops at the Bauhaus School, Dessau, Germany, 1926. From *The International Style* exhibition catalogue, curated by Henry-Russell Hitchcock and Philip Johnson. Museum of Modern Art, New York, 1932.

Walter Gropius: Bauhaus School, Dessau, Germany. 1926. Workshops
THE WORKSHOPS HAVE ENTIRELY TRANSPARENT WALLS. A GOOD ILLUSTRATION OF GLASS PANES AS A SURFACING MATERIAL. THE PROJECTION OF THE ROOF CAP IS UNFORTUNATE, ESPECIALLY OVER THE ENTRANCE AT LEFT.

found in his 'the theory of Ruin Value'.[184] The objective of the 'ruins value theory' was to design the future cadaver of a building by strengthening certain constructive elements and weakening others, so that even after hundreds of years of destruction, war and neglect, the building would function as an independent monument. Speer had been greatly impressed by the Roman ruins he had seen on his travels to Italy following his studies. Taking inspiration from both their antiquity and their contemporary significance, he sought to plot the degeneration of his own monuments, thereby controlling the way they would be received into historical record. Accordingly then, whenever he planned a construction, Speer also sought to map out its decline, keeping in mind a whole iconography of different images of different buildings in various stages of deterioration.

On a practical level, strengthening particular parts of a building beyond its natural proportions (making the stone walls three metres thick, for example) naturally results in the weakening of other sections of the construction. For Speer, these were either the parts which could be readily dispensed with or those which *had* to be dispensed with in order for the building to achieve the desired stage (and image) of ruination. This hinged on the notion of 'carving' out a future story from the building's present form, which was perceived as kind of raw material, analogous to those blocks of Pietrasantan marble from which Michelangelo would have 'carved' out his pietas.

There is no doubt that any building, of any form, is also, by default, a pattern of the destruction which may await it. This, after all, is the working premise of any structural engineer, whose job is not to verify that the building will stand, but only to ensure it will not fall in the wake of destructive forces (whether that be from its own weight, from an earthquake or a from a terrorist attack, for example). While the structural engineer strives to neutralize these destructive forces – looking to pre-empt instances of overburden, cracking, bending or collapse, and in some cases (in light of the building regulations for civil defence constructions, for example) building-in escape and survival passages – the novelty inherent in Speer's approach is his attempt to tame all these variables, to harness them, to include them willingly in the building's aesthetic and rhetoric of ruin, to turn them into architecture.

What makes this architecture so troublesome, however, is precisely the distorted and disturbing consciousness of time which frames it: the idea that the building never had a present, and therefore it will never have a future. Instead, it sits wedged awkwardly somewhere between a nostalgia for the glorious past of the neo-classical monument and a longing for the imaginary future of the Roman ruin. Folding this heterochronic time bomb into the contemporary (and temporary) exterior of the building, the architect turns the present into a kind of festive funeral procession, drifting off towards some endless and unavoidable future.

There is, however, an outstanding difference between Speer's 'ruin value theory' and the Etzel Museum which stands in the middle of what was once the neighbourhood of Manshieh. Speer's ruins were only ever potential; the theoretician planted images of the ruins he *envisaged* in his buildings – they were always mental, rather than physical, testaments to the culture he sought to memorialize. In the case of the Etzel Museum, on the other hand, not only were the destructive forces created by the building's own namesake, 'Gidi' Faglin, and at the hands of individuals who also designed it, but its aesthetics evoke something of a 'retroactive ruin value theory' – the idea that, throughout all the years that the old Arab house existed, it was merely waiting in earnest, building up to the moment of its destruction and its subsequent role as decoration within Sir Charles Clore Park. This feeling stems from the fact that the Etzel Museum, as the one remaining ruin of Manshieh, does not preserve even one moment or one historical occurrence which took place in or around the building prior to its destruction.

Within the museum itself there is no mention of the builder of the house, of its former owners, of its former residents. Neither the conquerors nor the curators saw it fit to detail or showcase what the neighbourhood of Manshieh was like at any point in its history, or in any corner of the museum. In stark contrast to Speer's ruins, which displayed fabricated remnants of the living, Niv, Schwartz and Schwartz's testament stands as an immortalization of death, forgetfulness, and little else. Its morbidity is striking, and much more so than any catacombs since the Etzel Museum is outside, in the sunshine, for everyone to see. It is a daytime memento mori without the candlelight.

In a certain aspect, it was as if the whole area prepared itself to be a ruin: in fact, the Zionist dialect of 'making the desert bloom', as formed in Ben-Gurion's rhetoric, was only a derivative of a similar European narrative that formed around the Orientalist tradition of the 'voyage to the East' in the nineteenth century. The ruin was a central image in this tradition and imprinted on all kinds of visual material during this period, in drawings, engravings and photographs. This iconography served Europe in its 'case' against the East, as the destruction of Hellenistic relics or those sites considered sacred to Christianity seemed to explain an Eastern inferiority, eventually providing justification for the continent's conquest. It was no different in Israel, where the image of the ruin was half a self fulfilled prophecy and half an indication of things to come: the ruins of 1948 quickly assumed the role of those historic sites which had encouraged Westerners to 'voyage East', a role seemingly preordained.

The Arab ruin became the natural state of Arab architecture, and came to be part of the Israeli Arcadia, along with the Eucalyptus groves, the Sabra cacti, or the scent of citrus orchards. The ruin had always been but a ruin – that way one could forget that it had actually been a house once inhabited.

Another Israeli take on the perverted manipulation of ruins is evident in the movie *Kazablan*, directed by Menachem Golan in 1973. According to the original story, penned for the stage in 1954, Kazablan is destined to become king of The Big Zone. But by the 1970s, 'The Big Zone' had already been transformed into the 'Garden of the Peak' and so, in their place, the ruins of Manshieh stepped in to fill the void; still waiting to be tarmacked and stuffed with artificial grass, she played the role of The Big Zone in the film's adaptation.

The Etzel Museum still stands out today as something unique, something completely distinctive from all those other 1948 ruins which have entered Israeli folklore and which mark destination points on youth movement pilgrimages, retracing the War of Independence. There is something astonishing about the unabashed manner in which the museum uses architectural means to dramatize the act of conquest, the takeover, the looting, the rape of the 'Bride of the Sea'. But the forced compression of the glass box onto the ruins of an emptied Palestinian home is not only chilling for what it represents historically; it lends the museum an expressive vigour which encourages this unbearably flippant usage of the 'old and new', detaching it

Written originally as a theatre play in 1954 by Yigal Mosenzon, *Kazablan* was produced as a stage musical in 1966. The musical's commercial success encouraged the film director Menachem Golan to produce a cinematographic version. But during the years between the theatrical production and the shooting of the movie, The Big Zone has been demolished and became Hapisga Garden. Therefore, the set was moved to Manshieh, which was still awaiting renovation at the time. As a result, it is possible to say that the ruins of Manshieh 'play the role' of historic Jaffa in the movie.

from the political context while still part of it. Strangely, the building uses the ruin and the aesthetics of the ruin in order to cover and conceal the full extent of the destruction done. The building tells the truth about the rape and murder of the city of Jaffa, but it lies at the same time by cloaking this bloody drama in 'architecture' and 'environmental art'.

In its use of architectural phraseology in order to conceal and whitewash reality, the Etzel Museum is the embodiment of architecturism. All of these make it an unbearable sight. Never before in the history of architecture has such an ugly truth been displayed in such a false, spruced up manner.

The Orange Route

Back to the prophecy: the black stain in the aerial photographs from the World War I period, marking the location of the 'black city' south of the white sands of Tel Aviv, has another name: JAFFA.

As noted, this dark blemish represents those orchards, which, in the two hundred years prior to the pictures being taken, garnered an international reputation as a site for cultivating world-class citrus fruits. Drawing evidence from various travelogues, Shmuel Tolkovsky claims these orchards were only planted at the beginning of the eighteenth century, despite the availability of Portuguese oranges across the Mediterranean from as early as the sixteenth century. Tolkovsky notes that only a quarter century after the first seeds were scattered in Jaffa, word spread among merchant traders that the port city was exporting a gigantic variation of the kind of fruits produced elsewhere across the region, in Sidon and Jericho. Tolkovsky is suitably vague about the established origins of this mysterious species and its particular appearance. He does note, however, a conversation he had with an inhabitant of Jaffa who told him that a priest from the Armenian Patriarch was specifically sent to China in order to retrieve samples of the Shamouti species of orange, now heavily associated with the city of Jaffa.[185]

Up until 1948, Jaffa oranges were for Jaffa what Bordeaux wine is for Bordeaux – not only the region's premier source of income, but also a premier source of pride and identity. For centuries, life in Jaffa centred around orchard farming and the burgeoning citrus industry it created – thousands were employed across the city's warehouses, box manufacturers and export services. Images of Jaffa captured in photographs taken before the War of Independence give an indication of the grip-like influence over the city; pictures detail the growers and pickers of the oranges at work in the orchards, logistical personnel frantically packing them onto conveys heading to the port and the markets, the array of camels, porters and cases used to load them onto boats in the harbour. Given the sheer numbers involved, it was considered a local, Palestinian operation. Arab inhabitants of Jaffa were fiercely proud of their produce and in much the same way that *since* 1948, Israelis consider the citrus fruit a distinctly *Israeli* export, once upon a time there was nothing more Palestinian than an orange from Jaffa.

But around the same time the aforementioned aerial photographs were being taken, Jaffa's citrus orchards had already lapsed into a state of decline. Gradually, tree by tree, they began to disappear – at first, due to the Turkish military and their desperate need for wood during the war against the British, then as a result of the 1921 riots and the Jewish settlement it encouraged, and finally thanks to the outbreak of World War I and later World War II and the cessation in citrus exportation to Europe. Local testimonies also point the finger at Bedouin immigrants, who had moved south from the Golan Heights during the 1940s, and who occasionally raided those orchards left unattended during the war in order to collect firewood.

During the War of Independence from 1947–1948, recently arrived Greek and Turkish immigrants joined forces with internal refugees from Jerusalem to take advantage of the siege on Jaffa, establishing a settlement on the orchards of Abu Kabir, one of Jaffa's largest orchard patches. Whatever the detrimental impact of these various instances on Jaffa and its citrus economy, the founding of the State of Israel signalled the end of any interdependent relationship between the city and its produce. The onset of the Absentees' Property Law in 1950 irrevocably sealed the fate of the orchards once and for all; they were transferred en bloc over to the Jewish National Fund, which proceeded to recycle them into new housing projects and neighbourhoods like Tel Giborim, Kiryat Shalom and Jaffa D. Other parts of this region have been replanned as industrial zones.

According to the Israeli Council of Citrus Fruit, the 'JAFFA' orange is now the most widely recognized Israeli brand in the world, and is protected as a trademark in over twenty countries.[186]

Many Israelis consider the JAFFA orange as the most Israeli product (just like the Sabra, another confiscated Palestinian symbol).

Somehow, the Israeli brand of 'JAFFA' oranges has seeped into national folklore without any connection with Jaffa, the city. Instead, the citrus culture in Israel is associated with other geographical locations situated across the Sharon and the Plain, with towns like Petach Tikvah, Rishon LeZion, Nes Ziona and Rehovot. The 'JAFFA' in the product's title has been accepted as

Jaffa's orchards after World War I as seen in a British aerial photograph of the region dating from 1924. The lighter zones in the black stain are dried or neglected orchards. Those plots were the first to be purchased by Jewish institutions or businessmen and later would become the new Jaffa's Hebrew neighbourhoods, alias the 'Black City'.
1924, Yad Avner Geographical Database, Department of Geography, Tel Aviv University.

Jaffa, as seen from north-east, 1905.

Turkish soldiers stationed at the orchards of Jaffa during World War I.

a brand logo and nothing more. According to the Israeli Council of Citrus Fruits, the 'JAFFA' trademark comes from the historic port which gave its name.[187] This may well be the case, but when one usually refers to agricultural products with site-specific titles – such as Burgundy wine, Parmesan cheese or rival oranges from Valencia – it comes with the ready acknowledgement that there is something specific about the environmental or cultural conditions in that particular geographical location which makes the product unique. This might be thanks to the quality of local soil for example, or a traditional, millennia-old method of distillation. Paradoxically, modernity and the emergence of commercial branding have only sanctified this age-old concept of *terroir* through national and regional norms. They have encouraged the creation of supervision systems and legal bodies like the Appellation d'Origine Contrôlée in France, which originally only protected the name/ place of different wine manufacturers, but which today grants certification to geographically indexed producers of agriculture, food and craftwork.

In the case of JAFFA, up until the foundation of the State of Israel and the occupation of Jaffa, the crop region corresponded with the specific Shamouti species of orange. But when Israel exports 'JAFFA' oranges today, it goes against global norms by weakening the relation between the brand and the place of origin. These oranges have nothing to do with Jaffa the old Arab capital or its soil or its people; despite their labels, they are cultivated in orchards based in *different* parts of the country or even different parts of the planet.[188] JAFFA oranges today are grown anywhere but in Jaffa.

At first, citrus cultivation moved to the Sharon and the Plain, but after several real estate spikes, they began disappearing from these regions as well. Even in the dizzy heyday of Israeli citrus exportation in the 1960s and 1970s, 'JAFFA' oranges were not even being dispatched from Jaffa port, let alone grown there – instead they were setting sail for the continent from the larger harbours of Haifa, Ashdod and Eilat (as in another Naomi Shemer song: 'Tomorrow maybe we'll go by ship / From the shore in Eilat to that in Shenhav / And on the old battleships they'll load oranges […]'. The 'JAFFA' brand has been expanded now to encompass other species of orange and other kinds of fruit, such as grapefruit, lemons and mandarins. After destroying citrus production in Jaffa, the Israeli government ineffectively ran production across the rest of the country into the ground before selling the 'JAFFA' brand to a variety of multinational commercial corporations across the globe![189]

Transforming 'JAFFA' into the purest form of trademark possible, with no relationship to reality, is only another aspect of the destruction of Jaffa. The 'JAFFA' sticker placed on today's orange is an accepted lie – historically, geographically and culturally, the 'Jaffa' to which it originally referred is no longer with us. The label is a signifier with no signified; it is only a simulacrum. With this in mind, it is interesting to see how this same simulacrum is intentionally manipulated as an alibi for the lie: Jaffa does not exist because it is nothing but a brand. And the brand is not under any obligation to tell the truth. On the contrary, sometimes the brand needs to lie. After all, this is our expectation of it – we acknowledge the need to market, the need to advertise. We accept, without question, that a 'good' brand will probably use deceptive tactics to sell its product. One can see how this same reversed argument works in a response to an article in *Ha'Ir* magazine, where Nitza Szmuk claims that she legitimately used the concept 'Bauhaus' in a commercial manner as a 'brand'.[190] In other words, as soon as the concept (Bauhaus, JAFFA or otherwise) is defined as a 'brand' and becomes commercially viable, it can legitimately break free from the shackles of reality, and there is no need to tell the truth. The Bauhaus moved from Dessau to Tel Aviv, JAFFA moved from the Mediterranean coast to South Africa. 'So what?' goes the argument. 'This is advertising; everything is up for grabs when it enters the public sphere.'

The black stain on the old aerial photographs of Jaffa and Tel Aviv is primarily important as a testimony, since it sheds light on Jaffa, and shows Jaffa as it was before it became a brand, an accepted lie, a trademark or a simulacrum. Whether we want it or not, the black stain is the signified of Jaffa.

As for Tel Aviv, the only prompt its citizens have to remind them of Jaffa, and the citrus economy which once governed the whole region, is 'The Orange Route' – a series of decorative orange-coloured steel poles, scattered across the White City in order to direct tourists from one Bauhaus building to the next.

The Children of Jaffa

After the War of Independence the black stains of Greater Jaffa were erased and a chaotic, degenerated urban backwater emerged in its place. All of the agricultural holdings which had once been reserved for citrus production were converted into metropolitan infrastructure for Tel Aviv, or became industrial areas, storage spaces, and other wasteful uses of land. The black stain morphed into a black city, and quickly became one of the most untended areas in the country.

The large masses of land that moved into the hands of the State of Israel allowed it to make Jaffa a collection of large-scale projects: new housing projects and neighbourhoods, the Eisenberg and Wolfson Hospitals,[191] massive industrial and commercial buildings like 'Merkazim' and 'Panorama', the Bloomfield football stadium.

Although Jaffa before 1948 was an Arab city, still there were a few Jewish neighbourhoods left within its territory – Kolchinsky, Givat Herzl, Shapira, Shafir-Klein, Gvat Moshe A and B, Shivat Tzion, Kerem Hateimanim, Ezra and Hatikva. Following the great Arab uprising in 1936–1939 their residents gathered in 1941 under a single representation, 'The United Committee of Hebrew Neighbourhoods'.

After Jaffa's annexation to Tel Aviv, the fate reserved for Jaffa's Hebrew neighbourhoods in becoming Tel Aviv's southern environs proved only slightly better than that dealt to Palestinian Jaffa and its Arab neighbourhoods; if before the founding of the State of Israel they were, regretfully, Jaffa's stepchildren, after 1948 they were punished alongside Jaffa and became stepchildren once again, this time Tel Aviv's. While their historic and geographic proximity to Jaffa undoubtedly encouraged a degree of antipathy, Tel Aviv's insouciance towards their brethren in the south was essentially rooted in what might be perceived as 'The Tel Avivian Idealogy'. And to paraphrase the American novelist Toni Morrison, the underlying premise of this ideology was that the white component would always be much more important than the Jewish one.

The literal translation of this ethos is simple: the 'White City' ignores anything and everything that is not white. Just as it had once been convenient for the largely Ashkenazi neighbourhood of Ahuzat Bayit to dismiss the largely Mizrahi neighbourhood of Mahane Israel/Kerem Hateimanim as an extension of Arab Manshieh, so post-war Tel Aviv disregarded the Hebrew neighbourhoods of Jaffa as distant, peripheral outposts; they may have been visible beyond the horizon of Jaffa-Tel Aviv Road but they were certainly not considered part of the White City's mental geography. The histories of the Black City's living quarters – neighbourhoods like Neve Sha'anan, Florentine, Hatikva, Ezra and Shapira, all of whom were either established a decade earlier than the White City, or around the same time – were not deleted in the same way Jaffa's was, but they were condemned to a lifetime of neglect. Not only were they discounted architecturally, but they were also deemed ideologically, geographically, economically and culturally irrelevant to the State of Israel's wider Zionist historical narrative.

Even from the most nationalistic point of view, they were considered unworthy of note. This, despite the fact that their strategic positioning had almost single-handedly ensured Jaffa's isolation and subsequent collapse; that the establishment of Hatikva neighbourhood in 1936 was basically not that different from the wall-and-tower settlements established at the same time; and that dozens of residents had died after Egyptian forces heavily bombed the central bus station in Neve Sha'anan in May 1948. None of these instances were considered important – they did not contribute to the deification of the White City and so there was no place for them in the municipal annals.

Removal from the story (as we well know) always takes physical form sooner or later. In the southern neighbourhoods it did not take long for the central thoroughfares, which had once linked agricultural routes from the orchards, to fall into a state of disrepair. Buildings and services were systematically neglected and the area's unique urban fabric was soon under threat of attack from 'evacuation and construction' schemes and real estate initiatives out to expand the new corporate 'Ayalon City' developments into the southern districts.[192]

There has been almost no reference to the history of these neighbourhoods in any of the municipal plans which have been presented or implemented over the last sixty years. On the contrary, in many cases (notably in Neve Sha'anan and Shapira) the most popular option has been the eradication of whole streets.

The Menorah

The story of Neve Sha'anan neighbourhood is another example of the urban process characteristic of Tel Aviv, according to which you first narrate and then do, or first erase and then demolish.

By all accounts, the neighbourhood's history should be more than enough to guarantee it a starring role in both Tel Aviv's regional narrative and the State of Israel's wider chronicle of Zionist settlement in Palestine.

Even when compared with other Tel Avivian neighbourhoods, the story of Neve Sha'anan stands out. Unlike Ahuzat Bayit and the opportune sea-shell lottery which determined who got which plot, the establishment of Neve Sha'anan was not a random event but a long-term, well-planned project. Unlike many of the other neighbourhoods in the Tel Aviv municipality, Neve Sha'anan saw itself as a pioneering collective, with shared values and a communal ethos, built on Zionist ideological and economic principles.

In many ways, Neve Sha'anan was the nearest Tel Aviv ever got to realizing the utopian image it projected for itself; one which strove to be both architecturally experimental and socially progressive. Other settlements established in the early twentieth century, such as Degania, Nahalal, Kfar Yehoshua and Kibbutz Ein Harod, all endeavoured to live out these same ideals but always remained as ethnically and socially monolithic enclaves. Neve Sha'anan, on the other hand, was from the outset a multicultural tapestry made up of people from a variety of backgrounds. In this regard, the neighbourhood was a realization of one of Zionism's central tenets – the 'Ingathering of Exiles'.

In contrast to those homogenous settlements which created and fostered social and political tension up and down the country, Neve Sha'anan showcased a different model of Zionism – one that isn't necessarily white. Its omission from the official history of Tel Aviv is revealing for what it tells us about the city's defining characteristic: that much more than a Zionist project or a Jewish project, Tel Aviv was a white, European project.

Neve Sha'anan was established in Jaffa in 1921 by a group of 400 Jews. Some were new immigrants, some were internal refugees having fled Arab neighbourhoods in the wake of the May Day riots, and nearly all were homeless, living in tents. In light of the increasingly untenable situation in Jaffa, which had been twitching with rancour ever since the Balfour Declaration in 1917, and the severe housing crisis developing in Tel Aviv, this displaced collective understood the necessity of starting over. The members

Neve Sha'anan in the 1930s, as seen from south to north-east.
The New Central Station would be built in the exact boundaries
of the orchards in the photograph three decades later.

of the association decided to unite as a collaborative corporation, to purchase a tract of land, and to build a new neighbourhood south of Tel Aviv.

They bought 260 dunams of orchard land for 30,000 pounds, which was a relatively low price at the time because most of the orchard's trees had been cut down during World War I.

Later that same year, the Neve Sha'anan association sent a report to the Zionist Congress in which it was noted that

> the members handle the building of the neighbourhood with trust and enthusiasm; one member donated 250 pounds towards the construction of a synagogue in the neighbourhood and another group of members took it upon themselves to assemble a library for the residents.[193]

Excitement at the manner in which Neve Sha'anan was developing was coupled with a great sense of pride at the unusually heterogeneous make up of the members involved. Rightfully eager to highlight this multicultural ethos, the same memo observed that 'the list of members is also interesting – the 400 are divided nearly half and half between locals and new immigrants, and among the locals there are about one hundred homeless Sephardi and Yemenites.'[194] Moreover, there was also an astonishing occupational diversity among the association's members, which included carpenters, doctors, librarians, locksmiths, police officers, construction workers, farmers, mechanics, merchants, clerks, drivers and teachers. They were joined and backed by twenty affluent industrialists, who, as it was noted, put down the guarantee on the association's loans: 'these people do not require loans themselves, and they are welcome among us, as the banks consider their involvement in the association given that the members' guarantee is reciprocal.'[195]

Regardless of their predominately urban background, the members of the Neve Sha'anan association sought to propose an alternative to the agricultural monopoly being run by Arab farmers and the Germans of the Sarona Colony (an area known today as the Kirya military base). They envisaged a new neighbourhood based on a unique mixture of city and village life, with a dual emphasis on both civil and agricultural work:

> The association of Neve Sha'anan is the first to attempt to find a practical solution to this problem (supplying basic products to Tel Aviv). The members of the association and their households are hard working in their nature; the orchard land we have purchased

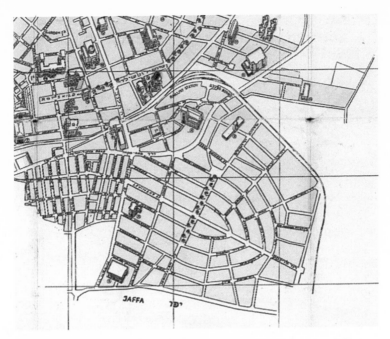

Neve Sha'anan in Tel Aviv's New City Map drafted in 1931 by Patrick Geddes. Although at the time, the neighbourhood's area was still divided between Tel Aviv and Jaffa municipalities, the new plan, as wishful thinking, included the entire 'Menorah' scheme of the neighbourhood as well as the northern part of Florentine neighbourhood in the city's map. 1931, The Technical Department, Tel Aviv Municipality.

is good for all kinds of crops; the neighbourhood is on the border of Tel Aviv – why should we not try to furnish the daily needs of our brothers in Tel Aviv, and thus allow our unemployed members a source of income?[196]

As befits any truly utopian project, the members declared an open contest among a group of local architects to determine how to best to design the structural layout of the new neighbourhood. The winning design was that of David Tischler who, in response to the cross-shaped outline of the Christian German Colony, proposed a Jewish equivalent. His Menorah composition positioned Levinsky Street as the central stem, with seven other streets – Yesod Hama'ala, Neve Sha'anan, Hagdud Ha'Ivri, Commercial Centre, Wolfson, HaKongress and Shivat Zion – sprouting off to form the emblem's branches. It may well have been a poor man's utopia, but it was a utopia all the same.[197]

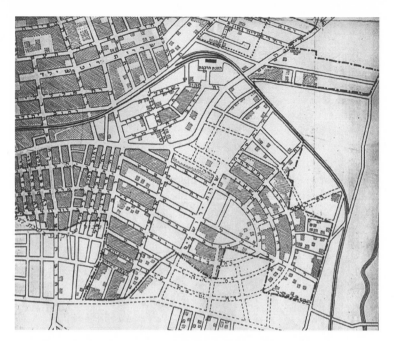

Neve Sha'anan in the 1930s. The border between Jaffa and Tel Aviv divides the neighbourhood's Menorah scheme. The southern parts of the neighbourhood are marked by hidden lines. Alter Droyanov, *The Book of Tel Aviv* (1938).

And yet, despite its powerful idealism and visionary semi-agricultural approach, Neve Sha'anan has always been historically overshadowed by the other Jewish settlements established around the same time. Lest we forget, Nahalal, perhaps the most lauded of all pre-State *moshavim*, was also founded in 1921. On the surface, there were several similarities between these two Zionist outposts: both settlements were naturally experimental in character; both were built on grand utopian principles; both sought to mirror their values in their physical design – Tischler's 'menorah' motif for Neve Sha'anan was just as clear and dogmatic as the 'circle' arrangement by Richard Kauffmann composed for Nahalal.[198] The year 1921 was also the founding year of Ein Harod, one of the largest kibbutzim in Israel, and of Ramat Gan, an agricultural garden-city near Tel Aviv that later became a city. That said, how many books have been penned about Nahalal, Ein Harod and Ramat Gan? And how many by comparison have been written about Neve Sha'anan?[199]

As is the way with many utopian projects, optimism got in the way of pragmatism and most of the founding members of the Neve Sha'anan association did not live to see the realization of Tischler's 'menorah'. The loans they had been promised proved insufficient or simply did not materialize, the money that was available was quickly used up and there were not enough funds to purchase all lands necessary to complete the design. In order to complete the project they needed to obtain two particular tracts of land, both of which were still prosperous orchards at the time of the first land purchase in 1921. These are visible from the 1918 aerial photographs: one sits in the north of the neighbourhood and the other, much larger lot is in the south. The smaller of the two was positioned on exactly the same spot where the first five Orient Fairs had been held from 1925–1932, a plot of land which, in 1941, would become Tel Aviv's first Central Bus Station. In turn, the larger lot in the south would eventually be chosen as the site of the New Central Station, to be constructed throughout the 1960s.

Notwithstanding the fact that right up until 1948 most of this southern zone was reserved for agricultural produce, each and every map of the neighbourhood produced prior to the State of Israel's establishment details (in an exercise of wishful thinking) a broken line demarking where the missing branches of the 'menorah' would, one day, come to fruition. This line was fleshed out slightly in 1927 when Neve Sha'anan was annexed to Tel Aviv, but the city's southern border still divided the 'menorah' in half; one side of the candelabra was tucked safely inside Tel Aviv while the corresponding branches on the other side (Wolfson, HaKongress and Shivat Tzion) remained in Jaffan territory. Only with the conquest of Jaffa did the menorah really begin to take form, as the 'missing' branches were gradually beaten out into dirt tracks and then the mass between them was covered with informal and illegal buildings.

Just as is the case today, Tel Aviv's borders did not correspond with the mytho-geographical boundaries of the White City, whose natural perimeters were already being defined by the buffer zone created by the city's train tracks – from Yehuda Halevi and Ibn Gvirol streets, to Jaffa Road and Petach Tikva Road. On the hem of this buffer zone, right in front of the train station, the municipality erected the Central Bus Station. Designed by the architects Werner Joseph Wittkower and Nahum Zelkind in 1941, the station cut off Neve Sha'anan from the rest of Tel Aviv. Hiding the neighbourhood behind a smokescreen of buses, it pushed Neve Sha'anan out of sight and out of mind; overnight Neve Sha'anan went from being Tel Aviv's agricultural rear-end to the White City's industrial backyard.

The split utopia of Neve Sha'anan (Jerusalem Boulevard is now known as Har-Zion Boulevard). Alter Droyanov, *The Book of Tel Aviv* (1938).

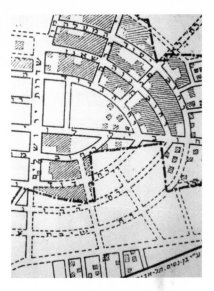

The border of Tel Aviv and Jaffa. Neve Sha'anan in 1936. Yad Avner Geographical Database, Department of Geography, Tel Aviv University.

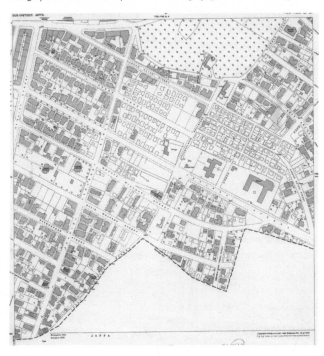

View in an advertisement brochure of Tel Aviv's New Central Bus Station project – General perspective view. Ram Karmi, architect, The New Central Bus Station of Tel Aviv (1963).

Ram Karmi, architect: Tel Aviv's New Central Bus Station project.
An aerial photo of the southern part of Neve Sha'anan from early 1960s showing a spontaneous reconstruction of the Menorah.

A drawing of the new station's footprint on top of the aerial photo of the southern part of Neve Sha'anan. 1963, Ram Karmi, advertisement brochure, The New Central Bus Station of Tel Aviv.

The Old Central Bus Station, as it is now known, was only the beginning. Considering the complete absence of Neve Sha'anan from the collective history, there is no wonder about what happened to it eventually. On top of the original sin of the Old Central Station, the New Central Station was built. Much more than just one of the most unsuccessful architectural projects in the history of the country, the New Central Bus Station also represented the first time that the city was successfully tempted into privatizing itself beyond all reason – passing responsibility for the city into the hands of private contractors, permitting them to wipe out buildings, streets, whole neighbourhoods at will, all under a banner of 'economic assessment'. So began an unhealthy readiness to accept 'poisoned gifts' on behalf of the public, whereby entrepreneurs and heavyweight donors received ample financial reward for supplying the public with an architectural treat which was not only unnecessary, but harmful.

Articles published in honour of the reopening of the station in 1992 state that in 1960 (the year of Naomi Shemer's *White City*) the entrepreneur and coffee shop owner Arieh Piltz began purchasing lots in Neve Sha'anan behind closed doors.[200] At first, Piltz had announced his intention to initiate a housing project for young couples, but disgruntled at the enlarged building rights he had received, he decided to switch his attention to developing a new central station in the area.

This idea was completely at odds with the expert advice offered by planners at the time, all of whom acknowledged that Tel Aviv was naturally linear in form, clearly lacked a centre and therefore had no use for a 'central' station of any kind (and the project's long coma is evidence of this). By all accounts, buses could be put to bed in small terminals on the outskirts of the city, near the Reading power station or in Tel Hashomer. The consensus argued that, if Tel Aviv was determined to invest in its infrastructure, it would do much better to invest the money in a modern metro system, similar to the network being developed in Cairo. Indeed, this was the recommendation even before the people of Neve Sha'anan, the communities who lived there, or the history of the neighbourhood were taken into consideration.

Piltz, however, was not preoccupied with such trivial debate. Nor, so it seemed, were Solel Boneh – the oldest, largest construction and civil engineering company in Israel – or the Egged Israel Transport Cooperative Society Ltd – the largest bus company in Israel. In 1963, all three – Solel Boneh, Egged and Piltz – joined forces to found the Kikar Levinsky Corporation (Levinsky Square Corporation), dedicated to building Neve Sha'anan a new central bus station, whether it wanted it or not.

Who's against who, from left to right: the remnants of an Arab well house, the New Central Station and the Mizrahi family home. When he built the station, the developer Arieh Piltz was keen to buy the home of the family that had lived there since the late 1940s.
To Piltz's offer to 'take 100,000 pounds and give me the house,' Abraham Mizrahi replied 'take 100,000 pounds and give me a break.' As a result of Mizrahi's stubbornness and that of a few other neighbours who insisted on staying, Piltz had to give up the expansion of the station eastwards, which culminated in its expansion southwards, moving Salame Road by diverting one of its lanes to pass through a part of the Arab well house mansion. Photograph: Roi Boshi.

A clean sweep of the surroundings: An aerial photo of Tel Aviv's New Central Bus Station in the early 2000s. Yad Avner. Geographical Database, Department of Geography, Tel Aviv University.

The architect Ram Karmi was the ideal choice for the design of the largest central station in the world. Karmi, who by then had completed the first and last stage of the 'Merkaz Hanegev' (Centre of the Negev) project, which was supposed to stretch over half of Beer Sheva, and would in time be responsible for the design of the 'Merkaz Hayekum' (Centre of the Universe) unrealized skyscraper project in Jerusalem, certainly liked to think big.[201]

If Piltz was the one to first envision the 'largest station in the world', Karmi was the one to give this vision both form and character. He also took the liberty of adding some extra dimensions to the construction programme; namely, image, theory, rhetoric, and inspiration: the top floors of this, the largest building in Israel, would house the intercity bus terminals and vehicles would arrive along bridges which criss-crossed the streets, a few metres away from the buildings' balconies. The basements would house the metropolitan buses, reached via a system of tunnels to be dug from the streets outside. Karmi claimed that inspiration for the planning of the station had come intuitively, from an almost divine source:

> the inspiration for the Central Station came to me from the
> biblical concept of the gate of the city. That is where the wise, the judges,
> and the elderly sat. The main idea derives from Damascus Gate in
> Jerusalem. It is meant to be the gate to the country.

As for the station's location in the southern area of Neve Sha'anan, in the south of the city, Karmi noted that 'it was a given [...] I was given a 44 dunams lot in the heart of a neighbourhood which was considered a ghetto. The primary intention was to make a clean sweep of the surroundings.'[202]

Even though planning of the station had taken place during Karmi's brutalist period, the architect claims that the station was never meant to be built from exposed concrete. In a photomontage he affixed to the project's commercial brochure, an aerial shot of the station reveals it as part-building, part-casting. Either way, in the photograph, this charcoal grey giant is painted completely white. Years later, Karmi would be the one to proudly parade the flag of 'white architecture', advocating its merits through a series of different projects, manifestos and declarations. And if we are to believe statements made soon after the New Central Bus Station was inaugurated, 'white architecture' had always been a predominant part of the building's design: 'The station was built with the conception of a productive society in mind, with housing project tiles and white ceramics, as a remnant of the innocence and the dream of the White City which was here.'[203]

Bus platforms making their way through Neve Sha'anan
to the New Central Bus Station: view from the platform.
Photograph: Roi Boshi.

Bus platforms making their way through Neve Sha'anan to
the New Central Bus Station: view from Levinsky Street.
Photograph: Roi Boshi.

תל אביב

על פי מחקר "גיאואוטוגרפיה", 54% מיהודי יפו משוכנעים:

בשעת מלחמה - ערביי
יפו יתקפו את תל אביב

"הדבר הזה"

מהומות
אוקטובר

פרויקט ענק • עמ' 24-80

Part III

WHITE CITY, BLACK CITY AND A RAINBOW

Everyone speaks of peace, no one speaks of justice
Muki, *Speak of Peace*

The principle of architecture is nothing but the humanization of space
Martin Buber, introduction to the Hebrew edition of
Architecture as Space by Bruno Zevi

Opposite: the title page of *Tel Aviv* magazine reporting the October 2000 Intifada. Byline: 'According to a Geo-Cartography Institute survey, 40 percent of the Jews in Jaffa are convinced'. Headline: 'At times of war – the Arabs of Jaffa would attack Tel Aviv'. Daniel Dor's *Newspapers Under Influence* (Babel, 2001).

The White City story progresses chapter by chapter, decade by decade: in 1984 there was the *White City* exhibition, in 1994 the *Bauhaus in Tel Aviv* events, and in May and June 2004 a calendar of celebrations in honour of UNESCO's declaration of the city as a World Heritage Site. Once again the city celebrated itself with dedicatory events, as Bauhaus-themed publications, honorary conventions, commemorative ceremonies and guided walking tours all satiated the municipality. News of the UNESCO 'victory' spread thick and fast through an unrelenting stream of catalogues, flags, pins and festive weekend supplements in the local papers.

On May 17, 2004, at the close of its twenty-year-long journey, the White City returned to the Tel Aviv Museum of Art with the inauguration of Nitza Szmuk's exhibition *Dwelling on the Dunes*, concluding her life's work as Tel Aviv's official conservation architect. By May 19, Bauhaus had returned home too (to Tel Aviv, that is). In a grand exercise in formal and symbolic pageantry, the Tel Aviv University School of Architecture held an academic conference in collaboration with the Bauhaus Institution (which had since reopened in Dessau) under the title *Critical Modernists: Homage to Tel Aviv, World Heritage City*.[204] Omar Akbar, the director of the Bauhaus School, concluded the ceremonial closing session with a lecture and led other professors and architects from Israel, Dessau and around the world, in a formal ceremony on June 8, under the banner 'White City: A Past in Renewal'. Other events incorporated into the celebrations included the screenings of various documentaries, architectural and painting showcases, a photography exhibition entitled *My White City* and even a sail-by from the navy (the White Corps) as they faced the Tel Aviv shoreline.

Nothing has really changed to alter the White City's historical narrative and its association with the International Style since the 1994 celebrations, other than the context: if in 1994, the discourse of the innocent White City was still believable, by 2004 the masks were off – the October 2000 outbreak of the Second Intifada that spread to Tel Aviv and Jaffa had occurred between the two celebrations and they had left their mark. It was the first time since 1948 that the simmering tension between the two cities had bubbled over into open, violent confrontation. Worse was to follow.

Between 2002 and 2004, Ariel Sharon's government instigated a programme of ethnic purification across the city. Under the supervision of the Minister of Interior Affairs, Avraham Poraz, of the Shinui party, the immigration police deported over 115,000 foreign workers, nearly all of them inhabitants of the 'Black City' of Tel Aviv-Jaffa and based in the southern Hebrew neighbourhoods of Neve Sha'anan, Chlenov, Hatikva,

Shapira and Ezra.[205] Their number was not much smaller than the number of Palestinians expelled from Jaffa in 1948.

At 12 noon on May 22, 2004, the citizens of Tel Aviv and their guests from the Bauhaus Institute in Dessau were congratulating each other at the end of another successful publicity campaign, safe in the knowledge that the celebrations would guarantee a steady flow of tourist-pilgrims to the White City over the next decade. At exactly the same time, the police blocked the streets in Neve Sha'anan under the false claim of a bomb threat. For over an hour dozens of policemen hunted down foreign workers, arresting individuals irrespective of their working or asylum status, stuffing them into buses brought into the neighbourhood especially for the day's activities.[206] Following these horrific scenes, which were described by witnesses as disproportionately violent and overtly aggressive, those lucky enough to escape a bludgeoning could be seen slipping through the backstreets of the Black City later that night, feverishly loading whatever belongings they had onto carts and into stray taxis.

A few kilometres away, the exact same spectacle was being enacted by the exact same governing authorities, albeit in a different context and with different victims. As the White City-UNESCO after-party raged and the streets of the Black City were being 'swept clean', the IDF executed 'Operation Rainbow' – a part-military, part-urban development operation in the grand old

Invitation card to the *Critical Modernists* convention, with the participation of Omar Akbar, Director of the Bauhaus School.

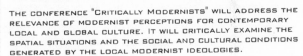

THE DAVID AZRIELI SCHOOL OF ARCHITECTURE, TEL AVIV UNIVERSITY HOSTS:

CRITICALLY MODERNISTS;
HOMAGE TO TEL AVIV A WORLD HERITAGE CITY
19-22/5/04

THE CONFERENCE "CRITICALLY MODERNISTS" WILL ADDRESS THE RELEVANCE OF MODERNIST PERCEPTIONS FOR CONTEMPORARY LOCAL AND GLOBAL CULTURE. IT WILL CRITICALLY EXAMINE THE SPATIAL SITUATIONS AND THE SOCIAL AND CULTURAL CONDITIONS GENERATED BY THE LOCAL MODERNIST IDEOLOGIES.

THE EVENT IS OPEN TO THE GENERAL PUBLIC

PLANING COMMITTEE: AMNON BAR OR, PETER KEINAN, MERON LEVI, MOSHE MARGALITH, DAFNA MATOK, AND ERAN NEUMAN

אריה סבינסקי   פרסקו   הברת אאו"ל בניה   מיסטר פיקס   הברה כרמית   NBI   הברת האחים שגראוי
ARIE SABINSKY   FRESCO-PRINTS LTD.   ONEAL CONSTRUCTION LTD.   CARMIT – MR. FIX   SHAJRAWI BROTHERS CO.

tradition of 'Project Anchor', circa 1936. The official objective of the mission was to reshape the physical order of the territory of Rafah in accordance with the tactical considerations of the army. The public justification provided was that this operation was a necessary means of preventing the construction of tunnels between Egypt and the Gaza Strip, which allowed for the exchange and passage of weapons right under the feet of those IDF soldiers stationed on the Philadelphi Route. While there were several engineering options available, if indeed this had been the objective, the army chose to demolish several huge residential blocks instead. The Israeli human rights organization, B'Tselem, reported that during the first days of 'Operation Rainbow' 183 homes were completely destroyed and thousands more were damaged.[207] Among the fifty-eight casualties, at least eight were children. Thousands of Palestinian civilians were left homeless as a result of the operation, with their possessions buried deep under the ruins of their collapsed houses.

A white city with a rainbow. The timing of these two spectacles was not coincidental. Neither was the lyricism which framed them. Even if one could picture Operation Rainbow taking place somewhere else, under another name, or for different operational purposes, it still would not have been coincidental, and it almost certainly still would have been poetically titled. This is because the White City celebrations and Operation Rainbow were connected events; on the one hand, Tel Aviv's past is still ahead of it, waiting to be unearthed, and on the other hand, Rafah's future is already behind it, buried deep under the rubble. In this sense the Palestinian city of Rafah is no different to the Palestinian city of Jaffa, or Salama, or Abu Kabir; they all share a long history as victims of military, urban and architectural actions whose sole goal has been to create a new geography in their place using processes of demolition and effacement.

The growing contradiction between the disturbingly coercive actions in Neve Sha'anan and Rafah, and the powerfully pastoral imagery of the 'White City' and the 'Rainbow', between the cruelty and brutality on the one hand and the self-righteousness on the other, these all form a crucial part of the Israeli reality. Neither is it a coincidence that these two images, which have both been carefully plucked and are powerful enough in their own right, have been welded together to create this graphically innocent vista. The terrible irony, however, is that those left to 'dwell on the dunes' were not the critical, modernist residents of Tel Aviv but the displaced inhabitants of Neve Sha'anan and Rafah. They were the ones left asking questions about how to preserve (what was left) of their city.

Perhaps more than any other architectural tradition, Israeli architecture has a tendency to reveal its own politics. The story of the international canonization of the White City of Tel Aviv hardly deviates from this rule. The White City's journey, from lowly exhibition to global certification, even demonstrates how Israeli architecture unveiled, rehashed and manipulated *other* political economies; in this instance, the politics of UNESCO and the politics of international architecture. From the Israeli standpoint, the practical meaning of the UNESCO declaration is that Tel Aviv is obliged publicly, vis-à-vis the world, to realize its own designation as a white city.

What exactly did Tel Aviv promise UNESCO when it accepted its stamp of approval? Essentially, it promised to be whiter, to bleach itself clean. Of course, had it already been white then this whole exercise would have been utterly superfluous. Establishing UNESCO's political positioning is all the more interesting then when we consider that Tel Aviv was not given a *carte blanche* as a prize for actually *being* white, but rather for *wanting* to be white.

There is obviously something politically unsettling about the portrayal of Tel Aviv's architectural white as an extension of a grander 'will *to be* white'. It is problematic at the very least, because only that which is not white can want to be white. Beyond the realms of traditional white racism as we know it, this concept of an architectural white could only have originated in Europe, where the white is hegemonic in any case. This 'will to be white' is unlikely to have originated from within Afro-American or Afro-European communities, and is even less likely to have stemmed from post-colonial Africa, where there would have been no benefit for black inhabitants to actively deny their own colour. Even if, as Frantz Fanon observes, the dialectics of the 'will to be white' and the resistance against it are a substantial and inevitable part of what it means to be a black man under European subjugation, this would not nor could ever qualify as a determined ideology or a publicly supported strategy. It might be a personal survival tactic at best, or a form of surrender at worst.

Plenty of ink has been spilled over the usage and quest for white in modern architecture, not least because the most contentious of all architectural images has been the flagship white box. For Le Corbusier, modern architecture's chief propagandist, white was the ideal base for the clinically sharp and beautifully accurate 'game of forms assembled under the light'. For Adolf Loos, it was a powerful ideological statement, which negated the cheap temptation of the decorative ornament. Among a whole generation of architects (and their clients), white has become almost the sole chromatic option worth working with, despite the availability of an infinite range of other possibilities. It became a 'default option' for the modern movement as it first traversed the field of architecture, there has been no reason to replace it and so it remains – always the safe choice, always in vogue. Of all the colours, it is presented as the 'natural' option that does not require explanation or excuse, in much the same way as the rectangle is considered a 'natural' choice for planners when compared with all other building forms.[208] 'You can choose any colour you want, as long as it's white' goes the cry, well-known across every architect's studio and building site in the land.

When it talks of the nudity of the wall, white is seen as a blank page, a base and a background, ideal to put on display the shapes in the sunlight on the outside, and to show the pictures, furniture and other objects in the electric light indoors. This white default had supposedly formed itself, organically emerging as the most minimalist pigment possible, as the standard, the neutral, the norm, the universal state of things. Over time, white was attached with new attributes and tagged with fresh labels: it became clean, hygienic, fresh, original, naive and virginal.[209] All of a sudden, what had once been the plain default option now became the basis for a wonderful array of different possibilities and reference points; white as ascetic as a Dominican monastery, as hedonistic as a Mediterranean villa, as classic as a Greek temple, as contemporary as a New York loft, as minimalist as a Japanese boutique.

As soon as white was transformed into an ideology, it ceased to be neutral. In this sense, white cannot be considered as a 'Degree Zero' of chromaticity but, similar in a way to the neighbouring concept of an 'International Style', is a sufferer of the very same trappings of European universalism.

The distance between the white box and the white gaze is minute: the gaze establishes the box; the box contains the gaze. White is not only the universal sum of all colours, but above all else, the colour to replace all others, to cancel them out, to erase them. White architecture became the fantasy reflection of the modern movement; a fantasy that suggested innovation and which projected an image of the world as European, international and universal, all at the same time. Since this fantasy had no place in Europe, it was destined to realize itself in the distant, heterotopic provinces of the continent.

If the white architecture which left Europe and made its way to North Africa, West Africa, South America and the Middle East was originally exported as examples of the 'Bauhaus Style' or the 'International Style', then it reached its destinations under an altogether different patronage;

it arrived under the auspices of colonialism, with all its spearheads, its backwinds, its programmes. This is precisely how white architecture was enrolled as one of the chief agents of Europeanism and Westernism and why, ever since, it has established itself as the architecture *of* the white, created *by* the white and *for* the white.

Evidence of this can be found all over the world. In the centre of Dakar, Senegal, for example, there is an area very similar in size, scale and architecture to the White City of Tel Aviv.[210] With streets decorated with grand Ficus trees like in Tel Aviv, Dakar boasts a whole range of modern architecture dating back from the 1920s and 1930s, complete with touches of French Art Deco and those early colonial designs which, in Tel Aviv at least, are described (for some reason) as being of an 'eclectic style'.

In particular locations, like on the island of Goree for example, this colonial architecture is reminiscent of Neve Tzedek, with its pebbled red roofs – here, as in Neve Tzedek, the roofs are covered with ceramic tiles (nicknamed 'Marseille tiles'), plastered with warm colours, fitted with narrow windows and furnished with wooden shutters. In the Place de l'Independence in central Dakar, a different, more urban architecture is visible; harking back to a classic use of plaster casts, its form is similar to Nachalat Binyamin and Ahad Ha'am streets in Tel Aviv. Prowling through Dakar and it becomes clear that there is really nothing revolutionary at all about the shift between these different styles. Any fluctuation is solely down to a change in taste of the white ruling elites. In fact, more accurately, the shift is just from one colonial style to another; both instances are representative of white, architectural power.

This is where Tel Aviv's real singularity lies. In comparison with other cities like Casablanca, Algiers or Dakar, where the white architecture represents a present–absent culture of white governance, in which the buildings remain but the rulers do not, in Tel Aviv the white rulers are still present and their culture remains, more than ever, *the* prevalent culture.[211] Tel Aviv stands today as the urban prototype of what Casablanca, Algiers and Dakar would or could have looked like had colonialism won out, had the French retained their colonies. Architectural historian Jean-Louis Cohen, who has researched Algiers and Casablanca extensively, claims that, in light of the trauma, humiliation and oppression that went hand in hand with French rule, it is too much to expect the Algerian or Moroccan public to push for the preservation of modern French colonial architecture.[212] And again, in this respect Israel is outstanding for being one of the few countries in the world to canonize its colonial architecture. Even in nation-states outside of Europe

International Style
architecture in Dakar,
Senegal, 2002.
Photos: Sharon Rotbard.

with a large concentration of International Style constructions, the emphasis on indigenous heritage and the natural antagonism towards commemorating periods of colonial subjugation means these buildings are rarely maintained.

While the political relevancy inherent in the whiteness of modern architecture may not have been obvious at first, the writing has been on the wall for a while now.[213] Primarily, it is important to recognize that many of the values ascribed to the modern movement came from its own propaganda, and that from today's perspective it is both possible, and necessary, to judge the movement by its actions and their outcomes, as much as by the intentions or ideas which encouraged them. When we do that we can see that the political colouring of modern architecture was always visible; it was always there to be seen, if anybody had actually wanted to see it. Perhaps in contrast to what we would have expected, or at least in contrast to what adherents of the preservation of modern architecture would have expected, the pioneers of the modern movement never considered architecture to be an autonomous discipline. They never dissembled nor hid their political colours and readily acknowledged the necessary link between their architecture and their politics. As far as the three central figures of the modern architectural movement – Mies, Loos and Le Corbusier – are concerned, it is a hard task to argue that the white colouring of their pieces reflected the progressiveness alluded to in, say, Tel Aviv's narrative: politically, there is no doubt that their white was always more brown than it was red; just as in Tel Aviv, white actually read as a translation for blue and white, the colours of the Israeli flag.

Adolf Loos never concealed his pioneering efforts, not only of modern architecture, but also of Westernization. As a firm believer in Western supremacy over other cultures, he was the one to identify, more than any other, modernity with Westernization. In his writings he never ceased to conduct a 'war of civilizations', where each nation battles for its place – in the hierarchy of evolution, when discussing the differences between a white person and a black person (the Papuans in *Ornament and Crime*); or in the hierarchy of Westernization, when discussing the differences within Western culture, between the German and the English (in *The Plumbers*, for example).[214] To Loos' credit, it should be noted that he assigned both the Papuan and the European the same simple, hygienic and functional modernity.

In his famous essay, *Ornament and Crime*, Loos claims that 'the primitive man had to differentiate himself from his fellow men through different colors.' In the same essay he also states that he 'preaches for aristocracy' and is willing to tolerate ornamentation as long as it is in its place: 'on the member of the Bantu tribe, the Persian, the Slovak farmer, and his shoemaker.' A

'Algiers, the White City'. Tourism poster of the French railway company advertising the white city of Algiers, from *Alger: paysage urbain et architectures, 1800–2000*, Cohen, Oulebsir and Kanoun (eds).

Examples of International Style architecture in Algiers. From *Alger: paysage urbain et architectures, 1800–2000*, edited by Jean-Louis Cohen, Nabila Oulebsir and Youcef Kanoun, Institut français d'architecture, Cité de l'architecture et du patrimoine, Paris, 2003.

closer inspection reveals that more than the wish of these to differentiate themselves from each other, the aristocratic European wishes to be differentiated from all of them. By isolating himself with this white appearance, Loos, the European aristocrat, manages to gather in Vienna all those individuals native to the four corners of the earth.

Mies van der Rohe was the director of the Bauhaus School before it was shut down. Even after the closing of the school in 1933, he tried with all his might to convince the Nazi regime of the necessity of modern architecture, and filed proposals for projects initiated by the Nazi regime. Only after his abstract proposals were turned down over and over again did he leave for the United States in 1935. In this regard, he differs from other non-Jewish German intellectuals, like Thomas Mann for example, who emigrated from Germany in disgust as soon as the National Socialist Party rose to power. Architectural historian Richard Pommer recognized this in his essay 'Mies van der Rohe and the Political Ideology of the Modern Movement in Architecture',[215] where he 'stained' the political whiteness of modern architecture by analysing the conduct of one of its leaders:

> *politically, Mies was the 'Talleyrand' of modern architecture: in less*
> *than ten years he designed the Monument to Karl Liebknecht*
> *and Rosa Luxemburg for the Communist Party, the Barcelona*
> *Pavilion for the Weimar Republic, and a project for a German pavilion*
> *for the World Fair in Brussels in 1935, that would have been the*
> *first Nazi monument of international significance had it been built.*[216]

Le Corbusier, who willingly cooperated with colonialism and the Vichy regime, proved no less scandalous within his own political context. Le Corbusier used his first book, *Toward An Architecture* (1923), to suggest that modern architecture be applied as a replacement or 'vaccine' against social revolution.[217] In his third book, *Decorative Art Today* (1925), he dedicated a key chapter to the 'the milk of whitewash, the rule of Ripolin' (a well-known paint manufacturer in France) in which he announced that the whitening of traditional and modern architecture was the trademark of 'harmonic culture' and a sign of 'the victory of the West'.[218] Le Corbusier closes the same chapter with the words 'there may be people who think on a black background. But the creation of a time so brave, so dangerous, so aggressive, so captivating, brings us to expect that we think on a white background.' To this statement he affixed a photograph of three African men holding spears, accompanied by an enigmatic credit: 'The Sultan Mahembe and his two sons. Three black heads on a white background, talented to rule, to reign. [...] A half-open door through which we can see true greatness.'[219]

Le Corbusier provided a more detailed indication of how he perceived the term 'greatness' in his 'Plan Obus', produced in 1932. In mirror of 'Plan Voisin' (which he had penned with Paris in mind a decade earlier), 'Plan Obus' suggested constructing one enormous, elongated building with a highway mapped on its roof, spread out along the entire coastline of Algiers, replacing the city. Jean-Louis Cohen interprets Le Corbusier's plan to conquer the 'White City' of Algiers and the warring metaphors he employs as part of a wider 'realization of the architectural revolution through modern technology.'[220] Le Corbusier continued in much the same vein for the next fifteen years, and in 1941 published *Sur les quatre routes* while he was in Paris during the German occupation. In this book, Le Corbusier deals extensively with his plans for the Nemours Project – a design he had mapped out for a new city of 50,000 residents while he had been in Algeria in 1933. It was a project economically dependent on the suppression of the last of the opposition forces based in the Atlas Mountains, as well as a railway link with equatorial Africa. 'Why should we not gain from these circumstances?' he asks unabashedly. After all, to Le Corbusier the Nemours Project was just another means of illustrating how 'urbanism is no longer a municipal matter, but the concern of states', noting how 'as always, colonizers are ahead of their time'. In the chapter entitled 'The Water Way', Le Corbusier outlines his vision for the Mediterranean Sea, confessing that the sight of naval ships excites him and bemoaning the lack of finances available to begin work on the project. He notes that after the suppression of opposition in the Atlas Mountains, the area would be evacuated, thus freeing up land towards the south in order to lay the railroads which would form part of a 'steel equator'.

The Nemours Project did not materialize for a number of different reasons but Le Corbusier blamed its failure squarely on the laziness of the 'Maltese, Castilians, Marseillaise' and all those 'other refugees of the casbah', who he accused of sitting around in cafés, playing cards and drinking arak. His conclusion was that 'a frontier should not separate the Northern people from the Southern ones'. Le Corbusier uses *Sur les quatre routes* to consider the scale of continents, claiming that the only way to harness them is through the 'four roads': the air, the sea, the steel and the land. The architect champions colonization as a means to link distant locations in Africa and considers a takeover of Europe, which had recently been 'unified' by the Nazis. The book includes several other troublesome commentaries and statements, including a very favourable analysis of Adolf Hitler, who apparently 'demands healthy

Le Corbusier's Plan Obus. Taken from *Alger: paysage urbain et architectures, 1800–2000*, Cohen, Oulebsir and Kanoun (eds).

materials and through a return to tradition aspires to instil the health every race deserves.'[221]

The link between European architecture and colonialism is not limited to the fact that European architects often planned work in, and for, the colonies. Many of the components of modern architecture – especially those 'white' elements, such as the white wall, the *brise soleil*, and the *pergola* – were imported to Europe *from* the colonies themselves, and more often than not through Le Corbusier's North African connection. The white Corbusian architecture and the 'folk architecture' of North Africa can be conceived in the same terms used to describe the ties between African Art and modern painting today: both would not have been possible in the absence of colonialism, both were its result.

It is also questionable as to how international the International Style actually was. A study of the *International Exhibition of Modern Architecture*, held at the Museum of Modern Art in New York in 1932, and the catalogue which went with it outlines precisely how geographically restricted the participating projects were: of the eighty projects Philip Johnson and Henry-Russell Hitchcock chose to showcase, only nine came from outside Europe – eight came from the United States and one from Japan. Not a single exhibit came from the Middle East, North Africa, Central Africa, South Africa or South America. The rest of the works came from Europe, with a disproportionate number from Central Europe in particular. Inspection of the listed architects involved only reinforced this concentration as even the majority of buildings which had come from the United States had been planned by Central European architects like Mies, Neutra and Frey.[222] Even putting curator Philip Johnson's dubious affiliations with Nazism aside, there is no doubt that his selection of architects mirrored an overwhelming bias towards European tastes.[223] Whether Johnson's curatorial decisions were justified or not, Europeanism became *the* defining characteristic of the modern canon after 1932. Ironically, many of those architects actually based in Central Europe had held completely the opposite opinion to Johnson, the American longing for Central Europe. For individuals like Loos, there was

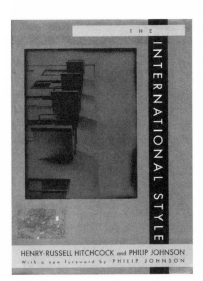

How international was the International Style? Most of the projects displayed in the exhibition catalogue are in Europe, and European architects designed the few buildings included from the United States. Beyond that, the catalogue shows only one building in Tokyo, planned by Mamoru Yamada.
The catalogue of the exhibition *The International Style*, curated by Henry-Russell Hitchcock and Philip Johnson. Museum of Modern Art, New York, 1932.

no modernity to be found in Austria or Germany – modernity was beyond the Channel and over the ocean, in England and the United States.[224]

These zealous ideologues were not wild thorns in the modern movement, they combined to make up its central branch and they reflected the views of white, male philosophy prominent throughout the twentieth century. Modern architecture also drew on an inherent violence, characterized by a principle of invasion, stemming from the scale of its economy and, occasionally, in light of the brute force used to make way for it. Illustrative examples include Le Corbusier forcibly plotting the Villa Savoye in the middle of a meadow in Poissy or Adolph Loos' description of the modern villa by the lake in his essay, *Architecture*.[225] Occasionally, this architectural invasion took a more explicit form – in the mobile homes of *Voisin*, in Buckminster Fuller's Geodesic domes, in Israel's very own 'Wall and Tower' settlements, in Jean Prouvé's *Tropical House* and *House of the Lone Settler in the Sahara*. In certain instances, architects were utterly unambiguous about this kind of architectural violence and how they intended to make use of it – Marinetti's Futurist manifestos carried the call for war, Albert Speer eagerly endorsed the 'ruin value theory', Claude Parent and Paul Virilio declared their intention to 'take over the site'.[226] These examples prove that the visual and stylized violence inherent in modern architecture, as much as the violence turned against it, did not just end with debate and academic commentary; it addressed something so fundamental that if pushed, people would willingly, literally, kill and be killed for it.[227]

White would play a unique role in all this: it had already seduced modern architecture and it would become the representative of both Mediterran-eanism (courtesy of Le Corbusier) and Easternism (as in the famous Nazi postcard showing the Weisenhof neighbourhood in Stuttgart as an Arab village). At same time, it also became emblematic of the European fantasy abroad, of the European *in* the Mediterranean, or the South, or the East. The white house became an extension of the white ruler, in much the same way that the white suit, the European apparel donned in these colonial outposts, also became a strong symbol of white supremacy. With this in mind, Le Corbusier's plans to whitewash Algiers cannot be separated from the pressed, white suit he wore while making them, nor can we divorce either whitewash or white suit from the French government's wider designs for North Africa in general. With this in mind, the architectural context needs to be extracted as far as is necessary, even if it does derive from the disciplinary definition. When we consider 'White Cities' like Tel Aviv or Dakar today, we do so in light of the fact that the best places to examine modern architecture remain outside Europe, in urban spaces which developed under colonial governance. These settlements were open fields for European experimentation in architecture and urbanism.[228] Therefore it is also important to consider this architecture within the context of anti-colonial and post-colonial thought – to recognize the considerable political and military power modern architecture provided imperial governments.

Criticism in this spirit started to form in the early 1950s, with Roland Barthes' literary and cultural criticism, and the theoretical and political writings of Frantz Fanon. Still, even though many architects read Barthes and even studied with him, his political lessons were not realized in the field of architecture. In 'African Grammar', Barthes attacked this same bourgeois obviousness, presenting itself as 'natural', observing how the formal discourse of the colonial state in North Africa was a 'cosmetic version' of the ruling power itself, in which the main objective was always to embellish reality.[229] Re-examining those 'White Cities' speckled across Africa and the Middle East in the light of 'African Grammar' we could say the same of architecture in general; isn't it a better definition of the overall role of architecture, to be a 'cosmetic version' of reality? Similarly, just as another one of 'African Grammar's key assertions was that axiomatic language had been employed by colonial regimes to stifle and deny the existence of any kind of conflict (let alone war), there is also no doubt that architecture, too, played a leading role in creating the semblance of normality which lay at the heart of colonial order. It is also interesting to note the way in which, even at this very early stage of anti-colonial debate, Barthes acknowledged the perverse dialectic between black and white and the multitude of different ways, masks, costumes and fictions in which this dynamic played itself out.[230] Writing on the myths of modernity from 1954, Barthes observed that there was a clear affinity between all whites (laundry detergents, milk etc.) which laced colonialism and inherently affected the way it was put into practice. In this context, there was little difference between the white of modern architecture and the white of colonial architecture, the white of plumbing accessories and the white of the colonial suit. Eventually, and not very surprisingly, the white is the sign of the white, and it is always placed at the top of a system of values, that the colonized must assimilate as well.

The psychiatrist Frantz Fanon expanded on this white system of values and explored the way in which it had 'entered the soul' of colonized communities through language, accent and culture, examining processes of 'internalized racism' and the development of a 'will to be white' within black identities.[231] Despite being a psychiatrist moulded in the French tradition, it seems that

Fanon's interest in the symbolic, visual and representative machinery of the colonial state stemmed from a desire to unravel the way in which the colonial order worked. He was eager to decipher how this order had manifested itself in such a practical and concrete manner and, more importantly, how one might challenge the same order in a practical and concrete way. Among his many inferences, Fanon demonstrated how violence and aggression were the beating heart of the colonization project. It is only a short distance from this acknowledgement to the conclusion that in order to create modern architecture, let alone to create whole new cities, a considerable amount of violence and aggression is also required.

In 'Concerning Violence', the first chapter of Fanon's last book *The Wretched of the Earth*, the author details how colonialism is first and foremost about order. The basic principle governing the colonial order is separation: 'The colonial world is a compartmentalized world.' And since this compartmentalization takes place within the actual space

> *there are cities for Europeans and cities for the Indigenous people [...] The European city is a solid city, built with stone and steel, it is lighted and asphalted [...] in the European city the coloniser's feet are never seen, except maybe at the beach. [...] The colonized's city is a hungry city, it is hungry for bread, for meat, for shoes, for carbon, for light.*[232]

Those two regions are opposite to each other and obey a principle of reciprocal exclusion. A concilliation is impossible. The logic of the colonial world is unilateral and simple: 'the cause is the effect – you are rich because you are white, you are white because you are rich.'[233] Fanon notes how the colonizing power also uses violence as a tool when it comes to organizing the space and history of the colonial order in its image:

> *The colonizer makes history, and knows that he is making history. And since he constantly refers to the history of the metropolis, he shows that even though he is here, he is the continuation of the metropolis. The history he writes is not that of the land he is using, but that of his nation, which loots, rapes, and starves.*[234]

Therefore, the only resource against this compartmentalized world is a total negation of it: total revolution, total chaos. The inevitable response to this threat is another, crushing wave of violence.

But perhaps it is not as simple as that; the replacement of one city by the other is not always possible and it was only with the development of post-colonial studies as an academic subject and the emergence of thinkers like Edward Said and Homi K. Bhabha that the principles behind effective programmes of resistance were outlined. As Bhabha notes:

> *The subversive move is to reveal within the very integuments of*
> *'whiteness' the agonistic elements that make it the unsettled, disturbed*
> *form of authority that it is – the incommensurable 'differences' that*
> *it must surmount; the histories of trauma and terror that it must*
> *perpetrate and from which it must protect itself; the amnesia it*
> *imposes on itself; the violence it inflicts in the process of*
> *becoming a transparent and transcendent force of authority.*[235]

Blue and White

Surprisingly, in the face of the complexity of these internal and external gazes, and the tangled system of reflections and representations they create, it is the supposedly learned professional architectural discourse that withdraws into the pure simplified 'History of Architecture' standing at the basis of the 'White City' thesis, thus concealing reality, erasing it and reshaping it simultaneously, all the while creating a whole new web of justifications and excuses.

This is precisely the violence that Fanon, Bhabha, and many other anti-colonial and post-colonial theoreticians refer to. The feigned innocence which weaves and frames the White City story does not solely derive from the white narrative that decomposes almost by itself, but from the eagerness to isolate the autonomous history of architecture from the 'general' history; to create spheres of consent between the autonomous history of Israeli architecture and the autonomous history of universal architecture, in order to recount the history of the region.

If the story of Tel Aviv's White City teaches us anything, however, it is that it is impossible to extract the architectural from the general. The reason that Tel Aviv does concentrate on the White City's architectural narrative, repeating it over and over again for its own citizens as much as for the rest of the world, is because it means we get to block out another story – the story of Jaffa. And as time and erasure goes on, and that story gets increasingly diluted and worn out, it also gets harder to tell.

And yet, these two stories are two sides of the same coin. Each turns the other over. This is something painfully reflected in the Israeli architecture erected in Jaffa since 1948 – the uneasy embarrassment, the confusion, the unclean consciousness. The architecture is obliged to translate political facts into action and, by implementing planning regulations such as those that had transformed the historical city of Jaffa into a colony for Jewish artists, the nature of these political facts can sometimes lay bare an intrusive, racist and bio-political character.

The Israeli architects who plan and build in Jaffa cannot ignore the looting of Arab property, as by virtue of their work they are forced to hold evidences of this in their hands. Architects, in their actions and their works, are the ones who finalize the occupation, making it irreversible. No Israeli architect has been unscathed by this.

Of course, this process of dividing reality into black and white – a process which may lead the architect into an ethical cul-de-sac or a state of moral bankruptcy – is not only a danger for those working in Jaffa: 93 percent of Israel's land mass reached the market in a similar way. Other red lines can be thrown down – what does it mean to build in the Occupied Territories, or for the army, or for corporations, or within the framework of problematic projects such as 'evacuation & construction'? It is important to note that these questions are relevant not only in Israel. The wild urbanism taking place in China, for example, as described by Rem Koolhaas in his study of the new cities being created in the Pearl River Delta, asks difficult ethical questions given that these projects demand the transfer of hundreds of thousands, maybe even millions, of inhabitants from their homes.[236] This is just one of an endless index of examples to choose from. Clearly simplistic divisions into black and white are not always useful in this context and establishing the dichotomy between innocent and guilty does not help tackle the issues at hand. But the world is still built on the actions of individuals and whether we like it or not, each and every attempt to grapple with these kinds of ethical dilemmas will, and should be, subjected to political criticism. Perhaps of all the architectural strategies employed by the State of Israel in Jaffa, the intrusive brutalism of the 1950s and 1960s housing projects was the most decent course of action. Identical in form to those projects constructed in Kiyrat Shmona, Beer Sheva and Dimona, at least this was architecture without pretence. Still, there is always an itch that comes with Israeli architectural projects in the old Arab capital; it is always covered with some surplus self-consciousness, with some kind of stylization, with some good, old-fashioned architecturalism. Like this modern villa Adolf Loos describes in his 1909 essay *Architecture*: 'what is it there? A fake sound in this peacefulness, like a redundant squeak.'[237]

The problematic nature of developing Israeli architecture in Jaffa is complicated further whenever official bodies like the municipality of Tel Aviv, the self-proclaimed 'gate-keeper' for construction in the city, stand behind the planning processes. Ajami's building style, for example, has been scanned, documented, sorted and catalogued in exactly the same way the municipality approached the 'White City'. The municipality of Tel Aviv published a prospectus that is in part an architecture catalogue with referential and historical pretence, in part a document of statutory validity. The prospectus attempts to showcase Jaffa's architecture through an array of postmodern architectural observations. These include the morphological and typological analysis of the structures, the indexing of characteristic parts and details of buildings, surveying the development of building in the city, and so on. This brochure, meant to ensure the authenticity of the Jaffa building heritage, has an almost obligatory standing with all questions and dilemmas that arise when building in Jaffa, and it acts as a sort of set of building rules.[238]

It seems, whatever it does, Israeli architecture can neither forget Jaffa nor console itself with Tel Aviv. Jaffa cannot but taint the narcissistic consolation of the White City, as the white of Tel Aviv is also the white of the eraser, the Tipp-Ex. Tel Aviv is a predatory city, a wolf in sheep's skin; the White City is the skin.

Multicultural City

Parallels with this 'White City, Black City' story can be found all over the world and in various different forms and scales: Tel Aviv and Jaffa, Israel and Palestine, Paris and Algiers, West and East, North and South, First and Third Worlds. In this story all places resemble each other, and so does the physical reality: the architectural, the urban, and the political intertwine and sustain one another. If we adopt Carl von Clausewitz's formula, complete with all its geometries and possible inversions, White City is an example of how architecture, like war, is the continuation of politics by other means. In turn, we can classify a Black City as an example of how war is the continuation of architecture by other means.[239]

Eventually, the division into a black city and a white city is the outcome of the perspective, the terms, and the rules of the game as dictated by the White

City. In Israel, this division is even more paradoxical if we acknowledge that only the non-whites could wish to be white. Moreover, Tel Aviv, as we have seen, is not really white. In fact, if we search for the initial authentic identity which, over the last century or so, has shaped the region's local identity, then we can only arrive at one conclusion: that Tel Aviv has always been much more of a non-white city, a multicultural city, than ever conclusively either a 'White' or 'Black' city.

If there is anything to celebrate in Tel Aviv, it is this – the collapse of the white into the non-white. The non-white is trace of the collapse of that same 'transparent and transcendent force of authority'.[240] In fact, this is exactly what we were taught in nature class at elementary school, when the teacher tried to explain to us that the white is not really white but simply an optical illusion created by the merging of all the colours of the rainbow. To prove this, we performed a little experiment: we cut out a circle from a cardboard box, divided it into different sectors and each one filled in with a different colour. Then we stuck a pin in the centre of the circle and spun it quickly in order to see how all the colours merged together and turned to white. Anyone lucky enough to take part in such an exercise will note that a complete white cannot be reached; it is unattainable however fast you try; that the white is more of a concept than a colour, and that the colour generated from the circle's spinning is never white, but a sort of greyish non-white. My teacher blamed this disappointing gap between the milky ideal and the murky result on the distinct lack of a colour named 'indigo' in our pencil cases (it should have been between the blue and the black pencils), and our inability to spin the circle fast enough. This may well have been the case but it did not matter; from our point of view we could have summarized the conclusion then: *white is the colour you see when you cannot make out the others.*

It is not really necessary to state again that the White City will be never be white enough – the earth simply does not rotate fast enough. With this in mind, it seems much more appropriate to try to take the time to discern all those other colours on show. After all, life, as they say, is not all black and white. Moreover, confronted with the monolith of the white Tel Avivian identity, supposedly made up of that starched middle class which all political powers long to bed, the Black City has never looked so colourful – it is by far the most vibrant, cosmopolitan space in Israel.[241]

Ultimately, what lies at the foundation of the White City story is more than just the chorus singing the praises of plain good architecture. It is a story anchored in an aspiration; an aspiration to isolate Tel Aviv from its surroundings, to transform it into an aristocratic European bubble, to detach it from Jaffa in order to ensure it is hygienic, to sterilize it if necessary. In this regard, the White City is the cultural incarnation of division, separation and disengagement. The consequences of this idea on the Tel Avivian are clear: Tel Aviv is out of it all. Judea, Samaria and Gaza are over there, they are there and we are here, far from the crazy in Jerusalem and Gaza, on the right side of the Green Line, on the right side of the Yarkon river, playing alone, completely alone and totally innocently with beautiful buildings and righteous white houses on the sand.

Maybe Brenner was wrong to call for 'no politics, only the touch of two souls', not taking into consideration the fact that there is no 'touch of souls' without politics, and that politics cannot but enter the soul. Still, he must have been more accurate than the adherents of the separation idea, who believe that both politics and the touch of souls can be ruled out in such a small place.

Given that in Tel Aviv writing always comes before construction, it did not take long for the act of definition to realize itself as an act of fencing: the Separation Wall skirting the West Bank is arguably nothing more than an outer wall of the White City.[242] And if this is Zion, how can one help but think wistfully about Babel as an alternative? If there is any moral to the story of the White City and the Black City, it is to be found in the collapse of these separations and definitions, in the impossibility of decanting the white from the black, in the natural range of pigments, in the multiplicity, in the potential to package a spatial model, much more complex than anything based on a binary division of black and white, which has been forced onto a particular tract of land because of its definition as a 'White City' or the 'State of Israel'.

The starting point for this new breed of politics can only be found in the city, and in the *ideal* behind the city. The author Hannah Arendt argues that the most celebrated value of the Greek *polis* was not democracy or the rule of the people ('the worst of all tyrants', according to her) but isonomy – the principle of equality of rights.[243] In other words, Arendt argues that what made the city a political hub was not the space allotted for government, but, on the contrary, that empty, ungoverned space which was open to all. In its historic course from the Greek *polis* to the Latin *urbs* to the modern metropolis, the city has been stripped of the political in the sense that equal rights, equal law, and equality before the law are no longer ideals, let alone certainties. Today, the spatial configuration of this loss – the loss of the political – is becoming more and more radical. Expressed through boundaries enforced by national authorities, who press prohibitions on bodies and block the movement of human beings, it has led to the re-ordering of public space into a network of territories and ex-territories, into a system of islands and enclaves, fences and barriers. Each new barricade imbues the physical reality with this same principle of inequality, making it easier to impose upon different categories of people.

Having said this, right under the nose of the political and cultural hegemony of the White City in the north-west of Tel Aviv, there are the sparks of a new southern, eastern, cosmopolitan melting-pot. These neighbourhoods are instantly reminiscent of Ben-Gurion's description of Jaffa in 1906 as a 'multicoloured and speckled population', made up of 'a rabble of races, nations and languages that one does not find even in the world's largest cities [...] natives of Egypt and Algeria, Tunisia and Morocco, Zanzibar and Madagascar [...] among them a large number of "Arabized Negros".[244]

History has shown how thirty years later, the same Ben-Gurion linked this rabble with the *fellahs* and turned them into the Palestinian nation by subjecting them all, regardless of religion, race and sex, to the same fate of exiled refugees. Therefore, if a continuous historic struggle takes place here, it is not that between the white and the black, but a struggle between the white and everybody else. The current 'rabble' also looks likely to unite under a new identity, as a coalition of minorities. And these politics are no less wilful than Herzl's legend, and not more legendary than Ben-Gurion's stories.

Among many of the inhabitants of the 'Black City', multiculturalism is seen as the key, defining component of the civilian, urban, and neighbourhood ethos. A visit to any public park in the southern neighbourhoods proves that the future is already here: the children that play together in Levinsky Park are made up of an eclectic mix of secular Jews, religious Jews, Palestinians, Russians, Ethiopians, Chinese, Eritreans, Colombians, Darfuris and Filipinos. They all speak the same Hebrew they learnt in kindergarten and at elementary school. *Their* city has nothing to do with the 'White City' narrative. The ethnic purification programmes which continue to terrorize their neighbourhoods and their families is proof enough that, in contradiction to the claim made by Dani Karavan, the 'White City' has yet to defeat the tenets of Nazism.

The cumbersome attempt of politicians and military establishments to arrange the space of the city may culminate in disaster. Their city will never be safe enough or shielded enough, just as it will never be white enough. The neglect, the imperviousness (literally), and the roughness of the Separation Wall – with all the spatial contradictions, local paradoxes, and the everyday injustice that it brings about in each and every metre of its path – only reflect the desperateness of the attempt to force the simplistic and binary interpretation of space, designed by and for nation-states of the nineteenth century, onto an area roughly the same size as a medium-sized European metropolis. Cleaving through an impossibly intricate constellation of inter-communal dynamics and inter-personal relationships, it advocates the artificial division of the region into segregated, homogenous, taxonomically contained, spatial units – Jews on one side, Arabs on the other, White City here, Black City there.

While conducting this colossal project of building and separation, the nation-state of Israel gradually becomes devoid of any value, content and role, and privatizes all of its public assets – education, health, and even the enforcement of the law. Given the strategic reality, that nation-states have already relinquished their monopoly over war the world over, the Separation Wall and the White City increasingly feel like the final act of Israel the Nation-State, or at very least, its rearguard battle.[245]

This book began with the acknowledgement that in order to change the city, we first need to change the city's story. We can only hope that after that, the rest would follow. Therefore, why should we build walls now, after we have learnt that we have the abilities to pass through them? Why knock down and rebuild reality, if its very interpretation could be altered? Instead of fixating on the formulation of the region into two enemy states, could the space not be reimagined as a city, or even a cluster of cities?[246] In lieu of the failed attempts to leave the mark of the nationalist delusion on the space, could the Middle Eastern conflict not be seen as a social and urban issue, rather than a national one? Perhaps disengagement and eternal division are not the only ways to put an end to the occupation; maybe it would be enough to simply stop being occupiers? These are processes which need to be realized everywhere but they need to begin in Jaffa.

We need to stop occupying Jaffa. It is time to strip the army barracks from the 'Bride of the Sea'; to remove the army from Jaffa, to give her and her neighbourhoods back their keys, back their history, back their language; to hand the Etzel Museum back to Manshieh. This is not a project of preservation or reconstruction, as was the case in the White City, but a project of repair which is as utopian and unprecedented as Tel Aviv and Zionism itself. It is a cultural, urban, national and international challenge which requires just as much, if not more, of the same energy, investment and idealism that has been used to sustain the White City campaign.

It could only come from Tel Aviv, and it needs to start in Jaffa, because that is where it all started. The sin of the murder of the city of Jaffa, its occupation and rape is at Tel Aviv's door, and it requires repair on a utopian scale. After truncating an urban continuity spanning thousands of years, it is Tel Aviv's responsibility to instigate this project of repair even if it is the first of its kind. Even if such repair has yet to happen anywhere else. This is because what has happened in Ajami, and in Manshieh, and in the Old City of Jaffa, and even in Neve Sha'anan and Shapira, cannot be repaired by anyone else and would never be repaired anywhere else; because in today's global village, Jaffa's exiles are the poor of Tel Aviv, and because the Jaffa-Tel Aviv problem lies at the heart of the Middle East conflict.

AFTERWORD

Booming Tel Aviv: A Few Notes to the Non-Hebrew Reader

I am not a historian, but in the problematic political contexts and difficult circumstances of any possible architectural practice anywhere, and especially in Israel, writing has always seemed to me one of the few decent and effective ways to be an architect. In addition to this, when I decided some twenty years ago to settle in the Black City, there had not yet been much written about it.[247]

Therefore I have always preferred to consider this first book of mine as part of a much larger engagement with the southern parts of Tel Aviv-Yaffo; it was a programme, a part of an architectural, urban, political project or counter-project for Tel Aviv and Jaffa and for Israel's architecture in general.[248] It was written with anger and the urge to bring justice to the city and to many of its people, and with the intention to generate changes in the reality of the city without the usual use of physical power and sometimes violence; to change the city just by telling its story in a different manner. Therefore, *White City, Black City* was indeed, and first and foremost, addressed 'to every Hebrew reader', as nicely worded by the late Adam Baruch.[249]

Did the book change the city? The Hebrew edition's cover showed the Gidi House with a caption that suggests recycling the building, the Etzel Museum, into 'A memorial home for the Manshieh neighbourhood and a place for studying the history of Jaffa and its surrounding villages.'

Well, this, unfortunately, did not happen.

But I heard of a few readers who moved their apartments, and now, when preparing this English edition almost ten years after its first publication in Hebrew, except for adding few notes and explanations for the non-Hebrew reader, I did not find any reason to revise the book's contents.

During most of the time that I have been writing these notes, once in a while I could hear the sirens and the booms and maybe see the little clouds of white smoke provoked by the destruction of the low-tech Palestinian rockets rebounding upon the Iron Dome defence system, Tel Aviv's new vertical separation wall. And at the same time, I could only guess that in this same city, not very far from me, young khaki-dressed people were sitting at their Tel Avivian desks and actually executing 'Operation Protective Edge' in Gaza, compared with which the 2003 'Operation Rainbow' seems almost like a humanitarian mission.[250]

Nevertheless, underneath the Iron Dome and despite 'Operation Protective Edge', Tel Aviv, the bubble, keeps on booming.

In the past decade Tel Aviv has accumulated a large number of trophies and titles in addition to its UNESCO diploma. The Bauhaus City, the White City, the city that never sleeps, is today the capital of the Israeli Start-Up Nation, one of the world's most gay-friendly cities, one of the world's most creative cities, one of the world's coolest cities, among the world's three best cities, among the ten best cities in the world for architecture lovers, among the top ten ultimate party cities, among top ten hedonistic city breaks, home to the world's most beautiful people, and among the top ten beach cities in the world.

Since UNESCO's declaration, the White City has undoubtedly become whiter. Tel Aviv's conservation plan with its severe regulations was approved to fit UNESCO's norms and is now transforming the White City into a wax museum. Unsurprisingly but still ironically, Tel Aviv's modernist heritage campaign engendered an overkill approach to old buildings' conservation that reminds one of the Iron Dome's approach vis-à-vis Palestinian rockets. In recent years, Tel Aviv has witnessed extravagant high-tech renovation projects in which old buildings were elevated in the air to enable the excavation of car parks underneath, and in order to make room for Kaplan street's enlargement, historical houses in Tel Aviv's German quarter of Sarona were cut from their foundations and pulled over steel rails to their new locations.

Ordinary working families owning an apartment in a building that figures in the conservation list may find that it becomes a real burden. Sooner or later, corporations are purchasing the White City buildings. The heavy cost of the strict renovation of historical buildings may be covered either by transforming them into boutique hotels and gourmet restaurants or by embalming them under glass as decoration in office buildings' lobbies. In both cases, as already defined through the Zion insurance office building precedent that enables the municipality to extend its building rights in exchange for the conservation of a historical building (which could be located elsewhere), the implementation of Tel Aviv's conservation plan has been one of the means of developing Tel Aviv's vertical expansion and pro-corporation politics. This vertical development is now taking place not only near the Ayalon freeway but in the city's historical centre too, and is about to separate Tel Aviv and the White City from Jaffa and the Black City by a row of tall towers that are being erected on the historical Jaffa – Tel Aviv Road (the first of them was the Neve Tzedek Tower, inarguably Tel Aviv's ugliest residential tower, planted in a Jaffa plot overlooking the historic neighbourhood of Neve Tzedek).

Every summer since the UNESCO declaration, Tel Aviv celebrates its whiteness on the occasion of the 'White Night' event during which, for a whole night, all the White City is lit up and open, and loud music is allowed everywhere. Needless to say that during this very same night, music is banned in the Black City, as in summer 2013 when the Tel Aviv Police violently repressed the annual Black Night street counter-party taking place at the Akhoti Feminist Mizrahi movement's headquarters in Chlenov neighbourhood.

Jaffa is still the most vulnerable prey for Tel Aviv's real estate speculation. In order to satisfy its thirst for the picturesque, Tel Aviv is now in the process of whitening Jaffa too. In order to encourage Tel Aviv's seafront hotels and luxury residential strip sprawling southwards (thus finally bridging the empty gap between Jaffa and Tel Aviv), Jaffa's entire northern part, where Manshieh neighbourhood had been located, was redefined as a leisure and tourism zone. Jaffa's Turkish railway station, occupied for more than half a century by the IDF, was restored and recycled as an open-air, gated luxury shopping mall.

All over Jaffa's city centre, as well as around the Jaffa port and in the Adjami neighbourhood, the city's gentrification by gated luxury projects such as that of Andromeda Hill has been spreading on various scales. The port was refurbished and let to shops, restaurants and art galleries; the flea market neighbourhood became a restaurant quarter.

The Palestinian Jaffa population, divided between religions and clans, is gradually constrained to emigrate to Israel's Arab slum hinterland in 'mixed' cities such as Ramla and Lydia.

But Jaffa's Arabic population is not the only one threatened by Tel Aviv's real estate industry. Inflated by its international reputation and luxury branding, and boosted by an officially encouraged speculative real estate economy, Tel Aviv is today one of the world's most expensive cities, expelling *de facto* its younger generations from the city's centre. Tel Aviv is unaffordable. To own an apartment in Tel Aviv, in most cases one needs to inherit one.

The Black City has certainly and literally become blacker, and this is not a metaphor anymore. In addition to the growing number of minorities, and fragmentary and split communities resulting from the accumulation of generations of legal and illegal immigrants from all countries and continents, which already spread across Jaffa and the southern neighbourhoods of Tel Aviv, in the past decade the Black City has absorbed a new population of some 60,000 refugees from South Sudan, Sudan and Eritrea. The Black City's geography is now composed not only of the phantom names of its dead

Palestinian past but also of new imaginary places such as 'Manila Avenue' and 'Little Khartoum'.

Many of the political subtexts described or pronounced in this book have become much more evident, obvious, violent and almost shameless.

If when writing the book 'Judea and Samaria is here' was only a slogan on a billboard campaign in Tel Aviv, now new right-wing colonies populated by West Bank settlers, fuelled this time by the slogan 'Settling within the hearts' as well as donations and governmental budgets, are being developed within Tel Aviv's Black City neighbourhoods, in the Adjami neighbourhood in Jaffa or in the Shapira neighbourhood in south Tel Aviv.

The Black City has become a privileged playground for far-right politics and politicians such as the former MK Michael Ben Ari who opened his headquarters in the Hatikva neighbourhood or MK Ayelet Shaked who did the same in the Shapira neighbourhood.

The refugees' arrival in Tel Aviv's southern neighbourhoods opened the way for new collaborations and coalitions between different Jewish religious factions and sometimes even between religious and secular Jews. In summer 2010, some twenty-five neighbourhood rabbis from south Tel Aviv gathered in the Shapira neighbourhood and issued a common decree forbidding their communities from renting or selling apartments and houses to non-Jewish people, in particular, to African refugees. Led by the new local settlers, neigh-bourhood activists and far-right politicians, the rabbis' decree saw the launch of a xenophobic campaign directed against African refugees and Africans in general, as well as against radical left activists or NGOs supporting the refugees' rights.

These two opposing developments within the White City, Black City dialectical relationship, as well as within each one of those parts of the city, were also the sources, the reasons and even the locations of only two moments of political and social unrest in the past decade in Israel.

In summer 2011, the increasing housing costs in Tel Aviv caused a huge wave of social protest (the tents protests). Rothschild Boulevard, the White City's main pedestrian spine, was invaded by thousands of youths and activists who occupied the boulevard and jammed the city for a whole summer. Despite a series of mass demonstrations (the largest one attended by half a million) demanding social justice, and despite the wide public and media support for its cause, the protest was put to sleep before winter by the entire political class.

A year later, in summer 2012, while everybody was waiting for the social protest to reawaken, a series of Molotov cocktail attacks against African kindergartens in Shapira neighbourhood led to anti-African riots in all the Jewish southern neighbourhoods of the city. Unlike the 2011 protest, this wave of xenophobia, fed by years of neglect and discrimination, armed with a Rabbinical decree, led by local activists and right and far-right politicians and organizations, resulted in real, substantial achievements: following the riots Israel erected a new 240km-long fence separating it from Egypt (in addition to the Wall that separates it from the West Bank). In 2013 the Knesset approved a reform of the forgotten Anti-Infiltration Law originally passed in 1954 to prevent Palestinian refugees from crossing the border and returning to their lands. The new Anti-Infiltration Law automatically changed the African refugees' status to 'Infiltrators', thus accepting de facto and *de jure* the anti-African activists' terminology and approach, and abandoning a huge community that was already in a legal black hole to racial persecutions and poverty.

Tel Aviv is certainly, and today more than ever, a predator city, just as Jaffa has been and still is its prey. I still, and more than ever, maintain that Israel is one of the most radical laboratories of modernity on earth, where the most explosive ingredients of our time in their purest form, modern utopias and ancient beliefs, are boiling together with no precautions.[251] When looking today at the bombarded isolated enclave of the Gaza Strip on the map, surrounded by the Israeli territory, one cannot help but feel a sense of déjà-vu. We already saw the similarly surrounded Palestinian enclave of Jaffa surrounded by the booming Tel Aviv of the 1930s.

The most obvious particularity of the Israel/Palestine situation resides in the fact that this is the only place on the globe where the Western world, the Arab world and Africa share a common terrestrial border. Except for the USA–Mexico border region, it is the only region where Westerners and non-Westerners can effectively cross the border on foot, as did the African refugees who crossed the border from Sinai, and the Hamas fighters who dug tunnels into Israeli territory.

Nevertheless, those situations of conflict between two homogenous territorial entities are becoming more and more rare. Today, the borders between a White City and a Black City may be located anywhere, behind your backyard, in the middle of my street, between two kindergarten classes or at the entrance of any nightclub. Borders might be erected in all places and very quickly – like the separation walls between Israel and the West Bank or between Israel and Egypt – and sometimes even instantly; they could be built like a wall, installed like a fence, created by an ad-hoc checkpoint or, just like the new Anti-Infiltration Law, a barrier might be established just by virtue of an arbitrary legislative or administrative decision regarding who is allowed to pass through the checkpoint and who is not.

For many of this book's non-Hebrew readers those local conflicts that divide Tel Aviv and Jaffa may at first seem far away, beyond the seas, borders and airport checkpoints. Nevertheless, although this book was indeed addressed to Hebrew readers in Tel Aviv and Jaffa, as well as in Israel and Palestine, I think that many of the processes, encounters and conflicts witnessed in my city concern directly other scales and other regions too, Western and non-Western alike. Questions such as whether we are to live together or separately, in one city or two, in one state or two and how to achieve it, may be posed each time on a different scale while revealing a different problematic.

From my own personal viewpoint, shaped by fifteen years' long experience of life and work in Tel Aviv's Black City, there is today no difference between neighbourhood politics, city politics, national politics and global politics.

Those struggles over territories and narratives and over geographies and histories have been shaping every city. Any city in the world could be a predator city or a prey city; in any city one may find victors and losers, a White City and a Black City; any city is made with stones, brick and concrete, but it is also made up of stories and histories; so, whether you will it or not, those legends of architecture and war might one day be your story too.

Acknowledgements

This book would not have come to the world without the support, help, work and encouragement of many organizations and individuals.

I am profoundly grateful to the Graham Foundation for Advanced Studies in the Fine Arts for awarding me an individual grant to support the publication of this English edition of *White City, Black City*. Knowing the immense contribution of the Graham Foundation to today's architectural culture and its irreplaceable role for more than half a century in the shaping and the wording of architecture, I can only express my deepest feelings of gratitude for being honoured by its support.

I want to thank the Writers Omi programme at Ledig House, which hosted me at its residence and enabled me to spend few necessary weeks in order to work on this book.

I am deeply grateful to the translator Orit Gat and to the English editor Ben Du Preez. I know that both of them could not have done this without a true personal interest and engagement in the topics raised by my book.

I would like to thank the architect and activist Abe Hayeem, who had the ingenious idea to introduce this book to Pluto Press. I feel very lucky for being in Pluto's good hands and cannot but express my deepest admiration and my highest esteem to Pluto's professional, serious and committed approach.

I would like to thank David Shulman, Pluto's commissioning editor who has been personally, almost religiously, dedicated to this book from the very first moment; Melanie Patrick, Pluto's design manager, who taught me to see my book differently; Robert Webb, Pluto's managing editor who directed me through the editorial and production process; Emily Orford, Pluto's marketing manager and Alison Alexanian, the publicity manager who followed the publication of this book from very early stages of work; and Thérèse Saba, the book's copy-editor, with whom I have been corresponding intensively for days and nights. For someone who has been involved in publishing for almost two decades, this experience of working with Pluto Press and the interaction with each of their team was a true lesson for me.

I would like to express my gratitude to my friends Eyal Weizman and Anselm Franke, who have also been close friends of this book since its writing and publication in Hebrew, encouraged me to publish it in English and who have been presenting and endorsing it for over a decade on numerous occasions.

I thank Ariella Azoulay for endorsing the publication of this book in

English and providing her extremely precious moral support; Jeremie Hoffmann, the Director of the Conservation Department at the Tel Aviv-Yaffo Municipality, who has endorsed this book too and who has been trying his best, against all odds, to implement some of its lessons on the municipal ground.

I would like to acknowledge (more or less chronologically) the organizations, institutions, magazines, newspapers and publications that published pieces related to this book or allowed me to present its case: *Studio Magazine*, *Shishi* weekly newspaper, *Ha'Ir* weekly newspaper, Israeli Association of Architects, Institut français de Tel-Aviv, Shapira neighbourhood Library, Tel Aviv Left Bank Club, Kunstwerke Berlin, With de With Rotterdam, BIMKOM – Planners for Planning Rights, Tel Aviv University, BINA Center for Jewish Identity and Hebrew Culture, Achoti, Bezalel Academy, The Van Leer Jerusalem Institute, Zochrot, City of Dublin, Centre de Cultura Contemporània de Barcelona, Warsaw Museum of Modern Art, Chandigarh College of Architecture, CEPT University of Ahmedabad, New Delhi School of Planning and Architecture, *Bauhaus* magazine.

I would like to express my personal gratitude to individuals (in alphabetical order) who encouraged, supported, helped, or inspired me during the writing of *White City, Black City* from its early stages: Sami Abu-Shehade, Suad Amiry, Amnon Bar-Or, Adam Baruch (RIP), Yoav Ben-Dov, Dror Burstein, Jean-Louis Cohen, Catherine David, Itamar Gil, Yossi Granowsky, Dana Halevi, Nadav Harel, Roi Hemed, Rachel Lea Jones, Shula Keshet, Ayelet Kestler, Tsafrir Kurtzia, Sergio Lerman, Mark LeVine, David Mendelson, Assaf Molcho, Jean Nouvel, Amnon Rabi, Rafi Segal, Fadiya Shakur, Ella Shohat, Ifat Teherani, Paul Virilio, Ines Weizman, Haim Yacobi, Avraham Yasky (RIP) and Muki Zur.

I am grateful to Zvi Elhyani, founder and Director of Israel Architecture Archive for helping me finding images for this book, and to my friend and neighbour the photographer Roi Boshi for allowing me to use some of his photos.

I am totally indebted to my friends and co-workers at Babel, my Hebrew press: I could not have done anything without Or Aleksandrowicz, my Hebrew editor at Babel and the director of Babel's Architectures Series, who once had been my best student and is today my best teacher. Or provided me with his wise remarks and with his precious, irreplaceable and extremely wide knowledge.

This book (as well as many other books) could not exist without the persistence and the devotion of my friend, my partner and my agent Roni

Meyerstein. In her discreet ways, Roni has been accompanying, criticizing and supporting my work for ages. I owe her so much, and I am so happy to know that this book will make her happy. None of this could have happened without the unconditional support of my beloved family: my parents, Naava and Mota Rotbard, who were always willing to follow me to the most extreme adventures and through the darkest times.

I would like to thank and to remember my beloved late uncle Avi Plascov (1945–82). Without him, this book could not have been even imagined. Sportsman in his youth, Avi was my childhood hero. In 1973, when I was fourteen, I saw him sitting in my parents' kitchen, his military uniform covered in dust and soot, recounting the horrors of the holding battle in Ras Sedr in Sinai. The 1973 War led both of us to the same conclusion. In the following years, in times when Israeli governments and mainstream politics were still maintaining that 'there is no such thing as a Palestinian People', Avi was one of the first Israeli academics to study the Palestinian refugees question and to acknowledge its importance. He was the first person I ever heard speak about the Nakbe and the forced exile to which the Palestinians have been subjected since the 1948 War and to advocate for a just solution and an independent Palestinian State. In 1978 Avi received his doctorate from the School of Oriental and African Studies of the University of London. He was a visiting Fellow of the International Institute for Strategic Studies (IISS) in London and contributed commentaries to the BBC World Service. Avi passed away in London in 1982 at the age of thirty-seven, from leukaemia, probably caused – as was the case with other members of his aerial defence unit who had died from the same disease – by the explosion of a nearby radar in the first days of the 1973 War. He left behind him a widow, two children and a few books and publications.

This book, my first, was and has always been dedicated to my two children, Mor Kadishzon and Adam Rotbard. I want to believe that it represents the values of the world I wish for them and for my three granddaughters born after the publication of the first edition – Shell, Sophie and Keshet.

And at last, I am endlessly grateful to my wife Amit Rotbard, she is my friend, my partner, my boss, my love. She is and she fills my entire life.

Sharon Rotbard, Tiruchirappali, 2014

Notes

1. See 'White City of Tel-Aviv – the Modern Movement' at: http://whc.unesco. org/sites/1096.htm
2. In fact, Tel Aviv was not the first settlement to adopt the translated title of Herzl's novel. It was preceded by a small settlement that had been founded in 1904 near the colony Nes Ziona but was united with the latter two years later.
3. The usage of an oxymoron to name the novel is in itself a typical, paradigmatic trope consistent throughout the Zionist Project, which also sought, for example, to revive Hebrew, a 'living dead language'. Even today, oxymoronic tags and paradoxical definitions remain a prominent part of the State of Israel's lexicon; evident in reference to the 'Jewish democratic state', 'Israeli Arabs', 'Peace in Galilee War' and 'unilateral separation'.
4. This is the title of a book penned by the artist Nachum Gutman, published in 1959. Gutman (1898–1980) was an author and illustrator, famous for his graphic and literary picturesque approach, and one of the establishment's most beloved artists. *A Small City with Few People in It* has long been considered the first, and most outstanding of nostalgic works published in the 'Little Tel Aviv' period of the 1910s and 1920s.
5. Edna Yekutieli-Cohen, *Tel Aviv as a Literary Place 1909–1939* (Tel Aviv: Society for the Protection of Nature in Israel, 1990), pp. 12–20.
6. Michael Levin, *White City: The International Style Architecture in Israel, Portrait of an Era* (Tel Aviv: Tel Aviv Museum of Art, 1984). The second part of the exhibition displayed photographs of Tel Aviv buildings by Judith Turner.
7. Nitza Metzger-Szmuk, *Houses from the Sand: The International Style Architecture in Tel Aviv* (in Hebrew) (Tel Aviv: Tel Aviv Development Foundation and The Ministry of Defense Press, 1994). Nitza Metzger-Szmuk, *Dwelling on the Dunes: Tel Aviv, Modern Movement and Bauhaus Ideals / Des maisons sur le sable: Tel-Aviv, Mouvement moderne et esprit Bauhaus*, Bilingual edition English/French (Paris: Éditions de l'Eclat, 2004b).
8. After decades of neglect, Sheinkin Street became an iconic symbol of Tel Avivian escapism in the 1980s. Today, it is one of the most commercialized streets in the city.
9. David Grossman, *See Under: Love* [Ayen Erech: Ahavah] (New York: Farrar Straus Giroux, 1989; Tel Aviv, 1986).
10. This observation was delivered while I stood with Jean Nouvel, who had been my teacher at the École Spéciale d'Architecture in Paris, on a Tel Aviv rooftop terrace overlooking the city, at a party organized in his honour by the French cultural attaché. Nouvel's disappointment in what he felt was false advertising led him to suggest a by-law be introduced in the municipality whereby all buildings *had* to be white – just as a similar British Mandatory regulation in Jerusalem requires all constructions to be coated with Jerusalem stone. Dreaming of a Tel Aviv gleaming in shades of white, he noted that 'with architecture like this you ask yourself why the buildings are so grey, so washed out. They told me Tel Aviv is called a "White City" so this is taken for granted,

and if it is taken for granted, they should ensure it is so. White and shades of white can be included in the building regulations to transform the city into a "symphony in white". See Sharon Rotbard, 'Interview with Jean Nouvel', *Shishi*, Globes; November 3, 1995.

11. Michael Levin, 'The Architects Who Brought the Bauhaus to Israel', *Kav* No. 2 (1981).

12. Michael Levin, 'Introduction', *White City*, exhibition catalogue, p. 9.

13. Nitza Szmuk, *Houses from the Sand: The International Style Architecture in Tel Aviv* (Tel Aviv: Tel Aviv Development Fund and Ministry of Defense Publications, 1994), p. 22.

14. This was a key dictum of Bauhaus ideology, laid down by Walter Gropius who, in 1925, published 'Principles of Bauhaus Production' in which he declared that form must derive from the object itself, and that the search for new forms is as objectionable as the use of decorative forms. In a later article entitled 'Project for Training Architects', Gropius referred to the relevancy of 'visual language', claiming 'there was no rule that could become a recipe for architecture.' See Walter Gropius, *Architecture et Société* (Paris: Éditions du Linteau, 1995), pp. 37, 165.

15. Dani Karavan, 'Tel-Aviv', in Nitza Szmuk, *Dwelling on the Dunes: Tel Aviv, Modern Movement and Bauhaus Ideals* (Paris and Tel Aviv: Editions de L'éclat, 2004b [1994]), p. 13. Marc Scheps, 'Foreword', in *White City*, exhibition catalogue, p. 7.

16. Nitza Szmuk, *Dwelling on the Dunes*, 2004b, p. 51.

17. In fact, more recent studies acknowledge that there have also been two more Jewish Bauhaus graduate architects, Chanan Frenkel, who worked as an employee, and Edgar Hecht, both absent from the official history of the White City of Tel Aviv, and one Muslim Bosnian Bauhaus graduate, Selman Selmanagić, who travelled to Jerusalem in the 1930s and worked there for Richard Kauffmann. See Daniela Schmitt and Ingolf Kern, 'Routes to the Promised Land', *Bauhaus Magazine* no. 2, November 2011, p. 15; see also Aida Abadžić Hodžić and Ines Sonder, 'A Communist Muslim in Israel: How the Bauhaus student Selman Selmanagić came to Jerusalem and became a wanderer between worlds', *Bauhaus Magazine* no. 2, November 2011, pp. 16–19.

18. 'In Favour of Scale – Yigal Tumarkin Interviews Aryeh Sharon on the Bauhaus and the Development of Architecture in Israel', *Kav* 2 (January 1981), pp. 80–84 [in Hebrew].

19. Rafi Segal and Eyal Weizman, 'The Battle for the Hilltops', in *A Civilian Occupation: The Politics of Israeli Architecture* (Tel Aviv: Babel; London: Verso, 2003), pp. 100–108.

20. LeWitt (1907–1991) was a Polish-born Jewish illustrator and graphic artist. He did not study at the Bauhaus, but gained a reputation as a modernist after emigrating to England in the 1930s, where in 1933 he founded a successful partnership with George Him.

21. Concepts of the 'missed utopia' became central themes in Israeli culture during the late 1970s and early 1980s. In 1977, Yaakov Shabtai published his novel

Zichron Devarim [Past Continuous], which was set in central Tel Aviv around the workers' housing project Aryeh Sharon had constructed in the 1930s. Still considered today as one of the most accomplished and ambitious Hebrew novels, the book depicts the steady decline of Cezar, an Israeli architect, and his group of friends. In 1978, the young Israeli artist Tamar Getter expanded on similar motifs in her first solo show, *Tel Hai Courtyard*, at the Israel Museum in Jerusalem. Presenting chalk drawings and collages, and drawing on works such as Pierro De La Francesca's *Ideal City*, she confronted local national myths with utopian imagery. Similar work was produced by the artist Moshe Gershuni in a series of projects from the mid-1970s, including his performance of *Yad Anuga* (Delicate Hand) at an exhibition held at the Tel Aviv Museum of Art in 1978, his *Who Is Zionist and Who Is Not?* at the Julie M. Gallery, and in his Israeli pavilion presentation at the 1980 Venice Biennial of Art.

22. According to Jewish European tradition, Ashkenaz was a region situated between Germany and Alsace that contained a massive Jewish population during the Middle Ages. By extension, all Jews whose origins are European are designated as Ashkenazi. The term Mizrahi refers to Jews of North African and Middle Eastern descent.

23. Ella Shohat was the first academic commentator to really explore how the Eurocentric conception of Zionism and the dream of European acceptance affected social hierarchy in the state of Israel. She illuminated how it had not only defined relations between Jews and Arabs and Ashkenazi and Mizrahi (Sephardi, 'oriental' Jews), but was also behind an inner hierarchical struggle among Ashkenazim themselves, which had encouraged the suppression of traditional Eastern European Jewish characteristics. Shohat demonstrated how, through the dictates of this hierarchy, the 'Ost-Juden' were Westernized at the expense of Oriental and East European Jews who, in turn, became another one of Zionism's victims. See Ella Shohat, 'Sephardim in Israel: Zionism From the Standpoint of Its Jewish Victims', *Social Text*, 19/20 (Fall 1988) (Special Issue on Colonial Discourse), pp. 1–35.

24. In his biography of Herzl, Amos Eilon outlined Herzl's Germanophilia in great detail, describing how Herzl had dreamt of becoming a German writer and considered German his first language. Eilon recounts how, as a student, Herzl returned to Budapest for a visit only to write to a friend that 'unfortunately, Hungary has became even more Hungarian', and that 'systematically, I have not spoken a word of Hungarian since being here.' Amos Elon, *Herzl* (Tel Aviv: Am Oved, 1975), pp. 48–49.

25. Szmuk, *Houses from the Sand*, p. 19.

26. Ziva Socholovsky and Batia Carmiel, *Tel Aviv in Photographs – the First Decade 1909–1918* (Tel Aviv: Eretz-Israel Museum, 1990), p. 59.

27. 'Descender' (in contrast to '*oleh*' [ascender], which is the word used to describe a Jew who moves *to* Israel) was another term coined to describe those Jews who chose to immigrate in the 'wrong direction'.

28. Born in Ukraine in 1898, Rechter immigrated to Palestine in 1919 where he became a central figure in Israeli architecture and head of what later became

an important architectural dynasty. After a short spell trying to establish a name for himself, Rechter left for Paris in 1929 by commission of the Jewish sculptor Hannah Orloff. There, he designed a three-story private house for her in the 14th arrondissement and studied at the École Nationale des Ponts et des Chaussées. He graduated in 1932 and returned to Tel Aviv commissioned to plan the Engel apartment building. This was completed in 1933 and stood as Tel Aviv's first building 'sur pilotis'. In an interview published in the *Contractor and Builder* magazine in 1959, Rechter proclaimed himself an 'apprentice of the French school and a pupil and adept of Le Corbusier.'

29. Sam (Shmuel) Barkai was born in Russia in 1898 and immigrated to Palestine in 1920. He collaborated with Rechter between 1922 and 1925 before leaving the country in 1926 in order to study architecture at the Venice Academy. In 1927, he traded Italy for France and continued his studies at the École Supérieur des Arts Décoratifs and the Institut D'Urbanisme de Paris. Growing in reputation, he designed the Indian pavilion for the Paris Colonial Fair in 1931 and, in 1933, began work in Le Corbusier's office. Barkai returned to Palestine in 1934, but maintained his French contacts by sending regular articles and reviews to *L'Architecture d'aujourd'hui* magazine, where Le Corbusier continued as one of the editors. According to his son, the architect Dan Barkai, his father kept a correspondence with Le Corbusier himself for many years. See Szmuk, *Dwelling on the Dunes* (2004b), pp. 166–167.

30. '*Sur pilotis*' built on support columns or pillars; it refers directly to Le Corbusier.

31. Aryeh Sharon, *Kibbutz+Bauhaus* (Stuttgart: Karl Kramer Verlag; Tel Aviv: Massada, 1976), pp. 48–49.

32. 'I am through with Frenchmen' remains a favourite line in 'The Cafeteria in Tiberia', a comedy sketch written by Nissim Alony for the popular comic trio 'Hagashash Hachiver'. The sketch featured in the 1967 'Cinema Gashash'' review directed by Nissim Alony.

33. Yosef Eliyahu Chelouche, *Reminiscences of My Life, 1870–1930* (Tel Aviv, 1931 [Babel, 2005]), p. 174.

34. '*Adrichalut*' is the Hebrew term for architecture. Its origin is Akkadian and literally translates as 'slave of the palace'. Both words – the Greek 'architecture' and the Acadian 'adrichalut' – coexist and are used in Modern Standard Hebrew. There is, for example, a Faculty of Architecture at the Technion University in Haifa and an Adrichalut School in Tel Aviv University.

35. The Land of Israel.

36. Edna Yekutieli-Cohen, *Tel Aviv as a Literary Place 1909–1939* (Tel Aviv: Society for the Protection of Nature in Israel, 1990), pp. 12–20.

37. Ibid.

38. Naomi Shemer (1930–2004) was one of Israel's most popular songwriters and composers, known for nationalist hymns like '*Yerushalaim Shel Zahav*' (Golden Jerusalem), which became the country's anthem during the Six Day War. Born and raised in Kibbutz Kineret near the Sea of Galilee, she was later identified with extreme right-wing factions of the settler movement based in the Occupied Territories.

39. Arik Einstein (1939–2013) is considered to be one of Israel's most popular singers and actors and certainly the most 'Israeli' and 'Tel Avivian' among Israeli singers. As with many Israeli popular culture figures of his generation, he made his appearance as a star within a military entertainment group and moved gradually after his release from the army towards a more counter-cultural notion.

40. This English translation is purely literal, with no rhyming.

41. Arik Einstein, *Nostalgia* (CBS 1984). The particularity of the *Nostalgia* album was that unlike the other albums of the series, Einstein chose to include in it some new old-style titles such as 'Eretz Israel' and 'Long Sad Days'.

42. Mayor Ron Huldai has long displayed a dogged appreciation for public singing as means of keeping Israeli folklore alive. During the 2004 UNESCO declaration celebrations, Shemer's 'White City' was on permanent loop and a special evening was dedicated to the re-warbling of 'Good Old Eretz Israel' classics.

43. Led by Uri Zohar and Arik Einstein, the '*Lul*' collective produced satirical television serials, avant-garde films and rock music albums. Their carefree and hedonistic lifestyles made them cultural beacons for the younger generations during the 1970s and 1980s.

44. The term *politruk* in this instance refers to those special officers within the Soviet Red Army, whose job was to indoctrinate wavering citizens and 'fine tune' their morals to fit the party line. Max Brod, who was more famous for rescuing the writings of his friend Franz Kafka for the sake of humanity, initiated the creation of the first Hebrew opera *Dan the Guard* and penned its libretto. The opera, composed by Mark Lavry, is based on a play by S. Shalom, *Shooting in the Kibbutz*, which tells the story of Zionist pioneers in a watchtower and stockade settlement in the Galilee.

45. Dan Ben-Amotz (1923–1989) was born in Poland as Moshe Tehilimzeigger. As a child, he was sent by his parents to Palestine and was educated in the Ben Shemen Youth Village with Shimon Peres. After his parents perished in the Holocaust, he fabricated himself as the archetype of the new 'Sabra' (Israeli native), first as a 'Palmahnik' and later as a radio broadcaster, actor, writer, journalist and celebrity.

46. Haim Hefer (b. 1925), a poet and songwriter, Hefer was Dan Ben-Amotz's friend and partner; in 1983 he was awarded the Israel Prize for his achievements as a songwriter.

47. Yitzhak Sadeh (1890–1952) was the founder and the first commander of the PALMAH, and one of the first generals of the newly formed IDF in 1948.

48. Nahal are the initials of Noar Halutzi Lohem ('fighting pioneer youth'), a military unit that combines military and settlement occupations formed by David Ben-Gurion in 1948, in order to replace the paramilitary Palmach unit.

49. Shmuel Dayan (1891–1968) was one of the founders of the first collective village Nahalal, and a senior member of Israel's first Knesset. His son, Moshe Dayan (1915–1981), was one of the foremost and feared Israeli generals and politicians. Assi Dayan (b. 1945), the son of Moshe Dayan, is a well-known

Israeli cinematographer (*Life According to Agfa*) and remains one of the most colourful characters in modern-day Israeli bohemia. Yehonatan Gefen (b. 1947), the cousin of Assi Dayan, is a celebrated Israeli writer and journalist, who gained recognition for his critical position towards the establishment. His son, Aviv Gefen (b. 1973), is a famous Israeli rock star.

50. It would be decent to note here that as an Israeli architect and publisher, the writer of these lines realizes Zionism's two main tasks: the building of the land and the revival of Hebrew. In both cases, Zionism is an inherent and compelling position. It would be hypocritical to argue that it is not.

51. By the end of nineteenth century Baron Edmond Benjamin James de Rothschild (1845–1934) had founded several agricultural colonies, which served as the beginning of the Jewish settlement in the country.

52. Aviad Kleinberg, 'In Her Dreams: In Memory of Naomi Shemer', *Haaretz*, July 1, 2004.

53. 'Seashores are sometimes longing for a river' – from a very well-known poem by the poet Nathan Yonatan.

54. Deliberate or otherwise, the Zionist project has been guilty of causing many disruptions between the old and the antique, the historical and the archaeological. These interferences occur in language as well, but are most telling in the way the physical reality presents itself. Thus, for example, the Old City of Beer Sheva, which was built as a modern city by the Ottomans in 1900, is officially named the Antique City. The ruins of Palestinian villages which had been emptied in 1948 were recycled and repackaged first as 'ancient ruins' and then, via some rich European iconography of their Orientalism, they became 'antique ruins', suitable for archaeological contemplation.

55. See Pierre Restany, 'Dani Karavan, Semiology and Behaviour', *Makom* [place] Exhibition Catalogue (Tel Aviv: Tel Aviv Museum of Art, 1982).

56. The new towns developed in France during the presidency of François Mitterrand in the 1980s, like Cergy-Pontoise or Marne-La-Vallée, were planned as a new ring around Paris's concentric scheme. Their building has been a huge manifestation of state power, what the French usually call *le fait du Prince*. The figure of Karavan's axis of Cergy-Pontoise corresponded with a well-known French tradition of such demonstrations, from Le Nôtre's gardens of Versailles to the Historical Axis of Paris, Mitterrand's favourite playground. In a similar manner, Karavan's laser beam in Florence does more than correspond with the idea of Peace, as suggested by its title *Environment for Peace*, it reproduces the special effects of Albert Speer's 'Cathedral of Light' which he designed for the National Socialist Party's Rally in Nuremburg in 1935. Both projects echo a certain influence of the French eighteenth-century architect Étienne-Louis Boullée.

57. See www.danikaravan.com/

58. Dani Karavan, 'Tel-Aviv', in Nitza Szmuk, *Dwelling on the Dunes* (2004b [1994]), p. 13.

59. Ibid.

60. 'The British conquered India in various ruses and control the land by the force

of the army, tyrannizing hundreds of millions of India's population. England and other monarchies conquered territories in Africa and Asia to get markets to sell their products. This occupation too, is destined to exploit the natives of the place. We – we demand Eretz-Israel not to gain control over the native Arabs, and we do not seek a market to sell the products from our economy abroad.' David Ben-Gurion, 'Matan Eretz' [Gift of Land], in *Al HaHityashvut* [Of Settlement] (Tel Aviv: HaKibbutz HaMeuhad, 1987), pp. 14–15.

61. From the early days of Neve Tzedek, Jaffa's first Jewish neighbourhood, construction sites have been a battleground for the national struggle. Despite continuing efforts by the Jewish workers' organizations to promote and even enforce Jewish labour, many Jewish contractors preferred to work with local workers. See Or Alexandrowicz, 'Gravel, Cement, Arabs, Jews: How to build a Hebrew City' (in Hebrew) in *Theory and Criticism* 36, Spring 2010.

62. Haim Hefer, 'Two Builders', from *Tel Aviv Haktana* (Little Tel Aviv), Israphon 1970, original production 1958.

63. Dani Karavan, 'Tel-Aviv', in Szmuk, *Dwelling on the Dunes* (2004b), p. 14.

64. Dani Karavan, radio interview in Galei Tzahal (the IDF military radio station) dedicated to the UNESCO declaration, edited by Alon Kish, 5 June 2005.

65. The gradual disappearance of these calcareous hills over the last few decades has caused mounting concern among environmental organizations in Israel. This has led the municipality of Tel Aviv to demand that architects and developers either preserve or commemorate them in new projects.

66. Boaz Berr (director and producer), Noa Karavan (producer), *Air, Light and Utopia* (Artel Productions, Great Britain, 1994). Noa Karavan is the daughter of Dani Karavan.

67. Avraham Soskin (1881–1963) was one of the pioneers of photography in Israel. Soskin opened the first photography studio in the country and documented the events and personalities of the early stages of the Jewish settlement. This famous photograph of the lottery appeared on the opening spreads of the Hebrew edition of Nitza Szmuk's book *Dwelling on the Dunes*.

68. The argument that sand was used as Tel Aviv's main construction material would be more believable had there been a tradition of 'clean' silicate brickwork in the city. As it happens, few buildings of this variety were ever produced, with Yosef Berlin's 1929 design for 83 Rothschild Boulevard still standing as a rare example. *Had* such a tradition developed, it would have undoubtedly supported the claim made by those who point to a German, Central European Modernist tradition in Israel. After all, as German architectural historian Winifried Nerdinger noted during a colloquium at the Tel Aviv Museum of Art in honour of the UNESCO declaration, works by Hans Poelzig, Ludwig Mies van der Rohe and Hans Kollhoff are evidence enough that clean brickwork was typical of the German Modernist tradition. In turn, the distinct lack of any such tradition in Tel Aviv (where, it should be noted, a silicate brick factory has existed since 1922) is proof enough of the superficiality behind claims of German influence on local Tel Avivian architecture, which has almost always been plastered.

69. Nitza Szmuk, one of the White City's main spokespeople has repeatedly emphasized this link between the sand as the *ground* of Tel Aviv and the concept of *tabula rasa*. She made full use of it for example in her interview with Noa Karavan in the latter's film, *Light, Air and Utopia*.

70. Originally called Abu Butrus, the Yarkon River is the biggest river on Israel's coastal plain and runs across the north of Tel Aviv. It was used to mark the city's historical frontier until the War of Independence in 1948.

71. YESHA in Hebrew is Salvation, as well as an acronym of Judea, Samaria and Gaza. Founded in 1980, the YESHA council is an organization gathering all the municipal councils of the Jewish settlers in the Occupied Territories.

72. Ruth Kark, *Jaffa: A City in Evolution, 1799–1917* (Jerusalem: Yad Itzhak Ben-Zvi Press, 1984), pp. 56, 111.

73. Tamar Berger, *Dionysus in the Centre* (Tel Aviv: HaKibbutz Ha'meuchad, 1998), pp. 80–82.

74. 1 Dunam = 1000 m^2.

75. Association for the Building Neve Sha'anan in Jaffa-Tel Aviv, Memorandum to the Delegates of the 12th Zionist Congress. Jaffa: Shoaham Press, 1921, 8.

76. Between the years 1936–1939, in what was planned as a 'Settlement Offensive', fifty-seven new settlements were founded in single-day or even overnight operations. The method, developed by Shlomo Gur and the architect Yohanan Ratner, was first tried in November 1936 in Kibbutz Tel Amal and was based on a quick erection of an observation tower surrounded by a wall made of concrete formwork filled with gravel. See Sharon Rotbard, 'Wall and Tower: the mold of Israeli architecture', in Rafi Segal and Eyal Weizman (eds), *A Civilian Occupation: The Politics of Israeli Architecture* (Tel Aviv: Babel; London: Verso, 2003), pp. 39–58.

77. Ruth Kark, *Jaffa: A City in Evolution*, pp. 140, 100.

78. Yaacov Shavit and Gideon Bigger, *The History of Tel Aviv (1909–1936)* (Tel Aviv: Tel Aviv University Press, 2001), pp. 70–71.

79. The main reason for Herzl's short and only visit to Palestine between October and November 1898 was to be received by the German Emperor, Wilhelm II, whom he had recently met in Europe and who was visiting the country during this same period. On the 29 October, Herzl sent the Emperor a speech from the Zionist delegation with a request to be received. That same day he waited for the Emperor on the main road between Jerusalem and Jaffa, near the Baron Rothschild's Mikve Israel agricultural school, hoping to catch him and his delegation on their way to Jerusalem. As the Emperor approached, Herzl conducted a local school's chorus in the national anthem before stopping the Emperor's horse. They shook hands twice and had a brief conversation but, to Herzl's mortification, the moment was lost. As Herzl himself recalled in his chronicles; 'Wolfson, brave man, took two photographs of the spectacle. At least, that was what he believed. He knocked on his Kodak nonchalantly [...] But later, when we went to the photographer in Jaffa to develop the plates, we discovered that the first one showed only the shadow of the Emperor and my left foot. The second plate was completely damaged.' A photomontage of the

Mikve Israel meet was quickly prepared, with a photograph of Herzl standing on a Jaffan rooftop assembled next to and glued onto another picture of the Emperor on a horse. This new photomontage was rapidly distributed all over the world. Herzl and his delegation were finally received for an interview with the Emperor on November 2, but (no doubt to Herzl's chagrin) this meeting was also not immortalized. See Theodor Herzl, *Chronicles*, Volume III (Tel Aviv: M. Neuman Publishing, 1950), pp. 176–178.

80. Feingold had five associates in this project: Yehezkel Danin (Socholovsky), Nessim Korkidi, Yehuda Grazovsky, Haham Yosef Moshe and Haham David Haim. See Mordechai Elkayam, *Jaffa – Neve Tzedek: The Beginning of Tel Aviv* (Tel Aviv: Ministry of Defense Press, 1990), p. 230.

81. David Ben-Gurion, 'Masa Hashemama [The Burden of Wilderness]', in *Al HaHityashvut* [Of Settlement] (Tel Aviv: HaKibbutz HaMeuhad, 1987), pp. 73–82.

82. David Ben-Gurion, 'Daroma' [Southwards], in *Al HaHityashvut* [Of Settlement] (Tel Aviv: HaKibbutz HaMeuhad, 1987), p. 130.

83. David Ben-Gurion, *The Burden of Wilderness*, p. 82.

84. Yosef Eliyahu Chelouche, *Reminiscences of My Life, 1870–1930* (Tel Aviv: 1931 [Babel, 2005]), p. 427.

85. Bonnie Angelo, 'The Pain of Being Black: Conversation with Toni Morrison', *Time Magazine*, 22 May 1989.

86. 'L'Histoire avec sa grande hache' – a pun by Georges Perec from his *W ou le souvenir d'enfance* [W or the Memory of Childhood], (Paris: Denoël, 1975).

87. ' Architecture is the masterful, correct and magnificent play of volumes in light.' Le Corbusier, *Toward An Architecture*, translated by John Goodman, Introduction by Jean-Louis Cohen (Los Angeles, CA: Getty Publications, 2007 [1923]), p. 246.

88. From the eighteenth through to the twentieth century, Jaffa evolved into a heavyweight within the regional and international system of trade, with citrus exports from her orchards providing the city with its primary source of income. However, this integral branch of the urban economy suffered during the two world wars, with serious consequences for Jaffa's economy. During World War I, a large concentration of military troops stationed in the area cut down the orchard trees for firewood while in World War II, cargo shipping ground to a complete halt. The effect, in both instances, was to strip Arab farmers of their revenue and to encourage increasing numbers of them to cash in on the real estate value of land.

89. Rabbi Mordechai Elkayam, *Jaffa – Neve Tzedek: The Beginning of Tel Aviv* (Tel Aviv: Ministry of Defense Publications, 1990), pp. 17–18.

90. Although the authenticity of this proclamation has been challenged, Napoleon's sympathy for the Jews and his project for a Jewish national solution in Palestine had been widely acknowledged in the Jewish tradition since the beginning of the nineteenth century. An official reference for such a proclamation appeared in *Gazette Nationale – Le Moniteur Universel, Constantinople, 28 Germinal* (22 May 1799). The proclamation was published in 1943 in the canonical

compilation *Zionism, Political Documents* edited by Chen-Melech Merhavia, prefaced by David Ben-Gurion. The publication was based on a previous English paper published in 1940 in *New Judea* by Franz Kobler, a Jewish historian who had claimed having received a copy of Napoleon's declaration in German from a certain Mr Ernst Foges from London, who had found it among his grandfather's papers and copied it. The manuscript was not available. Napoleon's proclamation was accompanied by a letter from 'the first Rabbi of Jerusalem, Aaron Ben Levi'. Kobler assumed that the declaration was translated and even prepared by Venture De Paradis, Bonaparte's orientalist. Franz Kobler, 'Napoleon and the Restoration of the Jews to Palestine', *New Judea* (London, 1940): 189–190. Chen-Melech Merhavia, *Tsionut, Otzar Hateudot Hapolitiot* (Zionism, Anthology of Political Documents), Ahiasaf (Jerusalem, 1943), pp. 15–16 (in Hebrew).

91. Shmuel Tolkovsky, *Annals of Jaffa* (Jerusalem: Ariel, 2001 [Tel Aviv: 1926]), pp. 122–124 (in Hebrew).

92. Charles Richardot, *Relation de la campagne de Syrie, spécialement des sièges de Jaffa et de Saint-Jean-d'Acre* (Paris: Corréard J., 1839), p. 51 (French, translated by Sharon Rotbard).

93. See Tolkovsky, *Annals of Jaffa*, p. 126; Richardot, *Relation de la campagne de Syrie*, p. 53.

94. Juval Portugali, *Implicate Relations: Society and Space in the Israeli–Palestinian Conflict* (Boston, MA: Kluwer Academic Publishers, 1993).

95. Yaakov Sharet and Yosef Milo may have popularized 'Nama Yafo' (Jaffa is Asleep) but it was Yoni Rechter, one of the most talented pop composers of his generation and the grandson of one of the White City's most famous architects, Zeev Rechter, who composed the song in 1980. It was penned for *A Legend in the Dunes*, a dance spectacle celebrating Tel Aviv's 70th birthday but it also appeared in Rechter's first solo album (*A Legend in the Dunes*, Hed Artzi, 1980). Its lyrics include the following lines: 'Jaffa is asleep / Silence in the streets / A camel caravan / Passing at midnight // Night falls and suddenly falls asleep/ The tired city is lying down / As if it were dead / But what are those sounds // The city has been working and had enough / In the daytime / Not in night time / Bells will ring.'

96. 'Love of the Land' appears to be an ambivalent phrase within Zionism rhetoric. Even if there have been (and continue to be) many declarations of 'love' for the land of Israel, and fierce and genuine drives to wed the Jewish people to it, there have also been numerous instances when the Zionist movement has demonstrated a very negative approach towards the country's physical body. Ever since Herzl described the land as 'ill' in conversation with the Austro-Hungarian Emperor at Mikve Israel in 1898, the Zionist movement has never ceased in its attempts to 'heal' the country by altering its geography. These have included, among many others projects, Herzl's own 'Two Seas Canal' plan which looked to replace the Suez Canal by connecting the Mediterranean and Red Seas, Ariel Sharon's notorious 'Separation Wall', the drying of Hula Lake and the Dead Sea, and the systematic foresting of huge swaths of the country.

However, when processes of pure destruction are also taken into consideration (as was the case in Jaffa, for example), the relationship can be more accurately described as a 'Love–Hate of the Land'.

97. Theodor Herzl, *Chronicles*, Volume III, translated by R. Binyamin and Asher Barash (Tel Aviv: M. Neuman Publishing, 1950), pp. 173–196.

98. Ibid.

99. Ibid.

100. Ibid.

101. Ibid.

102. Ibid.

103. In Hebrew, 'Neve Tzedek' literally translates as 'Oasis of Justice', whereas Neve Shalom means 'Oasis of Peace'.

104. In Hebrew, 'Ezrat Israel' literally translates as 'Aid to Israel'.

105. Shavit and Bigger, *The History of Tel Aviv*, p. 53.

106. Nachum Gutman (1898–1980) immigrated to Palestine from Russia as a child and was raised in Tel Aviv. Following art studies in Vienna between 1920–1926, Gutman developed parallel careers as an author and illustrator of children's books, as well as developing a reputation as 'Tel Aviv's painter'. In harmony with the sentimental approach which distinguished *A Small City with Few People in It*, his book on 'Little Tel Aviv' in the 1920s, Gutman's visual interpretations of the city – reproduced in sketches, drawings and paintings – were also characterized by a saccharine sweetness and nostalgic naivety. He is one of the few Tel Avivian artists who have been honoured with a municipal museum dedicated exclusively to their work, and many of his pieces have been reproduced in and for official publications, stamps, public places and official buildings.

107. Worryingly, there had been no note of this discrepancy – the organized omission of these two neighbourhoods – until the Hebrew publication of this book in 2005. None of the catalogues and publications issued regularly by the Nachum Gutman Museum (including, for example, the release of the exhaustive *Nachum Gutman's Tel Aviv, Tel Aviv's Nachum Gutman* [Tel Aviv: the Nachum Gutman Museum, 1999] which came with several academic commentaries on the artist's work) have ever mentioned the inconsistency. For a representative collection of various versions of this drawing, see: *Nachum Gutman's Tel Aviv, Tel Aviv's Nachum Gutman* (Tel Aviv: The Nachum Gutman Museum, 1999), pp. 26–27, 42, 45.

108. Nachum Gutman, *A Small City with Few People in It* (Tel Aviv: Am Oved and Dvir, 1959).

109. My mother, who studied at the Herzliya Gymnasium in the 1940s, recalls that access to the building's backyard, surrounded by tall walls, was forbidden. There was no gate facing Manshieh.

110. The term 'Bypass Road' became a well-used phrase in Israeli lexicon in the wake of the 1967 war, and came to designate those asphalt arteries created in the West Bank which connect Jewish settlements. This network of viaducts and tunnels has dramatically reshaped daily Palestinian life, tearing whole villages and cities in half, separating farmers from their lands and altering the West

Bank's topography forever.

111. Henri Lefebvre, 'Espace et politique', *Le droit à la ville* (Paris: Anthropos, 1968), pp. 276–277.

112. This distinct lack of centre has created numerous spatial contradictions, mainly due to municipal attempts to *force* new artificial centres onto what are otherwise inherently 'centre-less' spaces. The erection of the New Central Bus Station in the southern neighbourhood of Neve Sha'anan, for example, has proved, as we shall see, an archetypal failure in this regard.

113. Chaim Lazar, *Kibush Yaffo* [The Conquest of Jaffa] (Tel Aviv: Shelah, 1951).

114. Description of this housing crisis can be found in a memorandum written by the members of the 'Neve Sha'anan' association, addressed to the delegates of the XII Zionist Congress and published in Jaffa in the summer of 1921 by M. Shoham Press, see Neve Sha'anan Cooperative, p. 4.

115. This figure comes from an interim report submitted to the League of Nations by the British High Commissioner, Herbert Samuel. In this same document, Samuel notes that Palestine is clearly too small a country to absorb such a mass influx of immigrants. See Herbert Samuel, *An Interim Report on the Civil Administration of Palestine to the League of Nations* (June, 1921).

116. Yosef Haim Brenner (1881–1921) was born in the Ukraine and educated in an orthodox Yeshiva, where he became close friends with another literary giant, Uri Nissan Gnessin. In 1898, Brenner joined the Bund Jewish Socialist Movement and adopted Zionism as his *raison d'être*. In 1902 he was drafted into the Russian army only to desert in 1904 when war broke out with Japan. He was initially captured but managed to escape to London, where he founded and edited the Hebrew literary periodical *Hameorer*. In 1909, he immigrated to Palestine, where he worked in agriculture for a short period before devoting himself to literature and education. Brenner published four novels, two novellas, numerous short stories and essays, and regularly translated works from Russian into Hebrew.

117. 'The Red House', as this particular mansion was known, stood on the Lydda Road (today Kibbutz Galuyot Road), adjacent to Abu Kabir's old graveyard. After several unsuccessful attempts to renovate the building, it was demolished in the 1970s and a new structure designed by the Bauhaus-educated architect, Shmuel Mistechkin, was erected in 1978. Named after Yosef Haim Brenner, this new building continues to serve as the headquarters for the Socialist youth movement, 'HaNoar HaOved VeHaLomed' (Working and Studying Youth).

118. The word Bayara derives from the Arab word *beer* [well]. The Bayaras of Jaffa were huge water tanks, fed by an extensive system of wells and pumps, which irrigated citrus groves and by extension, also designated the region's orchard plots. In many cases, they were attached to mansions located within these orchards, fusing to form a unique local architectural typology. Maps created prior to 1948 show some 200 Bayara houses scattered across Greater Jaffa, the majority of which were demolished in the immediate years following the War of Independence. In an oral history project conducted in the Shapira neighbourhood of South Tel Aviv between 2002–2004, I collected numerous

stories from veteran inhabitants who recalled regular summer swims held in the Bayara tanks, in which Arab and Jewish children would play together. One of the outcomes of the Hebrew publication of this book was a renewed interest in the Bayara houses and a two-year architectural research project initiated by the respective heads of the conservation programme at Tel Aviv University, Amnon Bar-Or and Sergio Lerman. The subsequent success of their documentation and exhibition of their work in 2008 has helped encourage public debate on the conservation of the Palestinian-built heritage of Jaffa. See Dalia Karpel, 'Wellsprings of memory', *Haaretz* (February 14, 2008) http://web.archive.org/web/20090325111844/http://www.haaretz.com/hasen/spages/952270.html

119. Yosef Haim Brenner, 'Note, 20 Nissan 5681', *Writings*, Vol. IV (Tel Aviv: HaKibbutz HaMeuhad and Sifriat Poalim, 1984), pp. 1833–1835.

120. By choosing to use the word 'Arabized', Ben-Gurion punned on the resemblance between the Hebrew verb 'arav' (to mix) and Arav (Arabic). See David Ben-Gurion, 'Clarification of the *Fellahs*' Origin' in *We and our Neighbours* (New York, 1916), p. 13.

121. Founded in 1919 by David Ben-Gurion, Yitzhak Ben Zvi and Berl Katznelson, Ahdut Ha'avoda ('Unity of Labour') was the first Socialist Zionist party, which served, until the foundation of the Histadrut in 1920, as a workers' union. The party aimed to unite Jewish labourers and agricultural workers through a non-Marxist socialist programme defined by Katznelson as 'revolutionary Constructivism'.

122. David Ben-Gurion, 'Our Relations with Our Neighbors, resolution proposition for the Ahdut Haavoda convention, Tel Aviv, 1921', see David Ben-Gurion, *We and Our Neighbours* (Tel Aviv: Davar, 1931), p. 61.

123. David Ben-Gurion, 'The *Fellah* and his Land' (New York, 1920), see David Ben-Gurion, *We and Our Neighbours*, p. 56.

124. Mordechai Kushnir, 'The Last Time we went to the Brenner's Residence', in M. Kushnir (ed.), *Yosef Haim Brenner: Selected Reminiscences* (Tel Aviv: HaKibbutz HaMeuhad, 1944), p. 209.

125. The hypothesis linking the child's disappearance with the massacre at the Red House has been suggested by Muki Tzur – a former leader of the Kibbutz movement in Israel and also a specialist historian in the Zionist Labour movement – who based his analysis on several witness testimonies, including that of Rivka Yatzkar-Shatz, who had been one of the few to be evacuated just in time. See Muki Tzur, *Early Spring, Zvi Shatz and the Intimate Group* (Tel Aviv: Am Oved, 1984), pp. 82–86. Incidentally, other references to and testimonies of the 1921 events can be found in an extensive collection of research, edited by Brenner's good friend, Mordechai Kushnir. Kushnir claims he had met Brenner on May 1, and Brenner had recounted the story of the child's disappearance and told him not to join the May Day march. Kushnir was among the first to reach the Red House after the massacre and he collected Brenner's last two short stories, which were still wet with blood. Kushnir also reported a motley pursuit around the outskirts of Jaffa for the body of Yosef Luidor, which had been kidnapped and slung on a camel's back. In his testimony of the whole

episode, Kushnir reported fragments from Brenner's autopsy report and printed a photo of the dead writer's face. He probably chose to display the photograph horizontally in order to emphasize his friend's passing. See Kushnir, 'The Last Time we went to the Brenner's Residence', pp. 209–228.

126. Samuel, *An Interim Report on the Civil Administration of Palestine to the League of Nations* (June 1921).

127. Wyndham Henry Deedes, British Brigadier General and Chief Secretary to the British High Commissioner of the British Mandate of Palestine between 1920 and 1922.

128. Chelouche, *Reminiscences of my Life*, pp. 380–385.

129. Neve Sha'anan association, *Memorandum to the delegates of the 12th Zionist Congress* (Jaffa: M. Shoham Press, 1921), p. 5.

130. Shavit and Bigger, *The History of Tel Aviv*, p. 93.

131. A revealing anecdote concerning this specific orchard at the heart of Shapira neighborhood was supplied by the participants of the neighbourhood's oral history project that I initiated in the neighbourhood's library: at the twilight period of the British mandate, in the last days of May 1948, a rumour had spread among the neighborhood's people, that 'anyone can settle wherever he wants.' The entire population, old people and children, invested the abandoned Arab properties in the neighbourhood with strings and stakes, each one trying to grab his own piece of land. An officer on one of the last British patrols that passed nearby, noticed the colourful hullabaloo, and drove his armoured vehicle over the divided property in order to erase the inhabitants' instant urbanism.

There were other, more official instant settlements, mostly in the southern parts of the neighbourhood, that took place during the 1948 battles over Arab properties, mostly directed by local commanders or officials. In many cases, those operations created administrative and ownership complications that have not been solved to this day.

132. Etzel (*Irgun Tzvai Leumi* – 'National Military Organization in the Land of Israel'), a right-wing paramilitary organization founded by Beitar members in 1929. Between 1943 and 1948, the organization was led by Menachem Begin, who later became Israel's first right-wing prime minister in 1977.

133. Lehi (*Lohamei Herut Israel* – 'Fighters for the Freedom of Israel'), an extremist paramilitary organization also known as the 'Stern Gang' were composed mainly of ultra right-wing activists but also by extreme leftists. The Lehi was founded by Avraham ('Yair') Stern in 1940, as a result of a split within the Etzel. After Stern's assassination by the British police in 1942, the group was led by the leftist activist Nathan Yellin-Mor and by Yitzhak Shamir, who became Israel's prime minister in 1983.

134. Curated by Israeli architect Zvi Efrat, *The Israeli Project* was the title of an architecture exhibition mounted at the Helena Rubinstein Pavilion of the Tel Aviv Museum of Art in 2001. The show displayed the vast project initiated by David Ben-Gurion in 1949, planned under the supervision of the Bauhaus-trained architect Aryeh Sharon and executed by the various organs of the centralized state. The unhidden ambition of the exhibition was to position

the 'Israeli Project' and its brutalist architecture as a second chapter of Israel's official architectural history. The first one, if needed to be mentioned was the White City and its Bauhaus style architecture. The exhibition's catalogue was published in 2005 (although falsely dated from 2004). See Zvi Efrat (ed.), *The Israeli Project: Building and Architecture 1948–1973* (Tel Aviv: Tel Aviv Museum of Art, 2005).

135. The London grandmother of the author, who came to Palestine as a member of the first Maccabiah British delegation, is one close example.

136. Shlomo Gur-Gerzovsky (1913–2000) was a founding member of Kibbutz Tel-Amal and became a sort of national 'project manager' following his success as the founder of Homa Umigdal. Before the establishment of the State, he was responsible for planning the defence constructions of many settlements including those of the Old City in Jerusalem. Following the establishment of Israel, he was charged with the country's first Grands Projets: the Hebrew University, the National Library and the Knesset building in Jerusalem.

137. Yohanan Ratner (1891–1965), a trained architect and a former Red Army officer, was the chief architect and strategic planner of the Haganah, the pre-state predecessor of the Israeli Defense Forces (IDF). He later became a general in the IDF. As a member of the central command during the War of Independence, Ratner was the only general who received Ben-Gurion's permission to retain his non-Hebrew family name. Later he served as Dean of the Faculty of Architecture in the Technion in Haifa. As a teacher and dean in the 1950s, Ratner was considered a reactionary and one of the more ardent opponents of modernist architecture.

138. Keren Kayemeth LeIsrael (Jewish National Fund) was established in 1901 during the fifth Zionist Congress in Basel, in order to purchase land in Palestine – Eretz-Israel for the Jewish people. This organization became the most important factor in the land system of the country and until today: KKL-JNF is the main proprietor of lands in the State of Israel, and owns more than 90 per cent of them. As an organ of the Zionist movement, KKL-JNF became one of the state's most important instruments to make sure that lands in Israel would remain under Jewish (and not 'Israeli') ownership.

139. This paradigmatic form of settlement was largely discussed in one of my early essays, 'Wall and Tower: the mold of Israeli Architecture', in Rafi Segal and Eyal Weizman (eds), *A Civilian Occupation: The Politics of Israeli Architecture* (Tel Aviv: Babel and London: Verso, 2003), pp. 40–56.

140. See Dov Gavish, 'The Oppression of the Arab Revolt in 1936', in 'Jaffa and its Sites', *Kardom* – bi-monthly of the Knowledge of Israel, published by the Ministry of Tourism, Vol. 51 (March–April 1981), p. 60–62.

141. Ibid., p. 62.

142. Yosef Eliyahu Chelouche uses his autobiography to recount discussions held in as early as 1925, as to whether the Tel Aviv port should be built in the north of the city, where the Yarkon River meets the sea. The British originally rejected this idea in light of the effect it would have on the Jaffa port and local interests across the area. Moreover, they were already in the process of planning the

construction of another modern port in Haifa. This did not deter Menachem Ussishkin who, convinced of the absolute necessity of building a port in Tel Aviv in order to consolidate its economic independence from Jaffa, told Chelouche plaintively: 'There will be a port here, just like the one in Riga, and I will order Yehoshua Hankin to buy this place tomorrow.' See Chelouche, *Reminiscences of My Life*, pp. 411–412.

143. According to Plan D, the Haganah only planned to conquer the suburbs of Manshieh and Abu Kabir, and to besiege Jaffa. Benny Morris claims that even after the beginning of the violence, most members of the National Committee of Jaffa opposed the idea of initiating a riposte against Tel Aviv. Benny Morris, *The Birth of the Palestinian Refugee Problem, 1947–1949* (Tel Aviv: Am Oved, 1991), pp. 37, 135.

On the contrary, in the Foreword to Chaim Lazar's book on the conquest of Jaffa, Menachem Begin claims that if it weren't for the conquest, Jaffa's port would have served as the base for an Egyptian invasion. Menachem Begin, 'The Truth of Victory and the Victory of Truth', in Chaim Lazar, *The Conquest of Jaffa* (Tel Aviv: Shelah, 1951), p. 12.

144. Morris, *The Birth of the Palestinian Refugee Problem*, pp. 71–76.

145. Morris, *The Birth of the Palestinian Refugee Problem*, p. 57.

146. Among numerous examples, Lazar recounts the barrel bomb rolled into Café Venezia near the Al-Hamra Cinema by Etzel members, Chelbi Ben David and Shaul Bador, which killed forty individuals (who he refers to as 'bandits') and injured many more. See Lazar, *The Conquest of Jaffa*, p. 82.

147. For another detailed account of the attacks perpetrated on Jaffa and its surrounding villages see Walid Khalidi, *All That Remains: The Palestinian Villages Occupied and Depopulated by Israel in 1948* (Washington, DC: Institute of Palestinian Studies, 1992), pp. 230–264. Within this record one can read the testimony of former Jaffan attorney Shukri Salameh, who recounts five terror attacks in Jaffa's cafés, in spots where residents would gather in order to listen to the radio. In direct contradiction to Etzel and Lehi statements declaring these attacks had specifically targeted 'bandits' and 'rioters', Salameh notes that only unarmed civilians were harmed. In reference to the Seraya bombing, Salameh claims that between ten and twelve social workers from the American University of Beirut were killed, some of whom he knew personally. The same testimony appears in Shukri Salameh's internet project, the 'Oral History of Palestine'. See www.palestineremembered.com/Jaffa/Jaffa/Story202.html

148. See the testimony of Shukri Salma, in Khalidi, *All That Remains*, pp. 230–264.

149. See the story of Ghassan Kanafani on the escape from Jaffa to Lebanon through Rosh Hanikra. Ghassan Kanafani, 'Jaffa, Land of Oranges', in *Al Ahram: 1948–1998: Special Pages commemorating 50 Years of Arab Dispossession since the Creation of the State of Israel*, at: www.palestineremembered.com/Jaffa/Jaffa/Story153.html

150. On the link between urban planning and urban warfare (and Jaffa in particular), see Eyal Weizman, 'Military Operations as Urban Planning: A Conversation with Philipp Misselwitz', *Territories* (Berlin: KW, 2003), pp. 272–286. For a

more detailed, military analysis of the assault on Jaffa in 1948, see Benjamin Runkle, 'Jaffa, 1948: Urban Combat in the Israeli War of Independence', in Col. John Antal and Maj. Bradley Gericke (eds), *City fights: Selected Histories of Urban Combat from World War II to Vietnam* (New York: Ballantine Books, 2003), pp. 289–313.

151. Bugeaud wrote this text in 1849 in his mansion in the Dordogne, during forced retirement following his failure to subjugate the riots in Paris in June 1848. Unable to find a publisher for the book, he printed a smaller edition, which he distributed among a few military colleagues. The manuscript was considered lost for some 150 years, but its existence was verified by Victor Hugo, who mentions it in his journal (Bugeaud had approached him several times in an attempt to help him publish the material). The manuscript was later located by the historian Maïté Bouyssy and published in Paris in 1997. It stands as a kind of urban combat guide to the streets of Paris, penned in the short space of time between the riots of 1848 and Georges-Eugène Haussmann's renovation of the city in 1853–1870. Beyond the delineation of tactical manoeuvres, Bugeaud also mapped out the dangers and threats inherent within the French capital, exposing the social boundaries between the Eastern and Western districts and proffering a new perspective for the city, which actually reappeared in the Haussmann's work. The latter put a civic spin on the former's military approach. For example, Haussmann sought to spread a net of 'headquarters' across the city, only for him they were police and fire bases as opposed to Bugeaud's army barracks; where Bugeaud had wanted to destroy buildings located in strategic intersections, Haussmann trimmed off the edges in order to guarantee wider vistas; even the ditches Haussmann dug out from the urban mass – the new avenues, the metro tunnels –bear some similarity with Bugeaud's carved 'mouse holes'. See Maréchal Bugeaud, *La guerre des rues et des maisons*, [manuscript inédit présenté par Maïté Bouyssy] (Paris: Jean-Paul Rocher, 1997).

152. An online edition of *Manual for an Armed Insurrection*, translated by Andy Blunden, can be found at: www.marxist.org/reference/archive/blanqui/1866/instructions1.htm

153. One of the main characteristics of the barricade is that it is made from regular urban material, which has been recycled for another, sometimes opposite, purpose. This may be why Friedrich Engels claimed that 'the barricade produced more of a moral than a material effect'. See Frederick Engels, 'Introduction', in *Karl Marx: The Class Struggles In France* (1895). Translated by Louis Proyect, at www.marxists.org/archive/marx/works/1850/class-struggles-france/intro.htm. More often than not, for example, it meant reusing apparatus which had originally *facilitated* traffic, in order to *stop* traffic.

154. Lazar, *The Conquest of Jaffa*, p. 171.

155. Weizman presents Kochavi rightfully as a super-theorist and a super-practitioner of the city, one deserving to be taken seriously like other urban thinkers of our times, such as Rem Koolhaas. It seems that Kochavi's interpretation is not just about tactical measures designed to capture enemy territory; it is also a philosophy, which re-imagines a whole new spatial perception of the

city, similar almost in a way to video games like DOOM. This perception of the city seems to employ quite easily and intently strategies and concepts borrowed from critical theory and architectural theory and post-modern or deconstructivist architecture. Practically, it means using similar principles to that of 'superposition' in Bernard Tschumi's design for Parc de la Villette in Paris in the beginning of the 1980s or in Daniel Liebskind's early *Line of Fire* project in Berlin in 1988. The extreme abstraction of the simple geometrical law – that 'a straight line passes through two points' – and its immediate application in a space where a new order has been forced upon it, derive from the need to use selective measures or in order to attack specific targets (selective assassination is one of the more obvious instances, for example). But it also expresses a paradoxical state of things in a space where differences between state and city, and between army and police, have become indistinct.

156. Lazar, *The Conquest of Jaffa*, p. 236.

157. See Salim Abu-Shukri's testimony for Walid Khalidi, *All That Remains*, p. 581.

158. In his book *The Birth of the Palestinian Refugee Problem*, Benny Morris estimates that the original number of inhabitants in Jaffa was between 70,000–80,000 people, out of which only around 4,000–5,000 remained in the city at the moment it surrendered. Walid Khalidi estimates in his book *All That Remains* that only 3,600 people stayed in the city. Morris, *The Birth of the Palestinian Refugee Problem*, pp. 135, 143.

159. Tom Segev dedicates a whole chapter to the issue of the spontaneous and organized looting in his book *1949: The First Israelis* (Jerusalem: Domino, 1984), pp. 83–104.

160. Lazar, *The Conquest of Jaffa*, p. 220.

161. Binyamin Tamuz, 'Swimming Competition', in *Selected Stories*, (Jerusalem: Keter and The Association of Hebrew Writers, 1990), p. 62.

162. Details of government assembly, 11 Tishrey 1949 – October 4, 1949: The Annexation of Jaffa to Tel Aviv (with gratitude to Tzvi Efrat).

163. For a detailed analysis of the later developments in Jaffa and the special manners in which worldwide gentrification processes work within the Andromeda Hill project, see Roy Fabian and Daniel Monterescu, 'The "Golden Cage": Gentrification and Globalization in the Andromeda Hill Project, Jaffa', *Theory and Criticism* (Teoria Ubikoret) (Issue 23, Autumn 2003, guest editor: Ronen Shamir), pp. 141–178.

164. In a recent study, Or Aleksandrowicz claims that in spite of various attempts made following the war, by several parties who tried to leave the false historical impression that the military operations resulted in the total annihilation of Manshieh neighbourhood, the eradication of Manshieh was the result of a premeditated plan that had almost no relation to the damage caused by the military actions. The plan was concocted by Tel Aviv's mayor, Israel Rokah and the city engineer, Yaakov Ben Sira, who shared a common worldview that regarded city plans of massive destruction as a legitimate instrument for the reshaping of the urban landscape. Since they believed Manshieh was a hopeless slum, they initiated soon after the 1948 War a comprehensive destruction

operation that was believed to be the first step in the reconstruction of the whole southern Tel Aviv region. The operation came to a sudden halt when they failed to receive governmental financing for the acts because of their illegal nature, leaving behind an unrecoverable dilapidated urban scape. Or Aleksandrowicz, 'Harisa Ezrahit: Ha-Mehiqa Ha-Metukhnenet Shel Shekhunat Manshiya Be-Yafo, 1948–1949' [Civilian Demolition: The Premeditated Destruction of Manshiya Neighbourhood in Jaffa, 1948–1949]. *Iyunim Bitkumat Israel* [Studies in Israeli and Modern Jewish Society], 23 (2013), pp. 274–314.

165. For the story of Jabaliya, see Haim Bresheeth, 'Gebalyia as a Symbol: Three Perspectives', *Theory and Criticism* [Teoria Ubikoret] (Issue 16: Space, Land, Home; Spring 2000), pp. 233–238.

166. This figure is an estimate made by Eyal Segev, a student of architecture at Bezalel University, who made a comparative survey of aerial photographs of the region from 1936 to the early 1990s.

167. The Absentees' Property Law of 1950 meant that anyone who had left their place of residence at any time between November 19, 1947 and May 19, 1948 was considered 'absent' and their property was transferred to the Custodian of Absentee Property, the Israel Land Administration (ILA). It means that today, the ILA, which is part of the Israeli Government, owns some 93 percent of the country's land mass. Under current Israeli law, the ILA cannot lease land to foreign nationals, including Palestinian residents of Jerusalem, who have identity cards but are not citizens of Israel. While most Israelis consider this 'official' expropriation of Palestinian assets to be irreversible – (not least in light of the processes of erasure and re-inscription which have dramatically modified the nation's physical landscape since 1948) – the debate is far from over, not least in light of European reparations schemes which have returned property and paid compensation to Jewish victims of World War II. Even today, the Israeli press gets excitable whenever a new story detailing loss of Jewish assets during this period arises – whether it is an art collection in Germany, an apartment block in Holland or a Swiss bank account. It should be noted, that when it does comes to settling the reparations due Palestinian victims (which is a prerequisite for peace in the region), the loss of Jewish property expropriated by Muslim countries should also be taken into consideration. Yehouda Shenhav has written extensively on this subject, and dedicates a chapter to this debate in his book *The Arab Jews: Nationality, Religion, Ethnicity* (Tel Aviv: Am Oved, Sifriyat Ofakim, 2003), pp. 121–148, 185–192.

168. This same practice of Hebraizing the Arab city, changing their streets' names into numbers and names in Hebrew, is still employed by IDF forces when operating in today's West Bank's cities.

169. Lazar, *The Conquest of Jaffa*, p. 255.

170. Jaffa's open-top hill is actually demonstrative of a wider neurosis within Israeli planning, in which captured mountains or summits are quickly emptied of any Arab presence, and eagerly transformed into 'Jewish-Israeli' spaces. See Rafi Segal and Eyal Weizman, 'The Battle for the Hilltops', *A Civilian Occupation: The Politics of Israeli Architecture* (Tel Aviv: Babel; London: Verso, 2003).

171. *Kazablan* was a Jewish adaptation of *Romeo and Juliet* set in Jaffa, in which Kazabalan (a Sephardic Jew from Morocco) falls in love with Rachel (an Ashkenazi Jew from Europe). The lead character is named Kazablan after his native town in Morocco, Dar-El-Baide, which was rebranded Casablanca (meaning 'white house') by Spanish conquerors in the sixteenth century. There is, of course, a glorious irony in this double and inverted colonial connection between Jaffa and the 'white houses'.

172. According to this survey, only 13 per cent of the inhabitants of The Big Zone were dependent on welfare – a much smaller percentage than the average figure found in other neighbourhoods designated as deprived. See 'Old Jaffa (The Big Zone): social economic survey', *Housing and Building III*, Introduction: David Tane. State of Israel, Ministry of Housing, December 1962.

173. Taken from the Old Jaffa Development Corporation website, www.oldjaffa.co.il

174. The Hebrew title of the old Jaffa project is 'Yaffo Ha'atiqa' (Antique Jaffa).

175. Urban Building Scheme 606.

176. As for Ben-Gurion's attitude towards the sea, one could best describe the 'Old Man' as a 'freshwater sailor'. When he spoke in front of that Jewish fishermen convention in Haifa on December 23, 1943, he confessed that most of his knowledge about the practice of fishing stemmed from the tales of the Jewish fish market, as told by Isaac Leib Peretz: 'Here in this country we've learned that fish exist in the sea, and are obtained not by purchase but through fishing,' he noted. He went on to compare the Jewish return to the sea to the Zionist return to working the land, which explains his attempts to find Biblical references to Jewish seamanship, and the importance he put on marine activity. He was passionate about the construction of new harbours in Tel Aviv, Eilat and Ashdod. See David Ben-Gurion, 'The Fisherman and the Sea', *Of Settlement*, (Tel Aviv: HaKibbutz HaMeuhad, 1986), p. 90.

177. Lazar, *The Conquest of Jaffa*, p. 223.

178. Zvi Elhyani, 'Seafront Holdings', in *Back to the Sea* (November 2004). See, http://readingmachine.co.il/home/articles/1111445772 (in Hebrew).

179. Zvi Elhyani, 'Seafront Holdings', in Sigal Barnir and Yael Moria-Klein (eds), *Back to the Sea*, catalogue of the Israeli Pavilion, 9th Biennale of Architecture, Venice, 2004, pp. 104–116.

180. Ibid.

181. For more information on the Etzel Museum in Manshieh and the way in which it echoes the perception of the sea in Zionist and Revisionist ethos, see Amit Gish, 'Conquest of the Hebrew Sea: The Etzel Museum as an Expression of the Perception of the Hebrew Sea in the Revisionist Ethos', *Theory and Criticism* [Teoria Ubikoret], Vol. 42 (Spring 2004), pp. 113–131.

182. *Altalena* was an Italian ship purchased by the Etzel in 1947. The ship, loaded with some 900 new immigrants, medical supplies and weaponry destined for Etzel forces, approached the Israeli coastline in June 1948. Given the fact that at the time, the Etzel has been already dismantled and its fighters incorporated within the newly-formed IDF, Ben-Gurion demanded that the ship's cargo should be handled to the IDF. At first, it was agreed that the ship would set

anchor near Kfar Vitkin, a beach north of Tel Aviv. Upon its landing, the Etzel leader Menachem Begin came to greet the ship, but soon after the passengers disembarked it appeared that there was a disagreement about the fate of its military cargo. Following the refusal of Menachem Begin to handle the weapons, the ship was attacked by the IDF forces and sailed southwards to Tel Aviv in the hope of getting aid from the city's Etzel fighters. On June 22, 1948, it anchored near Tel Aviv's shore. Ben-Gurion, who considered this as a serious challenge to the newly-formed State's institutions, ordered an attack on the ship. The IDF forces, under Yitzhak Rabin's command, shelled the ship and set it on fire, killing ten Etzel members and injuring dozens.

183. This text is taken from the plaque in the museum itself. The fact that the architects donated the design of the project is also noted.

184. 'The idea was that buildings of modern construction were poorly suited to form that "bridge of tradition" to future generations which Hitler was calling for. It was hard to imagine that rusting heaps of rubble could communicate these heroic inspirations which Hitler admired in the monuments of the past. My "theory" was intended to deal with this dilemma. By using special materials and by applying certain principles of statics, we should be able to build structures which even in a state of decay, after hundreds or (such were our reckonings) thousands of years would more or less resemble Roman models.' Albert Speer, *Inside the Third Reich*, translated from German by Richard and Clara Winston) (New York: Macmillan, 1970), p. 56.

185. Shmuel Tolkovsky, 'The Origin of the Jaffa Orange', *History of Jaffa* (Jerusalem: Ariel, 2001; Tel Aviv: Dvir, 1926), p. 147.

186. The advantage of registering the product as a trademark (over a patent, for example) is that the ownership of a trademark is eternal.

187. The website of the Israeli Council of Citrus Fruit is entitled 'JAFFA: the Israeli Brand'. See www.jaffa.co.il (last accessed 2005).

188. Even more galling, when the season is out in Israel, these same 'JAFFA' oranges are plucked from growers in Spain, South America and the USA.

189. Yuval Dror, 'There's nothing like JAFFA in the World', *Haaretz Weekend Edition*, 15 September 2004, p. 56.

190. Nitza Szmuk, 'Letters to the Editor', *Ha'Ir*, 13 February 2003.

191. The Eisenberg Hospital designed by Avraham Yasky has never been completed, and its steel skeleton stood still until its demolition in 2003.

192. 'Evacuation and construction' ('pinuy-binuy' in Hebrew) is a Ministry of Housing relocation procedure, which permits partnership between municipalities and private contractors and is supported by governmental funding. While the rationale given for this procedure is the need to gather populations as a means of reducing open land and saving on infrastructure, in reality, these projects nearly always take place in areas where the potential commercial gain for private contractors is significant, and where the residents' capacity to resist eviction is negligible. The distribution of the workload is simple; the municipality approves and promotes the projects through its different committees and the contractor is responsible for the planning and the evacuation itself. The contractor's designs

are almost always at odds with the already existing urban plans in place, as set by customary standards, and the sole parameter of the project is something loosely defined as 'density promoting'. The Ministry of Housing remunerates the projects according to the speed in which the procedure is completed. Since 2001, all budgets allocated to neighbourhood restoration schemes have been handed to private contractors by their respective municipalities. This has proved a form of privatization of public and urban planning for low-income populations, without the populations themselves notified or involved in the decision-making process. Given that the evacuation itself is a privatized action, those residents targeted for eviction are exposed to large pressures – both from contractors and their agents (sometimes lawyers, sometimes more questionable personalities) and by their families and neighbours.

193. Memorandum to the 12th Zionist Convention, Jaffa, 1921. (Archive of the Municipality of Tel Aviv).

194. Ibid.

195. Ibid.

196. Ibid.

197. Following a design competition held in 1948, the Provisional State Council of Israel chose the figure of the Menorah designed by Gabriel and Maxim Shamir as the emblem for the State of Israel. The emblem received its official status on 24 May 1949, under a special law defining Israel's flag, anthem and emblem.

198. Kauffmann's circular scheme of Nahalal sought to express the equality of its members. Each one of the houses spread along the circle is equally distanced from the circle's centre in which all the public buildings were placed.

199. In the National Library of Israel's catalogue are registered 245 publications on Nahalal, 752 on Ein Harod, 6,894 on Ramat Gan. Only two publications are registered on Neve Sha'anan: the settlers' Memorandum from 1921 and a study on the neighbourhood's water supply from 1928.

200. The details are based on a number of chronicles: Nathan Roy, 'The Central Station Does not Respond', *Davar Hashavua*, 11 October 1985, 7; Roni Hadar, 'The White Elephant Suffers from Split Personality', *Tel Aviv*, 18 September 1992, 40–42.

201. Ram Karmi (1931–2013) was the son of Dov Karmi (1905–1962), one of the White City's leading architects. Trained in the 1950s at the London Architectural Association, Ram Karmi was one of the first architects to import Brutalist architecture to Israel. In 2002 he received the Israel Prize for architecture.

202. Hadar, 'The White Elephant Suffers from Split Personality', p. 42.

203. Ibid.

204. The White City's obsession with its own genealogy (let alone genetics in general) was evident throughout these celebrations. Perhaps the most famous example was when spectacle's organizers paid the airfare of a young computer engineer from Sweden, who was flown in especially to be paraded as Sir Patrick Geddes' great-grandson. To much fanfare, this poor individual was forced to participate in the main ceremony held in honour of the White City, in the presence of Mayor Ron Huldai, the mayors of Tel Aviv's twinned cities, and

other VIP personalities. The wonderful irony of this episode is that the exact same blood and family ties which had paid this gentlemen's airfare to the ceremony in Tel Aviv, were also precisely what had prevented him from living in the city his great-grandfather had planned. Tomer Shalit, the man in question, had been one of the children at the heart of the debate over 'Who is Jewish?', which raged throughout 1968 when his father petitioned the Supreme Court to recognize his son as Jewish even though his mother (who happened to be Geddes' grandchild), was not. A political maelstrom followed the Supreme Court's acceptance of this request and subsequently, after bitter wrangling, the law was changed in 1970 in support of the minority opinion – a decision made because it was supposedly in accordance with Jewish law. Following this judgement, the Shalit family left Israel for Sweden.

205. These numbers are correct up until the end of 2004, and are based on data provided by the Immigration Administration, as published on its internet site: www.hagira.gov.il. Specifications of time and place are not provided.

206. This description is based on witness statements, attesting that the operation carried out by the immigration police was unprecedented in both magnitude and violence. As was the case in other cities, the local newspapers did not report the hunt or the blanket deportations which followed. It is important to note that sporadic searches across the Black City – in and off buses, through the New Central Station, across Levinsky Park – were a regular, everyday occurrence during this period, to the point where they had almost become routine.

207. B'Tselem is an Israeli NGO whose stated goal is to document and educate the Israeli public and policymakers about human rights violations in the Occupied Territories.

208. See Rem Koolhaas' essay on the 'typical plan', Rem Koolhaas, 'Typical Plan', *S.M.L.XL* (Rotterdam: 010, 1995), p. 334.

209. Within this context, it is interesting to read Frederick Kiesler's attack on modern architecture and its obsession with hygiene, and then to consider the only building he ever built, the 'Shrine of the Book' in Jerusalem. A sort of parody of this hygienic fetish, the 'Shrine of the Book' is covered with white ceramic tiles (the same tiles that coat the interiors of metro stations and Henri Sauvage's salubrious residential buildings in central Paris), which supposedly enable the building to 'bathe' itself. See Frederick Kiesler, 'Le pseudo-fonctionnalisme dans l'architecture moderne', in *L'Architecte et le Philosophe* (Liege: Margada, 1993), p. 32.

210. The author and editor Benny Ziffer has also commentated on the similarities between Dakar and Tel Aviv. See Benny Ziffer, 'My myths', *Haaretz 2004 New Year's Supplement*, September 15, 2004, p. 31.

211. One cannot omit the name of Casablanca in this context. Founded by the Portuguese as Casa Branca in 1515, following the demolition of the city Anfa, which was an independent base for commerce and pirate action located in the same area, a few years earlier. The Portuguese city was destroyed in an earthquake in the middle of the eighteenth century, and was founded again by the Moroccan Sultan under the name of Dar-el-Beide. It received the

Spanish name Casablanca due to the extensive activity of the Spanish colonial corporations in the city.

212. Quote taken during a conversation with the historian in Tel Aviv, June 2004.

213. Mark Wigley, who dedicated a whole book to the role of the colour white in modern architecture, managed to skip over political or racial contexts, and instead decided to focus on issues of dress, representation, style, taste and fashion. Wigley, M., *White Walls, Designer Dresses: The Fashioning of Modern Architecture* (Cambridge, MA: MIT Press, 1995).

214. Adolf Loos, 'Ornament and Crime' and 'The Plumbers', in Yehuda Safran (ed.), *Spoken into the Void, After All*, trans. Aryeh Uriel (Tel Aviv: Babel [Architecturs], 2004), pp. 57, 102.

215. Richard Pommer, 'Mies van der Rohe and the Political Ideology of the Modern Movement in Architecture', in Franz Schulze (ed.), *Mies van der Rohe: Critical Essays* (New York: The Museum of Modern Art, 1989), p. 96.

216. Richard Pommer, 'Mies van der Rohe and the Political Ideology of the Modern Movement in Architecture,' in Franz Schulze (ed.), *Mies van der Rohe: Critical Essays* (New York: The Museum of Modern Art, 1989), p. 96.

217. Le Corbusier, *Toward An Architecture*, p. 225.

218. In this particular chapter Le Corbusier lays out his argument with the Surrealists, and in particular, a text written by Giorgio de Chirico from *La révolution surréaliste*. Scathingly dismissing what he considers to be romantic Surrealist naivete, Le Corbusier champions the 'realist object' – an object that 'works', that is 'beautiful *because* it is functional'. The white required by the 'Ripolin rule' is not only characterized by its aesthetics then, but again, by an innate morality – 'We will not allow the dead drivel of the past on the white Ripolin walls', the author declares. Incidentally, in the same chapter, Le Corbusier notes the struggle of the Young Turks to promote modernity and Westernization in Turkey and associates their endeavours with the white of the modern movement. See Le Corbusier, *L'Art décorative d'aujourd'hui* (Paris: Arthaud, 1925/1980), pp. 187–196, 291.

219. Le Corbusier designed and laid out his books by himself. See Le Corbusier, *L'Art décorative d'aujourd'hui*, p. 194.

220. Jean-Louis Cohen demonstrates how pre-World War II Algiers served as Le Corbusier's field of experimentation. In this regard, he was no different from a whole generation of French architects who, working under the wings of colonization, used imperial outposts as blank drawing pads. Jean-Louis Cohen, 'Le Corbusier, Perret et les figures d'un Alger modern', in *Alger, paysage urbain et architectures, 1800–2000* (Paris: Les Éditions de l'Imprimeur, 2003), pp. 160–185.

221. Le Corbusier, *Sur le quatre routes* (Paris: Denoël, 1941/1970), pp. 123, 127, 132, 165.

222. Henry-Russell Hitchcock and Philip Johnson, *The International Style: Architecture since 1922* (New York & London: W.W. Norton & Co., 1932/1995), pp. 265–269.

223. According to Johnson's biographer Franz Schulze, during the same period that

the International Style thesis was being conceived and promoted (from 1932–1940), Johnson was a regular contributor to extremist right-wing journals, in which he expressed his support for the Nazi regime and defended anti-Semitic opinions. Prior to the publication of his biography in 1994, practically nothing was known or published about his Nazi past, with the exception of two articles: one by the architectural historian Geoffrey Blodgett and the other by the architect Michael Sorkin, published in 1987 and 1988 respectively. These revelations are all the more embarrassing in light of Johnson's close relations with well-known Jewish architects like Peter Eisenman and Heads of State in Israel, like Shimon Peres (Johnson designed the nuclear plant in Nachal Sorek which Peres had advocated). See Franz Schulze, *Philip Johnson: Life and Work* (New York: Albert A. Knopf, 1994); Geoffrey Blodgett, 'Philip Johnson's Great Depression', *Timeline* (June–July 1987), pp. 2–17; Michael Sorkin, *Exquisite Corpse: Writing on Buildings* (New York: Verso, 1991), pp. 307–311; Kazys Varnelis, 'We Cannot Not Know History: Philip Johnson's Politics and Cynical Survival', *Journal of Architectural Education* (November 1994).

224. The contempt the Viennese Loos felt towards Germanic culture was only equal in loathing to the contempt the Viennese Theodor Herzl displayed towards Hungarian culture. Loos expressed his Americanophilia and Anglophilia tendencies throughout his large body of essays. An unconventional example can be found in *The Plumbers*, where he ranks and classifies the nations of the world according to their water consumption: 'the Germans, I mean most of the public, consume too little water for the needs of the body and the home. They do so only when they must, when told that it would be advantageous for their health ... in this aspect, the relation between America and Austria is similar to that between Austria and China.' See Loos, 'The Plumbers', in *Spoken into the Void, After All*, pp. 77–87.

225. There is an admiration of force throughout this essay and Loos' aggression is positively palpable: 'What is the discord, that like an unnecessary scream shatters the quiet? Right at the centre of the farmers' houses, which were not built by them, but by God, stands a villa. Is it the product of a good or of a bad architect? I do not know. All I know is that beauty, peace and quiet have been dispelled.' Loos, 'Architecture (1910)', p. 104.

226. Claude Parent, 'Dominer le site', in *Form follows fiction: écrits d'architecture fin de siècle* (Paris: Les Éditions de la Villette, 1996), p. 75.

227. A concept elucidated by the architect Mohamed Atta, the Egyptian mastermind behind the September 11th terror attacks in New York.

228. With this in mind, it is worth considering the parallels between those military conclusions drawn by Maréchal Bugeaud following the conquest of Algiers and Haussmann's urban strategies for the planning of Paris. Many of Bougeaud's strategic inferences took new form in the Haussmannic project, beginning 1850 – carving out the avenues in the urban mass, spreading barracks and bases in strategic areas, and sustaining a separation between the East and Western districts of the city (while structurally favouring the West in light of its rapport with Versailles). Validation for encompassing this militarily-inspired urbanism

into the Paris design came in 1871 when the Paris Commune was quickly and brutally suppressed. See Maréchal Bujeaud, *La guerre des rues et des maisons*, manuscript inédit présenté par Maïté Bouyssy (Paris: Jean-Paul Rocher, 1997).

229. Roland Barthes, 'Grammaire africaine', in *Mythologies* (Paris: Seuil, 1957), pp. 137–144.

230. For example, in his essay *Bichon chez les nègres*, Barthes explores a story printed in *Paris Match* which tells the tale of a young couple, both professors, who made an expedition into 'Cannibal country' in order to do some painting. Taking their baby, Bichon, along for the ride, the periodical goes into ecstasy at the courage of all three. Barthes, *Mythologies*, pp. 64–67.

231. Fanon often used humour as a means of both extracting and expressing these instances of 'internalized racism'. For example, in *Black Skin, White Masks*, Fanon recounts the following joke: 'One day St. Peter receives three men at the gates of heaven: a white man, a mulatto, and a Negro.
   – "What do you want most?", he asks the white man.
   – "Money."
   – "And you?" he asks the mulatto.
   – "Fame."
   St Peter turned then to the Negro, who said with a wide smile; "I'm just carrying these gentleman's bags."' See Frantz Fanon, *Peau noir, masques blancs* (Paris: Seuil, 1952), pp. 39–40.

232. Frantz Fanon, *Les damnés de la terre* (Paris: La Decouverte, 2002; François Maspéro, 1961), pp. 41–43.

233. Ibid., p. 43.

234. Ibid., p. 53.

235. Homi K. Bhabha, 'The White Stuff' in 'The Political Aspect of Whiteness,' *Artforum International*, vol. 36, no. 9 (May 1998), p. 21.

236. Chuihua Judy Chung, Jeffrey Inaba, Rem Koolhaas, Sze Tsung Leong, *Great Leap Forward*, 2002, Harvard Design School Project on the City, Taschen.

237. Adolf Loos, p. 312.

238. *Jaffa, A Look at Ajami: An Architectural Portrait*, Municipality of Tel Aviv-Yaffo, The Engineering Administration, City Planning and Building Branch. The Jaffa planning team: architect Doron Zafrir, architect Sergio Lerman, architect Dani Rabas, 'Architecture' (architects Shmuel Groberman and Rami Gil), architect Nahum Cohen, Moria-Skali Landscape Architecture (landscape architect Yael Klein-Moria). The brochure is not dated, but was published in the early 1990s.

239. Michel Foucault dedicated one of his classes at the Collège de France to the inversion of Claeswitz's paradigm: Foucault, M., 'La politique comme guerre', *Il faut proteger la sociéte* (Paris: Gallimard, 1997).

240. Bhabha, 'The White Stuff', p. 21.

241. In modern Israel, 'middle class' is actually more of a nostalgic slogan than a legitimate term used to described any specific strata of society. The term may have had some validity for the latter half of the twentieth century, when it stood for the option of a socio-economic lifestyle which was, if not exactly lavish, then secure. In today's economic reality, few are privy to such a degree of stability,

which in the past had been based on a employment guarantees and public and national security systems, such as health insurance, social security and pension plans. Today's class system is made of an endless overlapping of different proletariats, each exposed to the terror and caprices of the market economy in their own way.

242. While this might sound like poetic hyperbole, one only need map out the distance between the outline of Ariel Sharon's Separation Wall and the outline originally suggested by the left-wing politician, Yossi Beilin, in order to understand just how qualified a statement this is. The space between the two outlines represents the political arc in Israel. The Likud's military separation techniques are really just an extension of the Labour Party's civil separation techniques. Both are equally efficient in their own way. So, for example, the construction of Highway Six moved all Arab towns eastwards, towards the West Bank (inasmuch as that now the only way to separate Baqa-el-Garbieh from Tul Karem is according to the placement of the security wall between the highway and the city.

243. Arendt, H., *Essai sur la revolution* (Paris: Gallimard, 1967), p. 38.

244. See David Ben-Gurion, 'Clarification of the *Fellahs*' Origin' in *We and our Neighbours* (New York, 1916), p. 13.

245. The Israeli government's ongoing attempts to force the nationalization of space belong to a different era; the dark period of nationalism, ethnocentricity and jingoism which characterized the great wars of the twentieth century. Paul Virilio claims that, after an absence of nearly five hundred years, the personal conflict is returning to the history books at the expense of the national. In states where cities merge into one global city, war becomes a battle for information, and it is contained everywhere and is present in everything. For Virilio, the direct outcome will be a privatization of war where we 'head back to the fifteenth century, the "condottieri" and the masters of war.' Under these circumstances, what really scares me about Ehud Barak's famous statement – 'we are here and they are there' – is its complete irrelevance. Paul Virilio, 'De la géopolitique à la métropolitique', *La ville et la guerre*, sous la direction de Antoine Picon (Paris: Édition de l'Imprimeur, 1996), p. 226.

246. This sort of reality could easily be imagined in the structure of the European community. In this position, national contradictions such as that between the Jewish right of return and the Palestinian right of return would cancel themselves out and dissolve into a whole different set of identities, as in any case national fate would change into individual projects. Since the Middle East conflict is the direct outcome of Europe's two main sins, anti-Semitism and colonialism, one should hope that the European community would find it plausible to accept Israel/Palestine for full membership.

247. Since 2005, when WCBC was published in Hebrew, many of those gaps have been filled. In 2005 Mark LeVine published in English his seminal book *Overthrowing Geography: Jaffa, Tel Aviv, and the Struggle for Palestine, 1880–1948*. It is the only book on Jaffa and Tel Aviv that relies on sources from all languages used in Jaffa and Tel Aviv – Arabic, Hebrew and Ottoman. This

same year, Or Aleksandrowicz, the Hebrew editor of this book, published a new annotated edition with Babel, of his great-great-grandfather Yosef Eliyahu Chelouche's book *Reminiscences of My Life (1870–1930)*. This is a beautifully written autobiography by a Palestinian Zionist, a Jaffa-born Arab-Jew, who became one of Tel Aviv's most important builders. In 2006 Adam LeBor's book, *City of Oranges: Arabs and Jews in Jaffa*, recounts Jaffa's History through the stories of three families, a Muslim, a Christian and a Jewish one.

248. Some of the WCBC-related work is books like *Reminiscences of My Life* by Yosef Eliyahu Chelouche, ed. Or Aleksandrowicz (Tel Aviv-Jaffa: Babel 2005) or *Neither in Jaffa Nor in Tel Aviv: Stories, Testimonies and Documents from Shapira Neighborhood*, ed. Sharon Rotbard and Muki Tzur (Tel Aviv-Jaffa: Babel, 2009) and community initiatives like the Shapira Neighborhood Oral History project (2002–2007), the new Master Plan for Shapira Neighborhood (2004–2009) or 'The South of the City for People' planning initiative (2009–2012).

249. Adam Baruch, *Maariv* (daily newspaper) May 8, 2005.

250. Since the West Bank 'Defense Shield' operation and the relatively forgotten Gaza Strip 'Rainbow' operation mentioned in this book, there was a Second Lebanon War in 2006, the 'Cast Lead' operation (alias Gaza War) in 2008 and the 'Pillar of Defense' operation in 2012, and as these words are being written, in 2014, the devastating Operation 'Protective Edge' (in Hebrew 'Solid Cliff'), which has not yet come to an end.

251. Sharon Rotbard, 'Preface', in Rafi Segal and Eyal Weizman (eds), *A Civilian Occupation: The Politics of Israeli Architecture* (Tel Aviv-Jaffa: Babel; London and New York: Verso, 2003), p. 16.

Bibliography

Books, Essays and Articles

Abadžić Hodžić, Aida and Sonder, Ines. 'A Communist Muslim in Israel: How the Bauhaus student Selman Selmanagić came to Jerusalem and became a wanderer between worlds', *Bauhaus Magazine*, no. 2, November 2011.

Aleksandrowicz, Or. 'Harisa Ezrahit: Ha-Mehiqa Ha-Metukhnenet Shel Shekhunat Manshiya Be-Yafo, 1948–1949' [Civilian Demolition: The Premeditated Destruction of Manshiya Neighbourhood in Jaffa, 1948–1949]. *Iyunim Bitkumat Israel* [studies in Israeli and modern Jewish society], 23 (2013): 274–314.

Angelo, Bonnie. 'The Pain of Being Black: Conversation with Toni Morrison', *Time Magazine*, 22 May 1989.

Arendt, Hannah. *Essai sur la revolution*. Paris: Gallimard, 1967.

Barthes, Roland. 'Dikduk Afrikani' [African Grammar]; 'Bishon etzel Ha'kushim' [*Bichon* and the Blacks] in *Mitologiot* [Mythologies]. (English version, *Mythologies*, trans. Annette Lavers. London: Jonathan Cape Ltd, 1972). Trans. Ido Basok, scientific ed. Moshe Ron. Tel Aviv-Jaffa: Babel, 1998.

Begin, Menachem. 'Emet Ha'nitzakhon Ve'nitzcon Ha'emet' [The Truth of Victory and the Victory of Truth] in *Kibush Yaffo* [The Conquest of Jaffa]. Tel Aviv: Shelah, 1951.

Ben-Gurion, David. 'Le'veirur Motza Ha'falakhim' [The Origins of the *Fellahs*] in *Anakhnu U'shkheneinu* [We and Our Neighbours] (New York, 1916). Tel Aviv: Davar, 1931.

—— 'Ha'falakh Ve'Admato' [The *Fellah* and his Land] in *Anakhnu Ve'shkheneinu* (New York, 1919). Tel Aviv: Davar, 1931.

—— 'Hatsa'a Le'veidat Akhdut Ha'avoda' [Proposal for the Labour Unity Convention], in *Anakhnu Ve'shkheneinu* (Tel Aviv, 1921). Tel Aviv: Davar, 1931.

—— 'The Fisherman and the Sea', in *Al HaHityashvut* [Of Settlement]. Tel Aviv: HaKibbutz HaMeuhad, 1986.

—— 'Daroma' [Southwards], in *Al HaHityashvut* [Of Settlement]. Tel Aviv: HaKibbutz HaMeuhad, Yad Tabenkin, HaMerkaz LeTarbut UleKhinukh BaVaad HaPoel shel HaHistadrut, 1987.

—— 'Masa Hashmama' [The Burden of Wilderness], in *Al HaHityashvut* [Of Settlement]. Tel Aviv: HaKibbutz HaMeuhad, Yad Tabenkin, HaMerkaz LeTarbut UleKhinukh BaVaad HaPoel shel HaHistadrut, 1987.

Benton, Charlotte. *Erich Mendelsohn, Dynamics and Function: realized visions of a cosmopolitan architect*. Ostfildern-Ruit: Hatje Cantz Verlag, 1999.

Berger, Tamar. *Dionysus Ba'center* [Dionysus in the Centre]. Collection 'Hakivsa Ha'shkhora', Hanan Hever and Moshe Ron (eds). HaKibbutz HaMeuhad, 1998.

Bhabha, Homi K. 'The White Stuff', in 'The Political Aspect of Whiteness', *Artforum International*, vol. 36, no. 9 (May, 1998): 21–24.

Blanqui, Louis-Auguste. *Instructions pour une prise d'armes: L'Éternité par les astres, hypothèse astronomique et autres textes*, Société encyclopédique française, Éditions de la Tête de Feuilles. 1972, at: www.marxists.org/francais/blanqui/1866/instructions.htm

Blodgett, Geoffrey. 'Philip Johnson's Great Depression', *Timeline*, June–July 1987.

Bouyssy, Maïté. 'Présentation', in Maréchal Bugeaud and Thomas-Robert Bugeaud, *La Guerre des rues et des maisons*. Paris: Jean-Paul Rocher, 1997.

Brenner, Yosef Haim. *Ketavim* [Writings], vol. 4. Tel Aviv: HaKibbutz HaMeuhad, Sifriyat Poalim, 1984.

Bresheeth, Haim. 'Givat Aliya Ke'mashal: Shloshah Hebetim' [Gebalyia as a Symbol: Three Perspectives] in *Theory and Criticism* No. 16: *Merchav, Adama, Bait*. Yehouda Shenhav (ed.). The Van Leer Jerusalem Institute and HaKibbutz HaMeuhad, 2000.

Bugeaud, Maréchal and Bugeaud, Thomas-Robert. *La Guerre des rues et des maisons*, manuscrit inédit présenté par Maïté Bouyssy. Paris: Jean-Paul Rocher, 1997.

Chelouche, Yosef Eliyahu. *Parashat Khayai* [Reminiscences of My Life, 1870–1930]. Tel Aviv, 1931, 1973, 2005.

Cohen, Jean-Louis. 'Le Corbusier, Perret et les figures d'un Alger modern', in *Alger, paysage urbain et architectures 1800–2000*, sous la direction de Jean-Louis Cohen, Nabila Oulebsir et Youcef Kanoun. Paris: Les Éditions de L'imprimeur, 2003.

Dror, Yuval. 'Ein Kmo Jaffa Ba'olam' [There is nothing in the world like Jaffa], *Haaretz*, September 15, 2004.

Efrat, Zvi. 'Me'ever la'nireh, Miba'ad Lakatuv: Habitan HaIsraeli Le'adrichalut Ba'Bianale Le'adrichalut u'shelat Shikum He'arim Ha'historiyot' [Beyond the Visible, Behind the Writings: on the Israeli Pavilion and the question of Historical Cities' restoration]. *Studio*, No. 80, January 1997.

—— (ed.) *Ha'proyekt Ha'Israeli* [The Israeli Project]. Tel Aviv: Tel Aviv Museum for Art, 2005.

Elhanani, Aba. *Ha'maavak Le'atsmaout shel Ha'adrichalut Ha'israelit Ba'meah Ha-20* [Israeli architecture's struggle for independence in 20th century]. Misrad Habitakhon Ha'hotzaah La'or, 1998.

Elhyani, Zvi. 'Seafront Holdings', in *Back to the Sea*, Sigal Barnir and Yael Moria-Klein (eds), catalogue of the Israeli Pavilion, 9th Biennale of Architecture, Venice, 2004, pp. 104–116.

—— 'Seafront Holdings', in *Back to the Sea*, November, 2004, see: http://reading machine.co.il.il/home/articles/1111445772 (Hebrew).

Elkayam, Mordechai. *Yaffo – Neve Tzedek: Reshitah shel Tel Aviv* [Jaffa – Neve Tzedek: The Beginnings of Tel Aviv]. Tel Aviv: Misrad Habitakhon Ha'hotzaah La'or, 1990.

Elon, Amos. *Herzl*. Tel Aviv: Am Oved, 1975; New York: Holt, Rinehart and Winston, 1975.

Fabian, Roy and Monterescu, Daniel. 'The "Golden Cage": Gentrification and Globalization in the Andromeda Hill Project, Jaffa', guest ed. Ronen Shamir, *Theory and Criticism* [Teoria Ubikoret], No. 23, Autumn 2003, pp. 141–178.

Fanon, Frantz. *Peau noire, masques blancs*. Paris: Seuil, 1952.

—— *Les damnés de la terre*. Paris: La Decouverte, 2002 (François Maspéro 1961).

Foucault, Michel. 'La politique comme guerre', in *Il faut protéger la société*. Paris: Gallimard, 1997.

Gavish, Dov. 'Dikuy Ha'mered Be'yaffo Bi'meoraot 1936' [The Oppression of the

Arab Revolt in 1936] in *Yaffo Ve'atareiha* [Jaffa and its Sites]. Kardom, Du Yarkhon Li'Ydiat Ha'aretz, Beit-Hasefer Le'tayarut, Ma'arakh Ha'hasbara Minhal Hatayarut. Ariel, Jerusalem, March–April 1981.

Gropius, Walter. *Architecture et société*. Paris: Éditions du Linteau, 1995.

Grossman, David. *See Under: Love* [Ayen Erech: Ahavah]. New York: Farrar Straus Giroux, 1989; Tel Aviv, 1986.

Gutman, Nachum. *Ir Ktana Ve'anashim Ba Me'at* [A Small City with Few People in It]. Tel Aviv: Am Oved & Dvir, 1959.

—— *Hapardess Ha'kasum* [The Enchanted Orchard]. Yoav Dagon (ed.). Tel Aviv: The Nachum Gutman Museum, 1999.

—— *Tel Aviv shel Nachum Gutman, Nachum Gutman shel Tel Aviv* [Nachum Gutman's Tel Aviv, Tel Aviv's Nachum Gutman]. Yoav Dagon (ed.). Tel Aviv: The Nachum Gutman Museum, 1999.

Guyot, Adelin and Restelliny, Patrick. *L'Art Nazi, 1933–1945*. Preface: Leon Poliakov (ed.). Bruxelles: Complexe, 1983.

Hadar, Roni. 'Ha'pil Ha'lavan Sovel Mi'pitzul Ishiut' [The White Elephant Suffers from Split Personality] in *Tel Aviv Local Newspaper*, September 18, 1992.

Herbert, Gilbert, Heintze-Grinberg Ita, Sosnovski Silvina. *Bish'ifa Le'metzuyanut Ba'Adrichalut, Mivnim U'Proyektim shel Hevrat Ha'Khashmal Be'eretz Israel 1921–1942* [In search of excellence: the architecture and building projects of the electric industry in the land of Israel, 1921–1942]. Ha'Tekhniyyon – Makhon tekhnologi le-Yisrael. Merkaz mehqar le'moreshet ha'arkhiteqtura; Haifa (Architectural Heritage Research Centre, Faculty of Architecture and Town Planning, Technion) with Keter, 2003.

Herzl, Theodor. *Sifrei Ha'yamim* [Chronicles] *1895–1904*, vol. 3. Trans. R. Binyamin and Asher Barash. Tel Aviv: M. Neuman, 1950.

—— *Altneuland* [Old New Land]. Translations and Editions: Nahum Sokolov (Tel Aviv), Warsaw: Dfus Ha'tzfira, 1904; Shmuel Shnitzer (*Altneuland*), Haifa – Hevra Le'hotza'at Sfarim, Tel Aviv, 1961; Miriam Kraus (*Altneuland*), Tel Aviv-Jaffa: Babel, 1997.

Hinski, Sarah. 'Shtikat Ha'dagim: Me'komi Ve'universali Be'siakh Ha'amanut Ha'Israeli' [The Silence of the Fish: Local and Universal in the Israeli Art Discourse] in *Theory and Critisism* No. 4, Autumn 1993. Adi Ophir (ed.). The Van Leer Jerusalem Institute and HaKibbutz HaMeuhad, 1993.

Hitchcock, Henry-Russell and Johnson, Philip. *The International Style: Architecture Since 1922*. New York, London: W. W. Norton & Company, 1995 (1932).

Hugo, Victor. *Ha'giben Mi'Notre Dame* [Notre Dame de Paris, 1831]. Trans. Dan Soen. Tel Aviv: M. Mizrahi (n.d.).

Johnson, Philip C. *Mies Van Der Rohe*. New York: The Museum of Modern Art, 1953 (1947).

Karavan, Dani. *Makom – Dani Karavan* [Place – Dani Karavan]. Tel Aviv: Tel Aviv Museum for Art, 1982.

—— Preface, in *Batim Min Ha'khol – Adrichalut Ha'signon Ha'beileumi Be'Tel Aviv*. Tel Aviv: Keren Tel Aviv Le'phituakh & Misrad Habitakhon – Ha'hotsaa La'or, 1994.

—— 'Noldah Min Ha'yam' [Born in the City], in *Hair: Ha'ir Ha'levanah,* Special supplement 2004.

—— *Radio Galei Tzahal,* a special programme for the celebration of the declaration of the White City. Alon Kish (ed.), June 5, 2004.

Kark, Ruth. *Yaffo: Tsmikhtah shel Ir, 1799–1917* [Jaffa: a city in evolution, 1799–1917]. Jerusalem: Yad Izhak Ben-Zvi Press, 1984.

Karpel, Dalia. 'Wellsprings of Memory', *Haaretz,* 14 February 2008, at: http://web.archive.org/web/20090325111844/http://www.haaretz.com/hasen/spages/952270.html

Kedar, Benjamin Zeev. *Mabat Ve'od Mabat al Eretz Israel [Looking Twice at the Land of Israel].* Tel Aviv: Yad Izhak Ben-Zvi Press, Misrad Habitakhon Ha'hotsaa La'or, 1991.

Khalidi, Walid. *All That Remains: The Palestinian Villages Occupied and Depopulated by Israel in 1948.* Washington, DC: Institute of Palestinian Studies, 1992.

Kiesler, Frederick. 'Le pseudo-fonctionnalisme dans l'architecture moderne', in *L'architecte et le philosophe,* sous la direction de Antonia Soulez. Liege: Pierre Margada, 1993.

Kleinberg, Aviad. 'Bakhalomot Shela: Le'zikhrah shel Naomi Shemer' [In Her Dreams: In memory of Naomi Shemer], *Haaretz,* July 1, 2004.

Kobler, Frantz. 'Napoleon and the Restoration of the Jews to Palestine'. *New Judea,* London, 1940.

Koolhaas, Rem. 'Typical Plan', in *SMLXL,* Rotterdam: 010 publishers, 1995.

Kushnir, Mordechai. 'Ha'peamim Ha'akharonot Baderekh el Maon Brener', in *Yosef Haim Brenner – Mivkhar Zikhronot* [Yosef Haim Brenner – Selected Reminiscences], Mordechai Kushnir (ed.). Tel Aviv: HaKibbutz HaMeuhad, 1943.

LeBor, Adam. *City of Oranges: Arabs and Jews in Jaffa.* London: Bloomsbury, 2006.

Lazar (Litai), Chaim. *Kibush Yaffo* [The Conquest of Jaffa]. Tel Aviv: Shelah, 1951.

Le Corbusier. *Vers une architecture.* Paris: Les Éditions G. Crès et Cie, 1923.

—— *Sur les quatres routes.* Paris: Éditions Denoël, 1970 (Paris: Gallimard, 1941).

—— *L'art décorative d'aujourd'hui.* Paris: Arthaud, 1980 (1925)

—— *Likrat Architektura* (Toward An Architecture). Trans. Ido Baso, Sharon Rotbard (ed.). Tel Aviv-Jaffa: Babel (Architecturot), 1998.

——— *Toward An Architecture,* trans. John Goodman, Introduction by Jean-Louis Cohen. Los Angeles, CA: Getty Publications, 2007 (1923).

Lefebvre, Henri. 'Espace et politique', in *Le droit à la ville.* Paris: Anthropos, 1968.

Levin, Michael. 'Ha'adrichalim She'heviou et Ha'Bauhouse Le'Tel Aviv' [The Architects who brought the Bauhaus to Tel Aviv], *Kav* No. 2, January 1981. HaKibbutz HaMeuchad, 1981.

—— *Ir Levanah, Adrichalut Ha'signon Ha'beinlemi Be'Israel – Sipourah shel Tkufah* [White City: the International Style Architecture in Israel, Portrait of an Era]. Tel Aviv: Tel Aviv Museum for Art, 1984.

LeVine, Mark. *Overthrowing Geography: Jaffa, Tel Aviv, and the Struggle for Palestine, 1880–1948.* Berkeley and Los Angeles, CA: California University Press, 2005.

Loos, Adolf. 'Architecture (1910)', trans. Wilfred Wang, in *The Architecture of Adolf Loos,* Yehuda Safran and Wilfred Wang (eds). British Arts Council exhibition catalogue, 1985.

—— 'Kishut Ve'Pesha' [Ornament and Crime]; 'Ha'shravravim' [The Plumbers], in *Dibur La'rik, La'mrot Ha'kol* [Spoken into the Void, After All], trans. Aryeh Uriel, Yehuda Safran (ed.) [Ins Leere gesprochen 1897–1900, Trotzdem 1900–1930]. Tel Aviv-Jaffa: Babel (Architecturot), 2004.

Merhavia, Chen-Melech. *Tsionut, Otzar Hateudot Hapolitiot* [Zionism, Anthology of Political Documents], Jerusalem: Ahiasaf, 1943 (Hebrew).

Monterescu, Daniel and Roy, Fabian. 'Kluv Ha'zahav: Gentrifikatsia Ve'globalizatsia Be'proyekt Givat Andromeda, Yaffo' [The Golden Cage: Gentrification and Globalization in the Andromeda Hill Project, Jaffa], *Theory and Criticism* No. 23, Autumn 2003. Ronen Shamir and Yehouda Shenhav (eds). HaKibbutz HaMeuhad 2003.

Morris, Benny. *Leidata shel Be'ayat Ha'plitim Ha'Phalastinim, 1947–1949* [The Birth of the Palestinian Refugee Problem, 1947–1949], (Cambridge: Cambridge University Press, 1988), Tel Aviv: Sifriyat Ofakim and Am Oved, 1991.

Naor, Mordechai (ed.). *Tel Aviv Be'reshitah, 1909–1934* [Tel Aviv at the Beginning 1909–1934]. Sidrat Idan, Merkaz Rachel Yanait Ben Zvi Le'limudei Yerushalaim, Jerusalem: Yad Izhak Ben-Zvi Press, 1984.

Parent, Claude. 'Dominer le site', in *Form follows fiction: écrits d'architecture fin de siècle*, Sous la Direction de Michel Dénés. Paris: Les Éditions de la Villette, 1996.

Perec, Georges. *W ou le souvenir d'enfance* [W or the Memory of Childhood]. Paris: Denoël, 1975. (*W, or the Memory of Childhood*, trans. David Bellow. Boston, MA: David R Godine, 1988).

—— *W O Zikaron Yaldut* [W or the Memory of Childhood]. Trans. Aviva Barak. Ha'sifriya Ha'hadasha, HaKibbutz HaMeuhad / Sifrei Siman Kria, 1991.

Pommer, Richard. 'Mies van der Rohe and the Political Ideology of the Modern Movement in Architecture', in *Mies van der Rohe: Critical Essays*, Franz Schulze (ed.). New York: The Museum of Modern Art, 1989.

Portugali, Juval, *Yekhasim Mukhalim: Khevrah U'merkhav Ba'sikhsukh Ha'Israrli-Phalestini* [*Implicate Relations: Society and Space in the Israeli–Palestinian Conflict*, Boston, MA: Kluwer Academic Press, 1993]. Tel Aviv: HaKibbutz HaMeuhad, 1996.

Restany, Pierre. 'Dani Karavan: Semiologia Ve'hitnahagut' [Dani Karavan: Semilogy and behaviour] in *Makom – dani Karavan*. Tel Aviv: Tel Aviv Museum for Art, 1982.

Richardot, Charles. *Relation de la campagne de Syrie, spécialement des sièges de Jaffa et de Saint-Jean-d'Acre*. Paris: Corréard J., 1839.

Roy, Nathan. 'Ha'takhanah Hamerkazit eina Onah' [The Central Station does not Respond], *Davar*, 'Dvar Hashavua', October 11, 1985.

Rotbard, Sharon. 'Tel Aviv Ir Mulbenet Bli Hafsakah' [Tel Aviv Incessantly Blanched City], *Studio*, August 1994.

—— 'Tel Aviv Adayin Tinoket – Tel Aviv Haita Tzrikha Lihiyot Levanah – I-Efshar Lishlot Behitpatkhut shel Ir' [Tel Aviv is still a baby – Tel Aviv Should be White – You cannot control a City's development] (an interview with Jean Nouvel), *Shishi*, November 3, 1995.

—— 'Postface', in Le Corbusier, *Likrat* Architektura (Toward An Architecture).

Babel: Tel Aviv-Jaffa, 1998.

—— 'Wall and Tower: the mold of Israeli architecture', in *A Civilian Occupation: The Politics of Israeli Architecture*, Rafi Segal and Eyal Weizman (eds). Tel Aviv-Jaffa: Babel; London: Verso, 2003.

—— 'Ir Levanah, Ir Shkhorah' [White City, Black City], a series of 3 articles in *Ha'Ir,* February 2003.

Rotbard, Sharon and Tsur, Muki (eds). *Neither in Jaffa Nor in Tel Aviv: Stories, Testimonies and Documents from Shapira Neighborhood*. Tel Aviv-Jaffa: Babel, 2009.

Runkle, Benjamin. 'Jaffa, 1948: Urban Combat in the Israeli War of Independence', in *City Fights: Selected Histories of Urban Combat from World War II to Vietnam*, Col. John Antal and Maj. Bradley Gericke (eds). New York: Ballantine Books, 2003.

Safran, Yehuda. 'He'ashan Halavan shel Ha'Bauhouse' [Bauhaus' White Smoke] in *Tel Aviv Be'ikvot Ha'Bauhouse*, Rachel Sukman (ed.). Textim, Misrad Be'Tel Aviv, 1994.

Said, W. Edward. *Orientalism*. Trans. Atalia Zilber. Tel Aviv: Sifriat Ofakim and Am Oved, 2000.

Samuel, Herbert. *An Interim Report on the Civil Administration of Palestine to the League of Nations*, London: HMSO, June 1921.

Scheps, Marc. 'Foreword' in *Ir Levanah, Adrichalut Ha'signon Ha'beinlemi Be'Israel – Sipourah shel Tkufah* [White City: the International Style Architecture in Israel, Portrait of an Era]. Tel Aviv: Tel Aviv Museum for Art, 1984.

Schmitt, Daniela and Kern, Ingolf. 'Routes to the Promised Land', *Bauhaus Magazine*, no. 2, November 2011.

Schulze, Franz. *Philip Johnson: Life and Work*. New York: Albert A. Knopf, 1994.

Schur, Nathan. *Sefer Ha'nosim Le'Erettz Israel Ba'mea Ha-19* [The Book of Travellers to the Land of Israel in the 19th Century]. Jerusalem: Keter, 1998.

Segal, Rafi and Weizman, Eyal. 'The Battle for the Hilltops', in *A Civilian Occupation: The Politics of Israeli Architecture*, Rafi Segal and Eyal Weizman (eds). Tel Aviv-Jaffa: Babel; London: Verso, 2003.

Segev, Tom. *1949, Ha'Israelim Ha'khadashim* [1949, The First Israelis]. Jerusalem: Domino, 1984; New York: Free Press, 1986.

Sharon, Aryeh. *Tikhnun Phissi Be'Israel* [Physical Planning in Israel]. Jerusalem: Ha'madpis Ha'memshalti, 1951.

—— *Kibbutz+Bauhaus*. Stuttgart: Karl Kramer Verlag; Israel: Massada, 1976.

Shavit, Yaacov and Bigger, Gideon. *Ha'historia shel Tel Aviv: Mishkhunot Le'ir (1909–1936)* [The History of Tel Aviv (1909–1936)]. Tel Aviv: Tel Aviv University, 2001.

Shchori, Ran. *Ze'ev Rechter*. Hamoatsa Ha'tsiburit Le'tarbut Ule'umanut, Jerusalem: HaKibbutz HaMeuhad & Keter, 1987.

—— 'Hesed Neurayikh' [Your Youth's Grace] in *Tel Aviv Be'ikvot Ha'Bauhouse*, Rachel Sukman (ed.). Textim: Misrad Be'Tel Aviv, 1994.

Shenhav, Yehouda. *Ha'syehudim-Ha'aravim: Leumiut, Dat, Etniut.* [The Arab Jews: A Postcolonial Reading of Nationalism, Religion, and Ethnicity, Stanford University Press, 2006] Tel Aviv: Sifriyat Ofakim and Am Oved, 2003.

Shohat, Ella. 'Sephardim in Israel: Zionism From the Standpoint of its Jewish Victims', *Social Text*, 19/20 (Fall 1988), pp. 1–35.

—— 'MIzrakhim Be'Israel: Hatsionut Mi'nekudat Mabatam shel Korbenoteiha

Ha'yehudim' [Sephardim in Israel: Zionism from the Standpoint of its Jewish Victims]; 'Zikhronot Asourim Ve'hirhourim Galutiyim: Colombus, Palestine Ve'Yehudim-Aravim' [Taboo Memories, Diasporic Vidions: Columbus, Palestine, and Arab-Jew] in *Zikhronot Asourim: Likrat Makhashavah Rav-Tarbutit*, [Forbidden Reminiscences: Towards a Multi-Cultural Thought], Tel Aviv: Bimat Kedem Le'sifrout, 2001.

Sochovolsky-Kamini, Ziva and Carmiel, Batia. *Tel Aviv Be'tatslumim – He'asor Ha'rishon, 1909–1918* [Tel Aviv in Photographs, The First Decade 1909–1918]. Tel Aviv: Eretz Israel Museum, 1990.

Sorkin, Michael. 'Where was Philip?', in *Exquisite Corpse: Writing on Buildings*. New York: Verso, 1991.

Speer, Albert. *Inside the Third Reich*, translated from German by Richard and Clara Winston. New York: Macmillan, 1970.

Sukman, Rachel (ed.). *Tel Aviv Be'ikvot Ha'Bauhouse* (Tel Aviv in the Bauhaus' Footsteps), Textim: Misrad Be'Tel Aviv 1994.

Szmuk, Nitza Metzger. *Bauhaus Tel Aviv: Mapat Ha'atarim Le'shimur Be'Tel Aviv* [Bauhaus Tel Aviv: Plan of Conservation Sites in Tel Aviv]. Photos: Ytzhak Kalter, Lishkat Ha'adrichalim Ve'hamehabdesim Be'Israel Be'siyua Minhal Ha'handasa shel Iryat Tel Aviv Yaffo [Bureau of Architects and Engineers in Israel, with the aid of the Tel Aviv Municipality Engineering Administration]. Early 1990s (n.d.).

—— *Batim Min Ha'khol – Adrichalut Ha'signon Ha'beinleumi Be'Tel Aviv* [Houses from the Sand: International Style Architecture in Tel Aviv]. Tel Aviv: Keren Tel Aviv Le'Phituakh & Misrad Ha'bitakhon – Ha'hotsaa La'or [Tel Aviv Development Foundation and The Ministry of Defense Publications], 1994.

——— 'Letters to the Editor', *Ha'Ir*, 13 February 2003.

—— *Lagur al Ha'kholot* [Dwelling on the Dunes]. Tel Aviv: Tel Aviv Museum for Arts, 2004a.

—— *Dwelling on the Dunes: Tel Aviv, Modern Movement and Bauhaus Ideals / Des maisons sur le sable: Tel-Aviv, Mouvement moderne et esprit Bauhaus*. Nitza Metzger-Szmuk, Véra Pinto-Lasry, Vivianne Barsky, Dani Karavan. Bilingual edition English/French. Paris: Éditions de l'Eclat, 2004b.

Tamuz, Binyamin. 'Takharut Skhiya' [Swimming Competition] in *Mivkhar Sipourim* [Selected Stories]. Jerusalem: Keter & Agudat Ha'sofrim Ha'ivrim, 1990.

Tolkovsky Shmuel. *Toldot Yaffo* [Annals of Jaffa]. Preface: Gideon Bigger. Tel Aviv: Dvir 1926 (*The Gateway of Palestine: a History of Jaffa*. London: G. Routledge and Sons, 1924).

Tumarkin, Yigal. 'Bizkhut Kne Ha'mida' [In Favour of Scale], *Kav, No. 2*, January 1981.

—— *Binyan Ha'aretz* [The Building of the Land]. Tel Aviv: Misrad Ha'bitakhon – Ha'hotsaa La'or, 1998.

Tzur, Muki. *Aviv Mukdam: Zvi Shatz Ve'hakvutsa Ha'intimit* [Early Spring: Zvi Shatz and the Intimate Group]. Tel Aviv: Am Oved, 1984.

Varnelis, Kazys, 'We Cannot Not Know History: Philip Johnson's Politics and Cynical Survival', *Journal of Architectural Education*, November 1994.

Virilio, Paul. 'De la géopolitique à la métropolitique', in *La Ville et la Guerre*, Sous la direction de Antoine Picon. Paris: Les Éditions de l'imprimeur, 1996.

Weizman, Eyal. 'Strategic Points, Flexible Lines, Tense Surfaces, Political Volumes: Ariel Sharon and the Geometry of Occupation', in *Territories: Builders, Warriors and other Mythologies*, Anselm Franke, Eyal Weizman, Rafi Segal and Stefano Boeri (eds). Berlin: WDW, Kunst-Werke and Cologne: Walter König, 2003.

—— 'Military Operations as Urban Planning: A Conversation with Philipp Misselwitz', 'Urban Warfare as Urban Design', in *Territories: Islands, camps and other states of utopia*, Anselm Franke with Eyal Weizman, Rafi Segal and Stefano Boeri (eds). Berlin: KW; Cologne: Walter König, 2003.

—— 'Walking Through Walls: Soldiers As Architects in the Israeli–Palestinian Conflict'. *Radical Philosophy*, no. 136, 2006.

Wigley, Mark. *White Walls, Designer Dresses: The Fashioning of Modern Architecture*. Cambridge, MA: The MIT Press, 1995.

Yavin, Shmuel (ed.). *Hitkhdshut Ha'bauhouse Be'Tel Aviv: Shimur Binyanei Ha'signon Ha'beinleumi Ba'ir Ha'levanah* [The Renewal of Bauhaus in Tel Aviv: Conserving the International Style Buildings in the White City]. Tel Aviv: The Bauhaus Center Tel Aviv, 2003.

Yekutieli-Cohen, Edna. *Tel Aviv as a Literary Place 1909–1939*. Tel Aviv: Ha'Havra Le'Haganat Ha'Teva [Society for the Protection of Nature in Israel (SPNI)], 1990.

Yinon, Ya'akov. *Sviv Kikar Ha'shaon: Le'sayer Be'Yaffo im Yad Ben Zvi* [Around the Clock Tower: Touring Jaffa with Ben Zvi Foundation]. Jerusalem: Yad Izhak Ben-Zvi Press, 2001.

Yonah, Ilanah. *Kolot Mi'shkhunat Ha'Katamonim* [Voices from the Katamonim neighbourhood]. Tel Aviv: Andalous, 2002.

Ze'evi, Rehav'am. *Yaffo Bi'ri Ha'yamim* [Jaffa in the Mirror of Times]. Gania Doron and Zvi Sha'ham (eds). Tel Aviv: Ha'aretz Museum, 1985.

Zevi, Bruno. *Be'halala shel Ardichalut* (Architecture As Space, 1957). Jerusalem: Mosad Bialik, 1957.

Ziffer, Benny. 'Ha'mitosim Sheli' [My Myths], *Haaretz*, September 15, 2004.

Public, collective and official sources

Jaffa's Municipal Planning Team: Arch Doron Zafrir, Arch' Sergio Lerman, Arch' Dani Rabas, 'Architectura' (Arch' Shmuel Grubman, Arch' Rami Gil), Arch' Nahum Cohen, Landscape Arch' Moriya Skali, *Mabat al Agami, Dyokan Adrichali* [A gaze on Adjami: An Archtectural Portrait]. Municipality of Tel Aviv Yaffo, Minhal Handasa, Agaf Tichnun U'binyan Arim (n.d.).

Neve Sha'anan Cooperative. *Tazkir Le'tsirei Ha'knesiya Ha'zionit ha-12th*, [Memorandum to the 12th Zionist Congress]. Makhberet Binyan Batim Neve Sha'anan Be'yaffo-Tel Aviv. Yaffo, 1921.

Protokol Yeshiva 20/49' shel Ha'memshalah. 'Ikhud Yaffo Ve'Tel-Aviv' [Unification of Jaffa and Tel Aviv, Government Discussion], 11th Be'ishrei TSh'I – 4 October 1949.

Yaffo Ha'atika (Hashetakh Hagadol): Seker Calcali Hevrati [Old Jaffa (the Big Zone): Economical and Social Survey], *Shikun U'vniya* No. 3, Preface: David Taneh. Ministry of Housing, State of Israel, December 1962.

Index

Note: references to illustrations are in **bold**. References notes are in the format 210n14 (for note 14 on page 210). Names of places in Tel Aviv are indexed under Tel Aviv, except for specific references to Jaffa (under Jaffa). Places outside Israel/Palestine are indexed under country names.

Namir, Mordechai, 124
Napoleon Bonaparte, 66–8, 121, 201n90
National Corporation of Tourism, 121
Nazar, Salah, 104
Nazareth, 123
Negev Brigade, monument for, 39–40
Nemours Project, 168
Nerdinger, Winifried, 199n68
Nes Ziona, 135
Neutra, Richard, 170
Neve Sha'anan Corporation/ association, 47, 143, 204n115
New York, *International Style* (exhibition), 29, **30**, 170
Newspapers Under Influence, 157
Niv, Amnon, 125–32
'Nothing like Jaffa at Night', 120
Nouvel, Jean, 1, 16, 193n10

Occupied Territories, 15, 44–5, 115, 175
   see also Palestine
Old Jaffa Development Company, 121, 122
Omer, Hillel, 122, 125, 128
'Operation Anchor' *see* Project Anchor
'Operation Cast Lead', 220n251
'Operation Chametz', 100
'Operation Defense Shield', 220n251
'Operation Pillar of Defense', 220n251
'Operation Protective Edge', 184–5, 220n251
'Operation Rainbow', 159, 220n251
orchards *see* agriculture
Order of Tel Aviv Township, 92
Orientalism, 28, 72, 132, 171
Orloff, Hannah, 196n28
Ornament and Crime , 165
Oslo Accords, 15
Ottoman Empire *see* Turkey
Oulebsir, Nabila, 166, 169

Pain Song, 55
Palestine
   21st century Israeli military

operations, 102–3
   Arab residents before founding of Israel, 50–1
   Arab residents replaced in old cities, 123 (*see also under* Jaffa)
   British Mandate, 47–8, 81–2, 91–4
   bypass roads in, 203–4n111
   Highway Six, 219n243
   Jewish settlement in, *see* Israel
   national identity, 88
   Occupied Territories *see* Occupied Territories
   refugees from and to, *see under* refugees
   significance of Jaffa to, 5, 72, 98
   UN Division Plan (1947), 91, 98–9, 105–6
   Zionist counters to Palestinian claims of entitlement, 50–1
   see also Gaza Strip, Israel, Separation Wall
Parent, Claude , 171
Peace Now, 26
Peeping Toms (film), 35
Penn, Alexander, 37
people as focus of architecture, 8–9
Perec, Georges, 55, 201n86
Peres, Shimon, 217n224
Peretz, Isaac Leib, 212n177
Perlstein, Yitzhak, 124
Petah-Tikvah, 135
Pichmann, Yaacov, 6, 33
Piltz, Arieh, 149–51
piracy, 123
plague (in Jaffa), 68
'Plan Obus', 168, **169**
'Plan Voisin', 168
Plumbers, The, 165, 217n225
Poelzig, Hans, 199n68
politics
   and changes of national administration, 24
   and the city, 178
   democracy and isonomy, 178
   and discourse on architecture, 59–61, 161, 165, 176

136, 139, 140, 158–9, 177, 179, 186–7

Bloomfield football stadium, 140

Botrus district, 109

boundaries and conceptions, 56–7, 146, 147, 200n70

Brenner House, 83

British urban planning in, 91–2

Chlenov neighbourhood, 17, 46, 56, 64, 89

Commercial Centre (street), 144

Commercial and Grocery Center (neighbourhood), 46

comparative neglect of areas formerly in/near Jaffa, 56, 64–5, 140–1

conservation/urban plans, 9, 16, **58**, 92, 121–2, 124–5, 141, 144–5, 175–6, 185

Dizengoff Center, 8

Dolphinarium, 76

Eisenberg Hospital, 111, 140, 213n192

Engel House, 21

'ethnic purification' (2002–04), 158–9, 179

expensiveness of property, 186

Ezra neighbourhood, 64, 90, 140

Fedja village/district, 100

Florentine neighbourhood, 17, 64, 89, 140, 144

founding of, 5, 43–4, 46, 48–50, 60, 69, 73

Frug Street, **23**

Gan Hapisga (Garden of the Peak), 115, 122

German Vineyard, 46

Geula neighbourhood, 89

Givat Aliyah neighbourhood, 111

Givat Herzl neighbourhood, 140

Givat Moshe A and B neighbourhoods, 140

as 'global city', 15

Gush Dan, 107

HaArgazim neighbourhood, 64, 90

HaCongress, 146

Hassan Bek mosque, 127

Hatikva neighbourhood, 64, 90, 91, 140–1

Herzl Street, 74, 78

Herzliya district, 80

Herzliya Gymnasium, 74, 76, 78, 83, 124, 203n110

(al-)Hiriya district, 63, 100, 108, 112

historical centre, 17 (*see also* Jaffa)

Holon district, 80, 110

hospitals, 76, 106, 111, 140

housing in *see under* housing

Ibn Gvirol Street, 146

infrastructure, 64, 82

internal north–south division, 17, 56–8, 62, 64–5, 146

Jabaliya neighbourhood, 111, 125

Jaffa *see* Jaffa

Jaffa D neighbourhood, 135

Jaffa–Tel Aviv Road, 17, 56, 140, 185

Jammasin neighbourhood, 108

Jerusalem Beach, 16

Jerusalem (Har-Zion) Boulevard, 114, 147

Jerusalem Boulevard/Jamal Facha Boulevard/King George Boulevard, 114

Jewish settlements on site, 48

Kerem Hateimanim neighbourhood, 16, 48, 74, **77**, 78, 91, 94, 140 (*see also* Mahane Israel)

Kfar Shalem neighbourhood, 112, **113**

Kibbutz Galuyot Road, 204n118

Kiryat Shalom neighbourhood, 111, 135

Kolchinsky neighbourhood, 140

lack of natural centre, 204n113

Levinsky Park, 179

Little Orchard neighbourhood, 47

'Little Tel Aviv', 74

Mahane Israel neighbourhood, 48–9, **77**, 140 (*see also* Kerem Hateimanim)

Mahane Yehuda neighbourhood, 48, 73, 76